Livin' the Dreem

Livin' the Dreem

A Year in My Life

HARRY HILL

faber and faber

First published in 2010
by Faber and Faber Ltd
Bloomsbury House
74–77 Great Russell Street
London WC1B 3DA

Typeset by Ian Bahrami
Printed in England by CPI Mackays, Chatham ME5 8TD

A CIP record for this book
is available from the British Library
ISBN 978–0–571–26015–7

2 4 6 8 10 9 7 5 3 1

For Tom, Isabel and Gus

Everything in this diary actually happened. Only the facts have been changed.

'Tic toc, tic toc,
time goes by so slowly.'
Madonna

January

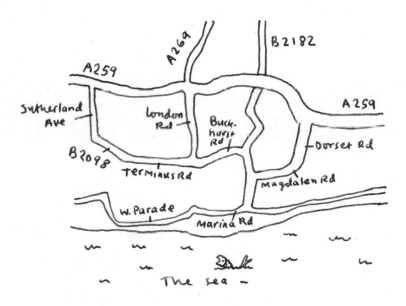

Map to show main routes
in & out of Bexhill

January 1st

Got a new diary for Christmas and decide to write in it with a view to having it published.

OK, this isn't strictly true. I was approached by a publisher who suggested that with my 'showbiz lifestyle and key position in British society' I could 'cash in like Piers Morgan has'. It seemed like a good idea at the time. Now, of course, I'm beginning to realise what a big commitment it is – 365 entries! Still, I suppose if I get really stuck I can always pretend to have been knocked out for a couple of days.

It's New Year's Day.* I spent Christmas at my mum's this year. By her own admission (and signed affidavits in my possession from countless visitors to her home) she's not the best cook in the world. She did turkey with all the trimmings. She got a different kind of turkey this year. Not free-range, no – a new line from Hugh Fearnley-Whittingstall's River Cottage outlet, the 'Free Spirit Turkey'. Not only does this turkey have the full run of the farm, it also doesn't hold with the conventional rules of society. These turkeys believe in free love, have no respect for authority and experiment with mind-altering drugs such as LSD, Calpol and Nurofen Max. The farmyard looks like Glastonbury, the air heavy with a mixture of cannabis and turkey droppings, as the turkeys lie

---

* I probably didn't need to mention that but I'm hoping that it's set our minds back to diary mode after that initial grumble about it being such a lot of work.

3

back, trying to entice ducks back to the coop for a listen to some cool vibes – Hendrix, the Grateful Dead, Peters and Lee . . . Hugh doesn't have to slaughter these turkeys; he just bides his time and eventually they OD and choke on their own vomit. The only slight drawback is that the breast meat is hallucinogenic, but you can't have everything in this world.

We did the usual this year and had Amanda Holden round for Christmas lunch. She's been coming to us for the last fifteen years, but she insists on keeping it a secret from her husband. Ever since she got *The Observer's Book of Bigamists* for her twenty-seventh birthday, she's fancied the subterfuge involved with bigamy, but without the legal implications, so she treats us – Mum and me – as her 'other family'. She starts Christmas Day with her own family – little Lexi and record-producer husband Chris. She then excuses herself for the toilet and escapes via the extractor fan to a waiting fast car. Up the A3 she speeds to join the M25, then round the M25 to the A21, up the A21 towards Hastings, then bears right along the A259 coastal road to Bexhill, where you'll find Mum's bungalow at number 4, The Close. All the time Amanda's real family are thinking, 'Where's Amanda?' and 'I hope she's all right.' As soon as we hear her car screeching up the recently laid drive (price £15,000 from Dave the cold-caller – 'It'll pay for itself in forty-three years'), Mum heaps up a fork with some hallu-cinogenic turkey and trimmings. In runs Amanda, gob wide open, and her freshly plumped lips tug on the morsel as she pulls a cracker with me with one hand and, proffering a sprig of mistletoe with the other, kisses Uncle Bob. Barely stopping to swallow, she heads towards the back wall, where Mum and

4

I have positioned a small trampoline, or 'trampet'. Amanda hits the trampet at speed and is propelled back through the

A Trampet, Like that used by Amanda Holden

dining room and out through the front door into the back seat of the waiting car. It's then straight back down the A259 to Hastings, bear left, A21, M25, A3, extractor-fan vent, taking care to flush the toilet before emerging back in front of her waiting family with a 'Phew, I must try and hit my five a day in the new year,' having been absent from the table for some four hours. Her husband and family put the whole thing down to a sluggish bowel. Amanda then joins in the Christmas celebrations as normal, allowing a couple of hours to pass, then makes her excuses and it's back to the car – A3, M25, A21, Hastings, bear right on A259, Bexhill, loaded fork, Brussels sprout . . .

'Aagh! She's choking! Quick, squeeze her from behind, eh? The Heimlich manoeuvre! Now!' yells Mum.

As I position myself behind Amanda and squeeze a sprout from her airway, sending it flying across the table and into the mouth of Hugh Fearnley-Whittingstall, who had just arrived to record the meal for training purposes, I vow to have a word with her perhaps later in the week about maybe skipping Christmas with us next year.

We watch the repeat of *Jools Holland's Hootenanny*, which was pre-recorded in December and which I attended, lingering for a good part of it on Lenny Henry's left knee – the right one accommodating the Welsh songbird Duffy. Duffy is not talking to me since I stood her up at Warwick Avenue tube earlier in the year. In my defence, there are two entrances to Warwick Avenue tube and I was waiting at the other one.

Mum can't understand how I can be sitting next to her and on TV at the same time, and asks me to leave the room as it's upsetting her.

I take out my iPhone with a view to phoning up a few mates, but the battery's died and the recharger is in the sitting room with Mum. Unable to remember any of my stored numbers, I resort to pressing redial on the landline handset in the hope that the last person I called is a friend.

'Hello Wing Wah! How can I help?'

It's Bexhill's premier Chinese takeaway.

'*Kung hei fat choi*!' I hear myself saying, which in Chinese means 'Happy New Year', but I back it up with a cry of 'Happy new year!'

'New year not till February, mate,' she says.

'Oh, sorry,' I say, and hang up.

Some new year this has been.

Cold hallucinogenic turkey for lunch.

January 2nd

Mum and I crack open a wine box at about 10.30 in the morning and take it in turns to suck from its little black tap. She asks to watch *Jools Holland's Hootenanny* again, so I activate

6

the Sky Plus for her. Then I break open the wine box, inflate the empty foil bag within and place it under Mum's head as she nods off to the strains of Lady Gaga. Mum looks so peaceful lying there in the dog's bed, but he's not going to be happy when he gets home from work.

I get a call from Duffy saying that she has now realised that she had in fact been waiting at the entrance to Warren Street tube and so has forgiven me. I write a letter to Transport for London asking for a full print-out of Duffy's Oyster-card activity so I can verify this, and will wait upon that before I agree to any further tube-station assignations. I suggest to her that in future we meet outside the WH Smith's at Charing Cross station to avoid any confusion. She says, 'Why can't we meet on Lenny Henry's knees, like at the Hootenanny? That seemed to work.' I explain that the position of Lenny's knees lend themselves to being a good meeting point only when he is sitting down, but that I will find out his whereabouts from his agent, with a view to a possible meeting. She's a lot of work is Duffy.

The dog gets home from its job at the airport, tired after a long day of sniffing strangers' bags. He has a quick bite to eat, then sees Mum in his bed. He starts to pull her from the bed but ends up dragging her around the freshly polished parquet floor as I clap along. This could be great entertainment, I think, and I text the controller of ITV, Peter Fincham: 'How about *Dancing on Wood Flooring*?' He texts me straight back. 'Already in production, with Schofield hosting and Holly W polishing! Hard lines, try again! Peter F.'

You've got to be quick to out-think the ITV format machine.

Wine for dinner.

I get a phone call from Rebekah Wade at the *News of the World* asking whether I was prepared to comment on the controversy surrounding this year's Queen's Speech.

Breaking with tradition, the Queen had decided to deliver her entire speech in the form of a rap. Trying to engage with the younger generation, she'd employed Dizzee Rascal and myself to write it for her. Her equerry had phoned me at home to sound me out. In instances like this where I'm not sure whether to take a job on, I recall the words of Bob Geldof: 'Wot's da wedge?' I say in broad Irish.

'There is no fee as such,' replied the equerry, 'but pull this one off and there might be a little something in the New Year's Honours List for you, but don't tell no one I told you.'

That would be nice, some sort of honour. It was me that started up the 'Get Bruce Forsyth a Knighthood' campaign. We'd hatched the plan over a coffee at my London-based medical practice The Showbusiness Disease Centre, which I still run in Penge (more of that later, probably – I mean, I don't know, because obviously I don't know how the year will unfold). He'd come in for CRT – chin-replacement therapy. His trademark chin had been noticeably less prominent all through the last series of *Strictly*, and the Chinese whispers were saying that he had started to reabsorb it rather than taking a lunch break, so he'd come to me. It was clear to me that he was indeed living off his chin, as a camel might live off its hump. He would not admit it, though, so I was injecting it with a special chin extract, donated by a prominent-chinned celebrity who cannot be named (all right, it was Jimmy Hill.

Jimmy was unhappy with the size of his chin and I was drawing off a pint of chin juice every other week. The beauty was I was charging both Jimmy and Brucie, merely acting as a chin-juice middleman).

Twice a week Brucie would come to me, and I would set up a drip directly into his chin to reinflate the organ, while he listened to that American crooner who had a big hit with a number of tunes on the Billy Crystal film *When Harry Met Sally*. Brucie kind of enjoyed the treatments – well, everyone loves the occasional Chin and Connick. What? Come on! Allow me one beautifully crafted gag! That's a beauty, what are you talking about?

Me and Bruce agreed that I would start up a campaign to get him a knighthood. Then, when that was successful, he would start up a campaign for me to get a Duke of Edinburgh Bronze Award.

We hadn't bargained on Her Majesty being an *X Factor* fan.

She rebuffed all attempts to knight him, even when Gordon Brown threatened to cut her Tupperware allowance. The Archbishop of Canterbury, a *Strictly* fan, had been asked to mediate and had managed to get Len Goodman a CBE. 'It's the best I can do. She's quite determined,' he reported back to Brown. 'I've never seen her like this, except when Jedward lost out to Olly Murs in last year's *X Factor* quarter-finals.'

So when the call came re. the Queen's Speech I jumped at it.

If I'm honest, I did find Dizzee Rascal a little difficult to work with initially. We are, you might say, from different sides of the tracks. Don't get me wrong, he's a nice bloke, but he wears his trousers very low, exposing his pants, as is the fashion – perfectly acceptable at a nightclub, MTV awards ceremony or Rotary Club annual dinner, but quite inappropriate when penning a monarch's national Yuletide address.

'Mash up! Dis am da Queen!' Her Majesty yelled at the top of her voice, throwing shapes like I'd never seen an eighty-two-year-old make since Nan caught her thumb in the washer-dryer.

'That's the royal jelly kicking in,' said Mum, nudging me, convinced that Her Majesty was serviced by bees.

'I liked the speech, and so did a lot of people, judging by the ratings,' I said to Rebekah when she called.

'S'pose you're right,' she said, kind of giving up on the idea of any potential controversy. 'But how the hell am I gonna fill this flaming paper?'

'Bigger cartoons?' I said, and she ran off to look into it.

Mum takes me to one side and asks me to go over how *Jools Holland's Hootenanny* works again. 'I don't understand, you're either there or you're not there,' she says, a look of panic on her face.

I give her a squirt out of the wine box, and before long she is asleep.

Burgers and leftover Jimmy Hill chin juice for dinner.

January 4th

I should explain that I am living with my mother in The Close in Bexhill while work is being carried out on a property I purchased during the great house-price slump of 1989. It has been a long project and that's partly because I really want it to be right and will not be rushed, but also because, if I'm honest, I really like living with my mum, even though she has on occasion tried to get me to leave.

The thing is, I've got it really good at The Close. I've got my own lockable room, decorated just how I like – magnolia over woodchip wallpaper – plus I've added those little personal touches: a free-standing shelving unit, the Kadvar from IKEA; a Postzin – that's a low table; a Malik – that's a lamp; and a Stachybotrys chartarum – that's a patch of mould on the ceiling that I need to get looked at.

Since the purchase Channel 4 have got interested, and I'm now doing the project as part of their series *Grand Designs*, presented by Kevin McCloud. It's a converted windmill just down the coast near Dungeness in Kent, and my plan is to convert it back into a windmill, then convert it into a fully functioning railway station.

I know what you're thinking: 'Why the intermediary "working windmill" stage? Why not convert it straight into a station?' Well, I'll use the electricity generated by the rotating blades to power the tools for the work.

The first stage was supposed to have been completed by Christmas, but the last time I went down it didn't look any different to me at all. I couldn't get in because I hadn't brought the key for the padlock. Every time I phone the builder I can hear flamenco dancing in the background and he says it's inconvenient to talk. Kevin spends his time sniggering at me, like he does, and saying, 'What was your budget again, Harry?'

No doubt, as Kevin says, 'it'll be great telly' when it comes out.

Mum and I share the house with Uncle Bob. He's not

really my uncle, but Mum encouraged me to call him that after Dad died. I was never really sure what their relationship entailed, and now Uncle Bob very rarely comes out of his room. When he does, he insists on clinging to a shopping trolley full of his stuff – bundles of magazines, rolls of gauze, a selection of ladies' knickers and a tin of pineapple chunks. We only really see him for twenty minutes at Christmas. This year he came down to get his present, had a mince pie and a snowball, then was back up to his room to watch his VHSs of *Countryfile*. Mum leaves his dinner outside his bedroom door. As she points out, he has tea- and coffee-making facilities in his room, and every three months she'll force a small bar of soap under the door. He has a sink, so God only knows what he gets up to in that. Certainly not shaving – his beard is long and knotted, like his hair.

When probed, Mum says she met him at a pub quiz thirty-three years ago. There seemed to be an intellectual bond, so she invited him in for a nightcap and he'd never gone home. Then she got bored of him and her love turned to pity as the break-up sent him into a downward spiral of madness and needless eBay purchases – sometimes he's watching thirty or forty different items at a time. At one time the doorbell seemed to be going constantly with recorded deliveries and parcels sent from all four corners of the globe. But not recently, no, not since his feedback turned 97 per cent negative. Now pretty much no one on eBay will give him the time of day.

Mum suggested last night that we try and get Uncle Bob out of the house and into some sort of warden-controlled flat.

'Warden-controlled?' I said. 'You mean, prison?'

'No!' she laughed. 'Somewhere that'll keep an eye on him, make sure he's OK so he's not a danger to himself – the sort of things we can't really do here with our limited facilities. And it would also have the added benefit of freeing up that room and getting him off our backs for good.'

'You sentimental old fool!' I said, and dived for the *Thompson's Directory* and started looking up local warden-controlled accommodation.

January 5th

I get a phone call from the controller of ITV Peter Fincham. The ratings for the Queen's Speech were so high that they have offered her a series: twelve shows on a Saturday tea time after *You Been Framed Yet?* and *Do Animals Always Make the Funniest Injuries?*

She's said yes on condition that me and Dizzee write it.

'Whaddya say, H?' says Peter F. 'You on board? Queenie wants it.'

I'm reminded that this is the bloke who quit the BBC over the trailer for that Queen documentary in which, by editing the footage in a certain way, she was seen apparently pushing photographer Annie Leibovitz into the path of an oncoming bus.

'I'll get back to you,' I say, bouncing on Amanda's left-over trampet.

I phone Dizzee. 'Not sure, H, it's a big commitment, innit?' he says. 'And what happens if her voice gives out?'

'Strepsils?' I venture, looking at the dog, which is still dragging Mum, who is awake now but clutching onto the plastic dog bed with all her might as he swings her around, the hard plastic cutting into the glossy wood floor.

'Nah, I done the speech, got her through that. She ain't up to a series, blud, and for that reason I'm out.'

He was right, it had been a nightmare getting her match fit. Her upper body was really strong but her thighs and calves were way out of shape, and we'd had to get Madonna in to really work on them using electric-shock pads. Madge would connect Her Majesty up to these gel pads – two on each leg – and bounce around to her hit song 'Into the Groove', and on every third beat she'd activate the pads. Her Majesty's legs would shoot out and Madonna would try to jump over them. Then me and Dizzee had a go. Then the Emperor of Japan, over on a state visit, wanted a go, but we could all see the breach in protocol and called time on the session, but it was fun while it lasted.

'Sorry, Peter, it's a "no" from me,' I say to Finchy, who I can hear choking back a sob. 'Why don't you try Alexei Sayle and Andy Abraham, the singing bin man from *X Factor*?'

'Hey, that's not a bad idea!' he says, brightening. 'Did you get your Christmas present?'

'Yes, loved it, thanks.'

'Well, I know you like tin frogs and jazz, so when I saw the tin-frog jazz band at my local garden centre it had your name written all over it.'

'Yes, they're great.'

'Where are they now?'

'Um, they're by the pond, Peter.'

'Cool! I'd love to see a photo! Can you send me one?'

'Sure. Listen, I've got to go now.'

This is a problem. The fact is I do like tin frogs and jazz, but there was something about that tin-frog jazz band that gave me the creeps, and so I sent Mum straight down the charity shop with them.

Hopefully he won't press for the photo.

Chicken supreme for dinner. Mum made a joke about having 'Chicken Diana Ross' tomorrow night. When I asked her what Chicken Diana Ross would be, she faltered and spluttered something about 'touching it in the morning'.

It's not as easy as it looks, this humour lark.

January 6th

Received Lenny's schedule from his agent, and he's in *Othello* at the West Yorkshire Playhouse in Leeds. There is a scene in the third act where he kneels and laments the loss of his Desdemona, which would be perfect for me and Duffy, so I contact her and we agree to meet there on his knees next Wednesday.

I send off for the entry forms for the Duke of Edinburgh Bronze Award. It seems the only way I'm going to get it now is under my own steam.

Chicken and noodle soup for dinner, which I have to spray into Mum's mouth using a water pistol as she is still being dragged around by the dog. Pretty successful, until a noodle blocks the nozzle.

January 7th

Spent the morning trying to get that noodle out of my water pistol's nozzle. I thought a paper clip would do it, but it had too wide a bore. Tried a needle but could only get the point in. Then, just as I was about to give up and consign the pistol to the dustbin, a butterfly alighted upon the nozzle and licked out the noodle with its long, semi-prehensile tongue. It attempted to fly off, but with its tummy packed full of noodle it must have developed cramp in its wings. Either way, it crashed into the TV, where the static electricity stuck it fast to the screen. The programme playing at that moment was *Bear Watch* (Bill Oddie watches a pride of bears as they hang around outside the flagship Kentucky Fried Chicken store in Marble Arch), just as a bear appeared on the screen in close-up, causing the butterfly to suffer a heart attack and die. I feel guilty about it but I didn't ask the butterfly to get involved, and at the same time I'm very glad to have my water pistol back to normal.

Peter Fincham texted me saying he hadn't received the photo of the tin-frog jazz band *in situ* in the garden yet. He's obviously not going to drop it. I'm going to have to try and get them back.

Breakfast for dinner due to delays.

January 8th

Mahesh the plumber is due round to fix the macerator blade on the toilet. We're not on main drainage and thus have one of these odd toilets that mash up the effluent, allowing its free passage through a narrow-gauge pipe. The poor thing can really only cope with bog paper, and despite a sign on the cistern to that effect, during the holiday season Mum tried to flush down a chocolate brazil. No one is really sure why, but when pressed she claims she was 'putting the system through its paces' so she could 'find out what its true boundaries are'.

Mahesh works for a company called Zen Plumbers, a group of Jain Buddhists who have got together and formed a plumbers' co-operative under the slogan 'We fix your pipes without killing a living thing'. They walk everywhere because they believe wheeled vehicles inevitably squash bugs (or, in Mum's case, wing toddlers! But that's a different story . . .). The combination of the heavy tools and the walking everywhere does mean that the time slot they offer you is between 9 a.m. and 6 p.m. over three days. But we've never had a problem with any of their work.

Went to the boot fair and bought a two-thousand-piece jigsaw of Peckham. I've never been to Peckham and thought this the perfect and safest way of acquainting myself with the colourful London borough made famous by the TV sitcom *Only Fools and Horses,* which I've never seen either.

I've found myself thinking about that poor butterfly. Mum says it probably didn't suffer, but what is a worse way to go than dying of fear? God only knows what went through its tiny mind as the giant image of a bear reared up towards it as it lay helpless on the TV screen. I hope it was quick.

Mahesh the plumber arrives just as I'm carrying my sleeping mother from the dog's bed up to her own. He looks knackered and in view of the late hour I offer him the spare

A chocolate Brazil

bed, but he says, 'No, I'll be fine here,' and curls up in the dog's bed. The dog is absolutely furious. What is it about that dog's bed that is so attractive?

Cheesy biscuits and soup for dinner.

January 9th

Take Mahesh the plumber breakfast in bed. Just some toast and a cup of tea, but he does look grateful.

The butterfly is still playing on my mind. Mum says we should perhaps have some sort of funeral which could help to act as closure for me. But what do butterflies favour? Burial or cremation? Mum points out that cremation is easier and spears the little critter on a pin, turns the gas ring on and sticks it over the flame.

At this point Mahesh walks into the kitchen brandishing a half-macerated chocolate brazil and stands open-mouthed at the scene before him: Mum with a flaming butterfly on a pin, the air thick with burning butterfly flesh. He bursts into tears and starts to flail his bare back with a length of copper pipe. I tried to explain but, to be honest, as I started the story it did sound a little far-fetched, even to me.

We are now blacklisted by the Zen Plumbers. The macerator is, however, back to normal, and I've hidden the choccy brazils.

Vegetarian pasta bake for dinner.

January 10th

Duffy has been in contact. She has managed to get backstage passes for *Lenny Henry's Othello Show*, and he has given permission for us to meet on his knees in the second act. It turns out he's not sticking strictly to the original Shakespeare script, hence the retitling. The principal difference is that he's play-ing Othello *and* Desdemona and thus ends up killing himself. The role of Iago is being taken by Kermit the frog. Listen, I've always rated Kermit's acting and I think he could bring a lot to the role, but it's led to a lot of discussion in the broadsheet press about whether it's right for an essentially green actor to 'white up' and play a Caucasian character. I don't have a problem with it personally. If Lenny's cool with it, then so am I. For the first time, Kermit is attempting to act without sticks attached to his hands, so it'll be quite a show. There is a disco at the end too, which is another way it differs from the original.

Great to have the bog working on full power again.

Turkey twizzlers and McCain oven chips for dinner.

January 11th

Am having difficulty finding the corners to the Peckham jigsaw. I've got two of them but the other two seem to be missing. Is it worth continuing with the rest of it? Mum says I should just cut the picture on the front of the box up into two thousand pieces for spares, but then the pieces I have got would be more likely to fall out of the box and get lost. She suggests that I should go to Peckham to see if the two remaining corners are in the positions they should be on the jigsaw. While I can see that this is extremely unlikely, there is something so profoundly elegant about the idea that I resolve to take a trip out there tomorrow, but I need to get the rest of the puzzle done so I can use it as a map.

The dog gets home from work and seems a little distracted,

and if I didn't know better I'd say he was depressed. The fur around his eyes is wet, which suggests to me that he has been crying. When I ask him about it, he says, 'You see things on this job that others don't, and it's hard.'

He's very buttoned-up for a golden retriever and just won't talk about his experiences on the job.

'It helps to talk sometimes,' I say, but he just shrugs and walks over to his bed. 'Has Mum been in my bed again?' he asks. 'It's just that there's loads of grey hairs in it.'

It's true, Mum has been using the bed in the afternoons when he's not there and has moulted into it. 'She knows I'm allergic,' he says, sneezing.

'Guzzentheit!' I cry.

'Don't change the subject,' he says.

I tell him I'll have a word with her about it.

Leftover vegetarian pasta bake for dinner, Greek yoghurt for pud.

January 12th

Brought up the subject of the dog's bed with Mum over breakfast, and she flew off the handle. She says she likes the bed and if he's not using it, where's the harm? I suggest that

Dog's Bed in situ
under the stairs

we buy a new dog's bed that she could have solely for her own use, but she says that what she likes about this dog's bed is that it belongs to a real dog, so it's more authentic.

I suggest to her that she might be suffering from a cuckoo complex, but when she asks me what I mean by that, I can't really answer because I'm not sure myself. I think it's something to do with her lying in another's nest but I clearly need to firm up the idea.

She agrees to take a look at the bed issue once I have formulated the cuckoo-complex idea properly.

How come I've come out of this with extra work to do? I've got enough on at the moment without having to research and write up a paper on the cuckoo complex. I'm starting to wish I hadn't got involved.

Stephen Page from Faber, the publishers, phones, saying he's enjoying the diary so far (that's a relief, as I've cashed the cheque in the town!). He says he particularly likes the Christmas stuff and suggests I 'weld it more to the diary format – you know, the changes in the seasons, the public holidays. It might just help to punctuate it, orientate people and remind people that it's supposed to be a diary.'

I suppose he's got a point.

As it is the holy day of The Circumcision of Our Lord, me and Mum celebrate in the usual way – a cucumber sandwich and a gherkin in front of *Antiques Roadshow*.

A Gherkin

January 13th

Set out for Peckham to try and find the corners to the 2,000-piece Peckham jigsaw puzzle. I'm using the actual jigsaw as a map and am having to stop to complete the next bit before I can work out where to go next. Then, as I get on a bus which I believe should take me to the bottom-left corner of Peckham, we are bus-jacked. A group of about five youths who'd been sitting on the back seat started going amongst the passengers demanding their wallets and mobile phones. When they got to me and saw the puzzle they were immediately intrigued. Having been brought up on video games and internet porn they'd never seen one before. I explained how a puzzle works, and they started fighting over it, each trying to identify a piece of Peckham with cries of 'Yo! That's my crib!' and 'Look, there's the library, innit!'

In the ensuing fight the jigsaw became upturned, and they lost interest and got off the bus. The problem was, I was stuck in Peckham with no means of finding my way home. I had to book into a bed-and-breakfast and start the puzzle all over again. This time I think I'll leave the sky to last.

Starburger and chips for tea.

January 14th

I wake up a little disorientated, before realising that in the night I have sleepwalked back to Starburger, and so I immediately order a fried breakfast. The manager asks me to leave as I am naked. I try to fashion a pair of pants out of two napkins, but my origami skills are not what they were and somehow being naked with a napkin around my waist just seems to draw attention to my indecent state. The owner's mother kept shouting 'Nookie! Nookie!' and tried to drag me upstairs, but I managed to run out of the shop towards the bed-and-breakfast, leaving her with a napkin in her hand.

I can't find the bed-and-breakfast because I haven't got the puzzle. Peckham is beginning to wake up and my nudity is raising a few eyebrows. I grab a black bin liner from outside the Sue Ryder shop and retire to a back alley to see if there is anything suitable for me to wear. It doesn't contain a tin-frog jazz band but there is a trilby and a scarf. I tear two holes in the top of the trilby and put my legs through them, and then loop the scarf under the hat and pull it up and tie it round the back of my neck to keep it in place.

When I get back to the bed-and-breakfast the landlady takes one look at me and bursts into tears, and between sobs explains that the hat and scarf belonged to her dead husband and she'd only just felt able to part with them and take them down the charity shop. I shift awkwardly from one leg to the other for a while, which tilts the trilby from side to side and just attracts attention to it. I make my excuses, go to my room, get changed and leave. On the way out I notice a small triangle of blue. It's a piece of a jigsaw puzzle, a corner of sky. It could have come from any puzzle. I'll never know.

I get a black cab home and watch *The Apprentice*. My money's on the shrill one.

January 15th

The phone rings, and it's Peter Fincham explaining that the tin-frog jazz band he sent me as a Christmas gift is, in fact,

The Tin-Frog Jazz Band

part of a rogue batch. The paint on the frogs is toxic and will kill all life if positioned next to a pond, which is kind of the obvious place to position the tin-frog jazz band; indeed, the photo on the front of the packet shows them in exactly that setting, along with a grey-haired bloke who looks a lot like Derek Nimmo and a Home Counties wife in a head-scarf pointing and throwing their heads back in laughter. Of course, I chose to position my tin-frog jazz band in a black bin liner outside a charity shop, but he doesn't know that. I explain to Peter that I have moved the frogs next to the down-stairs shower cubicle, at which he becomes extremely agitated and says that if they become wet and a child or dog licks the frog clarinet player, then death could ensue. I promise to move the amphibious tin musicians and return them to him. Oh, what a tangled web, eh?

Butternut squash and chips for dinner.

January 16th

Terrible indigestion in the night. I don't know whether it was the butter, the nuts or the squash, but I was burping like a polar bear from one in the morning right up to breakfast. Got up and took some Rennies – the indigestion tablets designed in the neo-classical style by Scottish designer Charles Rennie Mackintosh – which helped a bit. In the end I went downstairs and watched the News 24 channel on the BBC. I'd never watched it at night before but obviously news-wise there's pretty much nothing going on because it's the night and for a couple of hours the presenters, Bill Turnbull and Sophie Raworth, did the usual filler stuff, repeating the news from the day before and getting Melinda Messenger on to review the morning's papers. Then, as the hours ticked by, they got more and more desperate. Bill phoned his mum and asked her to recite a poem, Sophie attempted to predict the next day's news by reading the tea leaves in the bottom of her cup, and then the floor manager was dragged in front of the camera to do a magic trick with three cups and a ball. Then Sophie and Bill played snap for forty-five minutes.

It was actually pretty gripping TV. When Bill won, I found myself shouting at the TV, 'Best of three! Best of three!'

It turns out that the switchboard was flooded with calls, and as day broke the fact that they'd played snap live on TV had become news in itself – and was the lead story on the BBC's rival station Sky News. It was one of those rare 'water-cooler moments' that TV execs crave, even though people don't really have those water coolers over here like they do in America. A better term would probably be 'tea-pot moment'.

January 17th

I was just nodding off when Peter Fincham phoned, asking

me what did I know about this snap phenomenon and do I know the rules of snap, and as one of ITV's family-friendly entertainers, would I be interested in fronting snap live on TV? I tell him I'll get back to him.

Later on, Bill and Sophie appear as the main story on the BBC lunchtime news, along with slow-motion highlights of the earlier game (basically the bits where one or other of them said 'Snap!'). The pair announce that they will be playing snap again tonight at the same time. You can see the look of naked jealousy in the eye of lunchtime presenter Kate Silverton.

My interest in snap suddenly revived, I ask Mum to get me a pack of snap cards from Martin's the newsagent's, but when she gets back she says they've sold out, and missing the point rather she'd bought me some Torville and Dean Panini stickers and the album.

I stay up and watch snap live with Sophie and Bill, but it was virtually exactly the same game as last night's. The 'Snaps!' came in the same place and Bill won. Someone had forgotten to shuffle the pack.

Start sticking the Torville and Dean stickers into the book willy-nilly just to keep Mum happy. Well, no one's going to check, are they?

Red snapper in batter and sugar-snap peas for dinner.

January 18th

The overnight ratings have come in for last night's snap game and they are the highest for a news channel since the Queen Mother's arm-wrestle fiasco.

There are three messages on my machine from Peter

Fincham asking me to get back to him. I phone him back straight away and explain to him the rules of snap.

'So it's a bit like spot the difference, is it?' he says.

'Kind of . . .' I reply.

The BBC announce that they will be moving *Live Snap!* to Saturday prime time and that it will be hosted by Graham Norton, with a panel of judges consisting of John Barrowman, Claire Sweeney and Christopher Lee (who it turns out wrote a book about snap in the sixties).

'It's clear that we've missed the boat as far as snap goes,' I explain to Peter.

'How about spot the difference live?' he suggests.

I can't really get my head round how this would work.

'Well,' he explains, 'we have a group of celebrities and we show them pictures that are subtly different. They have to spot the difference and stand to win small amounts of money for a charity of their choice, especially children's ones.'

'Yes, I know how spot the difference works. What I meant was, how would that be entertaining?'

There is a long silence.

'OK, not pictures but actual people.'

'Spot the difference between the actual people?'

'Yes,' he says, 'twins, identical twins dressed pretty much the same, only with subtle differences that celebrities have to spot in order to win money for their charitable interests.'

'I think it's got real tea-pot potential,' I say.

'Eh?'

'You know a tea-pot moment, like the American water-cooler moment,' I say, trying to get my own phrase off the ground.

'Oh, right, yes.'

'Let's make a pilot,' I say, and hang up.

I love his dogged enthusiasm.

Feel bad about the Torville and Dean stickers and try to steam them off, but the paper tears and the stickers lose their adhesiveness. I use Pritt Stick and put the stickers (although they're not really 'stickers' now) in their proper places in the book.

Chicken with flaked almonds for dinner, marzipan fruit for afters.

January 19th

Really must try and track down that tin-frog jazz band (Finchy texted first thing with an 'Any news?').

'Perhaps they're on tour with *Jools Holland's Hootenanny*,' says Mum, rather unhelpfully.

I explain that while Jools *is* on tour, it is with his big band and not with the Hootenanny show, which only occurs a week before New Year's Eve.

'Maybe the frogs are part of his big band.'

Maybe, Mum, but probably not, but I put a call in to Jools's manager anyway.

A representative from Panini, the sticker company, comes round before lunch. He says he's doing random checks on people who had bought the Torville and Dean album and asks to see what I've done. While he disapproves of my use of an alternative adhesive, he is broadly pleased with the positioning of the stickers and enters 'satisfactory' next to my name on his database. That was a close one! If he'd come round yesterday it would have been a very different story!!

Dog got home from work last night and was absolutely furious to see Mum still asleep in his bed. I'm going off the idea of a cuckoo complex now and erring more towards a Goldilocks complex, but don't know what the parameters of that are either. More work!

The dog started on its bed-dragging ritual once again, with Mum holding on for dear life and me squirting it with mint sauce.

Went down the charity shop on the high street but there's no sign of the tin jazz frogs. I enquire within, but the proprietor is nowhere to be seen. I notice two old ladies hovering behind a bead curtain over which a sign hangs bearing the legend 'Staff Only Beyond This Point'. I hang around for a while but no one comes to my aid. I start calling out 'I say!' and 'Hello?', but there's no response, so I start smashing plates. I suppose I'd smashed about twenty before the curtain was pulled aside and Auntie came out to investigate.

'What were you doing back there, Auntie?' I ask.

'Sorting through the best stuff, of course,' she says, beckoning me in. 'Come!'

What met my eyes was little short of a second-hand Aladdin's cave: Fern Britton fitness videos vied for shelf space with Dale Winton's autobiography; a Bullworker sat next to a pair of size-eight Ugg boots which looked brand-new, a dress shirt – size 14-inch collar, still in its cellophane – and a child's dolly, its hair matted by play.

'What do you do with it all, Aunt?' I ask her.

'We take it up the boots, the boot fair on Cooden Common.'

Her accomplice nods as she stuffs a wig into a brogue.

'Don't worry about her, she's brain-damaged,' says the Aunt.

I ask whether she's seen the tin frogs.

'Still in the packet?' she asks.

'That's right.'

'Sold them last Saturday at the boot. A kindly man, lives at Lower Dicker,' she says.

At this rate I will never get any work done. As Auntie moved in for a kiss I made my excuses and left.

Dog has been crying again. Might have a word with the vet about it.

Stuffed vine leaves and tzatziki for dinner.

January 20th

Not sure how to get mint-sauce stains out of carpet tiles. Mum seems sure that you use horseradish, but it just seems to make it worse. 'I meant mustard,' she says, back-tracking, so in the end I take up the carpet tile and swap it with an unstained one from under the sofa.

'Leave the jigsaw of a carpet alone,' says Mum.

After the dog went to work this morning I crept into his bed to see what the attraction was, and before I knew it I was fast asleep. I dreamt that all the world were holding hands for just one day, but rather than living in harmony what actually happened – in the dream anyway – was no one got any work done, leading to a stock-market crash, the meltdown of several nuclear power stations, a huge build-up of casualties in accident and emergency departments, and a big rise in cases of leprosy.

An odd dream, even for me, but it is comfy that bed. I start thinking that maybe there's a way to adapt it for humans.

I set to designing one using a blue crayon and swatches of material snipped from the hem of some of Mum's summer dresses (it'll be months before she realises) and phone up the BBC for an application form for the inventor show *Dragons' Den*. There's not really been any advances in bed technology since the four posts were cut off to save wood back in the nineteenth century. This could be massive! Maybe I shouldn't go on *Dragons' Den* because what if they will only back me for a large percentage of the business? Or what if I have to deal with two or three of the dragons sharing the business, or what if none of them want to invest and belittle me, tarnishing the product in the process? I spend some time trying to come up with a name for the product. Harry Hill Man-Bed? No, too gender-specific – I want women to enjoy the dog bed too. Human Dog-Sleeper – no, too technical sounding. Homo Slumber Device – too gay sounding. Then I stumble upon it – the God Bed, yes! It's brilliant because (1) it sounds like it's been designed by a higher power, that it is infallible. In fact, I think this should be the strapline – 'The God Bed – a design made in heaven'; (2) it's the word 'dog' back to front; and (3) it suggests that it's like sleeping on a cloud.

I'm getting so excited about the God Bed that I'm thinking, 'No, stuff *Dragons' Den*! They don't deserve it! I'm going straight to Richard Branson.'

I send off for the *Dragons' Den* forms anyway, figuring I'll only settle for fifty thousand and 5 per cent of the business, and no, Deborah Meaden, I don't care if you are involved in the leisure industry in the south-west, I'm not popping corks with you for a percentage point more.

I think on balance I'd better keep the God Bed drawings

hidden from the dog. I don't want to upset him further.

I get several texts throughout the morning from Peter F asking whether he can send a bike for the frogs, which I ignore.

Set out after lunch and tour Lower Dicker on Mum's disability scooter, scouring the gardens for the jazz frogs. All I see is a man wearing my hat, but when I challenge him he explains that it is not my hat but a similar hat and is able to produce the receipt as proof.

With battery getting low on the scooter I head for home.

Spend the afternoon doing a little light research on the life cycle of the cuckoo on the computer. What a fascinating bird!

Dog doesn't come home until very late, and I swear I can smell booze on his breath.

There's a message on the answer machine from Jools Holland's manager asking me to call him back.

Gala pie and salad for dinner.

January 21st

Mum says the blue-crayon drawing of the God Bed looks a bit amateurish. She's got a point. What I really need is a photograph of someone in a very large dog bed, asleep. I phone up the Great Dane Society of Great Britain and ask if they know where I can get hold of a big moulded-plastic dog bed, ideally blue. Secrecy is of the utmost importance if I'm to stop a rival inventor from beating me to it, so I put on a voice, that of Trevor McDonald. 'Hello, this is Trevor McDonald,' I say. 'How do your dogs sleep at night?'

'Why, what they done?' comes the reply.

'No, I don't mean that they might be kept awake by a guilty conscience. I mean physically, what receptacle do they use? Some sort of giant dog bed, I suppose?'

'Is this Deborah Meaden?' says the voice.

Oh my God! I think, she's onto me already!

'No. Trevor, Sir Trevor McDonald.'

'As I told Debs, the thing with the Great Dane is that you can't get a conventional moulded-plastic dog bed to fit, so most of us make up a human bed in the spare room, or there's the sofa bed, which requires a little more manual dexterity.'

There's that name again – Manuel Dexterity.

'Thank you, *Señor*, and good night.'

I hang up. My head is reeling . . . How could Deborah have found out so quickly? A mole at the den? I need to work fast.

I call Jools Holland's manager, but it goes straight to answer machine.

Mum asks me to give her a hand dismantling Amanda Holden's trampet. It's bad luck to leave it up into February.

Fish cakes and green beans for mains, candy floss for puds.

January 22nd

Went swimming at the leisure centre, and Susan Hampshire was in the training pool with a dolphin, in an attempt to cure her dyslexia. As they swam round the pool she tried to read from a waterproof book, and the dolphin would follow shouting out the correct version.

I chatted to the dolphin in the changing room afterwards and he expressed his misgivings about the process. He's not convinced that it's working. I ask him why he's got involved, and then he tells me how much she's paying him. He explains that it's much more than he ever got acting.

'There's just no work about at the moment, not since computer-generated imagery took off. I mean, why work with a real dolphin when some computer can make one for you that doesn't communicate through a system of high-pitched whistles and squeaks and doesn't smell of fish?' he says, via a system of high-pitched whistles and squeaks, while simultaneously smelling of fish. I felt for the guy.

'Have you got a twin brother?' I ask.

He nods.

'And can you play snap?'

He nods again.

'Hmmmm. Put your showreel in the post and I'll see what I can do.'

I leave him trying to retrieve his pound coin from the locker with his pectoral fins.

Croque monsieur for lunch, croque madame for tea.

January 23rd

I try to book my train tickets to Leeds for the *Lenny Henry Othello Show* using National Rail Network Enquiries, but keep getting a machine. I don't like talking to these phone machines. They have that funny intonation, putting the emphasis in the wrong places: 'Where are you going TO? On what DAY are you RETURNING?'

But I do need the tickets and would really like to get seats with a table so I can pretend to work on the way up. Quite by chance I find that blowing very hard down a trombone into

34

the phone automatically puts you through to an operator, and I purchase the tickets with my credit card in the usual way. I suggest you try that yourself next time.

Trevor Nunn called to ask whether we could meet to discuss 'an exciting new project'. He won't go into any more detail other than saying that 'Imogen might play the lead'.

Monkfish stew for dinner.

January 24th

I read in *Broadcast*, the trade magazine for the TV industry, that the Queen has been poached by Sky TV for a new series of speeches and 'other tomfoolery' that's being written by Richard Blackwood and Charlie Brooker, from that Channel 4 show and those two BBC3 shows. 'Good luck to 'em,' I think, because she was a bit tricky to work with. Not being allowed to speak to her until she speaks to you may be fine at a garden party but not at a creative meeting for a muck-about show.

Latest on the God Bed: Mum says I should try to get a baby or a midget, dress him up as a man and photograph him in the dog bed. That way it will make the dog bed look bigger – as long as there's nothing else in the shot to suggest the real scale.

I pop round to see my mate Matt Bradstock, who, while not strictly a midget, does just nudge five foot. He's not keen. He says that people locally have only just started accepting him as being normal-sized, and a photo of him in a dog bed will just focus their attention back onto his height again. I offer to pay him seventy-five quid and raise it gradually in increments of five pounds until eventually I reach my top limit of £115. 'No, sorry, mate, not this time, not for a hundred and fifteen quid.'

I can see his point and we part on good terms, still friends.

But where am I going to get hold of a baby in Bexhill? Where the average age is over seventy?

'You could try going to Africa, like Madonna,' Mum suggests. But I haven't the time, what with Deborah Meaden on my tail.

'There was a girl in the village had one!' she says. 'She usually parks it up in a buggy outside Martin's the newsagent's first thing on a Wednesday while she does her lottery.'

'That doesn't give me long,' I say, looking at my watch, which bears the legend 'WEDNESDAY'.

'It's OK, she has a complicated lottery-number-selection process,' she says. It seems that like a lot of Bexhill locals she relies on birds' entrails.

I head straight down to The Parade on the disability scooter and stake out Martin's the newsagent's. I park up behind a Wall's ice-cream sign and crouch low in the seat of the scooter, peering over the top only occasionally to check for my quarry. Sure enough, at eleven on the dot along troops the baby lady. She parks up the buggy, retrieves a dead wren from her shopping bag and enters the newsagent's. I head for the buggy, pull the baby to me, do a quick three-point turn and head back to Mum's. I text her on the way and ask her to sterilise a bottle and teat.

The baby is as good as gold on the way home, and once ensconced seems even to enjoy being dressed up as a man – starched white shirt, trousers, frock coat, bowler hat and spats

– but will not fall asleep in the dog bed for love nor money! I've got my iPhone on camera setting, and Mum holds the standard lamp at an angle to give it a moody feel, but the little critter is wide awake.

I've got one eye on the time. It won't be long before its mum comes out of the newsagent's, and she'll start to wonder where it is. I try a medley of lullabies. Just as it seems to be nodding off there's a crash as the standard lamp falls to the floor. I look up to see Mum asleep on the rug.

'We need more time!' I cry.

'Let's just keep it,' says Mum, yawning and wiping the sleep from her eyes. 'We haven't had a new baby in the family for ages. Let's just keep this one.'

I know it's wrong but what choice do I have? If the God Bed business takes off, with the money and improved lifestyle that it will bring maybe the baby will one day forgive us.

'Pass the brown sauce, Dad,' says Mum.

'I'm not its dad,' I say.

'But what is Baby to call you then?'

'It'll have to call me Uncle, Uncle Phillip . . .' I say, attaching a teat to the brown sauce and passing it to her.

'Phillip?'

'We must preserve our anonymity, Mum,' I say. 'When we're around the baby it would be best if you call me Phillip and I call you Shirley like on *EastEnders*.'

'Can't I be Peggy?'

'Yes, OK – Peggy.'

'No, Denise.'

'But Denise is black, Mum.'

'I can black up.'

'No,' I say, firmly, 'stick with Peggy, otherwise if you're black and the baby's white it might raise suspicion.'

'It's Chinese though,' says Mum.

'What?!' I say, realising that I hadn't really looked closely at the kid. I peer under its bowler hat and, sure enough, the little swine is Chinese!

'If anyone asks, he's a visiting dignitary!' I bark, snapping the bowler hat back over his head. This is already far too complicated for comfort.

Later, we huddle guiltily in front of the TV as the baby's mother appears on *News South-West* and appeals for any information about her missing offspring, but it's too late. It is done. Our lives are going to be very different from now on.

Jools Holland's manager has left another message, saying something about 'phone tennis'.

Leftover rusks and brown sauce for dinner.

January 25th

Up all night with the baby. Ran out of brown sauce in the early hours and had to go down the petrol station to get a new bottle. They don't sell brown sauce. The lady on the till, who claims to have had a baby herself once and shows me the scar to prove it, says that a jar of Nutella should tide us over till sunlight if we water it down.

I water down the Nutella and put it in the brown-sauce bottle, but there's no fooling this baby. It pushes it away and screams at the top of its voice what I think is 'HP!', but maybe it's Chinese.

I think I have agreed to meet Jools Holland's manager for a game of phone tennis.

Sweet and sour pork and pot noodle for dinner to make Baby feel at home, fortune cookies for afters. Mine said: 'You will need to service your car at some point,' which I thought was a rather safe bet as far as predictions go. Mum's said: '*X Factor* winner will get Christmas number one.'

January 26th

There's a lot of heat around this baby-napping lark of ours and I'm beginning to wish I'd never got involved. Mum and her stupid ideas, eh? Of course, she's loving every minute of it – sewing Polaroids together to make booties, mixing up and sterilising the brown sauce – but it's stopping me from getting any work done. I'm absolutely drop-dead knackered. I've been meaning to fill in this bloomin' *Dragons' Den* form, but every time I get going I fall asleep around page 12. It's a big form. They want all sorts of information off you, things like 'Have you ever bought a pen from Ryman's?', 'Have you ever stayed on one of Deborah Meaden's caravan sites, and if so how did you find the foot-operated tap?' and 'If you were to meet Peter Jones would you be tempted to say, "Never knowingly undersold, eh, Peter?"' It just goes on and on. I suppose the form itself is part of the selection procedure. It sorts out the men from the boys. Only the serious business-men and women get through.

Since Mum and me are lying low and don't want to draw any extra attention we can't really go down the shop to buy nappies, which means that Mum spends most of the day chasing Baby around the house with a wad of cotton wool on a stick. Nightmare.

Findus savoury pancakes for dinner, toasted marshmallows for pud.

Matt Bradstock phones and asks whether the offer of £115 is still open for the dog-bed shoot, and I have to tell him no. Then he starts probing as to who I got instead of him, and I have to flannel him. He wasn't buying it, so I actually had to go round to his place with a flannel and rub his face with it while I retold him the story until he accepted my tissue of lies.

I have another go at the *Dragons' Den* application form and get to page 250 before I realise that I've been filling out a copy of Duncan Bannatyne's autobiography *Banana Time!* and not the form at all. They must have got mixed up. The *Dragons' Den* application form is actually only one side of A4 and just requires your name, the details of your invention and whether or not you would say 'Never knowingly undersold, eh, Peter?' to Peter Jones – which of course I would. Well, you would, wouldn't you?

As I'm filling it in I fall asleep halfway through. I'm afraid I am now associating the idea of the form with the idea of going to sleep.

I wake up. It's dark and I can't get back to sleep. I stay awake till morning, but as it gets light I am so tired that I fall asleep again. I realise that if I carry on like this I will become nocturnal within a couple of days.

I fashion an anti-sleep alarm. I glue a big piece of tin foil to my head with Copydex and attach it to a piece of wire, which in turn is attached to the mains. I attach another piece of wire to a metal tray in front of me, which is also attached to the mains via the standard lamp. The idea is that if I nod off, the tin foil will hit the tray, completing the circuit and turning on the standard lamp, which will wake me up. However, what actually happens is I nod off, my head touches the tray and I get 240 volts through my brain, which does indeed wake me up. It's pretty painful, but you know what? I face the day in a much more cheerful mood.

Mum says she wants a go, but I say no as I believe it will play havoc with her pacemaker and/or hearing aid.

Chicken fritters for main course, banana fritters for pud.

January 28th

Meet Jools Holland's manager for a game of phone tennis and break his serve in the first set, beating him 6–4, 7–6, 4–6, 6–3. He was using a Nokia N97, a slim, lightweight phone, and I an iPhone, broad and flat, and although slower it has a much bigger surface with which to hit the ball. In the locker room afterwards I tackle him about the tin jazz frogs, and he admits that Jools did have them for a while but had given them to Terry Wogan as part of his birthday present.

'But Terry's birthday isn't until August,' I say.

'Yeah, but you know Jools, he likes to get in early, and if you're in the music biz it doesn't hurt to butter up Britain's top breakfast DJ, does it?'

'But he's given up the breakfast show,' I say.

'Eh? Yeah, well, he's still got that show on a Sunday.'

I see what he's getting at now – the tin frogs were not a birthday present at all but a bribe! A bribe to get Terry to play Jools's latest boogie-woogie releases! I can't say I approve, because I don't, but I do have to say that I admire his style!

We arrange to meet some time in the future for a game of TV remote control badminton and go our separate ways.

January 29th

I leave Mum with the baby and head up to the West Yorkshire Playhouse to meet Duffy. On the train I put in a call to Terry Wogan's people to try and track down the jazz frogs, as ITV supremo Peter Fincham just will not let the matter drop. I'm starting to think that maybe there's more to it than he's letting on and resolve to examine the frogs in detail when I get them back.

It's a pleasant enough trip, except someone is sick on me. It was in a tunnel so I can't be sure who it was, but I strongly suspect it was the man sitting next to me. Basically, before we went into the tunnel he didn't smell of sick and when we emerged from the tunnel he did smell of sick. Mind you, so did pretty much everything. I was in a reserved seat as well. Fortunately I was wearing a broad-brimmed hat which I was able to scrunch up and throw out of the window.

I book into a Travelodge on the outskirts of town. I've got the Baywatch Suite – not because it has a surfing theme or has anything to do with the long-running American coastguard drama, but because it has a lovely view overlooking the loading bay for Marks and Spencer.

It's fascinating to see the comings and goings of that great, long-running store. Lorries bringing in produce from all over the country, everything from food to undergarments – fascinating! I watch for about an hour, I suppose, then suddenly realise that Lenny's show is due to start in twenty minutes! I run from the hotel and stow away on the back of an M&S sandwich truck, which I figure will take me straight into town. Exhausted from the day's travails I fall asleep amongst the soft, downy baps and plump, cushiony wraps. When I awake I glance at my watch – half past nine! I've missed the first half completely! Fortunately Lenny's knees do not make their appearance until late in the second half, so there's still time. I pop my head up above the tailgate and try to get my bearings. What can I see . . . trees of green . . . red roses too – oh Christ, I'm in a Louis Armstrong song! No, hang on, there's a sign – 'Next lyric eight bars'. I bide my time, and when he starts on the instrumental break I make a jump for it. I hit the hard shoulder and roll across the grass verge and down a hill. Gaining momentum I roll through the outskirts of Leeds, and by parting my legs slightly I am able to steer a course towards the Playhouse. I roll up the steps of the theatre and into the stalls just as Lenny is taking his bow. I fight my way to the front of the stage, my head spinning.

'Dizzy?' says Lenny.

'No, Duffy,' says I.

'She left,' he says. 'She seemed pretty upset. You staying for the disco?'

'Um, no, I'd better get back. Did she say where she was going?' I ask.

'Not sure, but I know she has to fill in the breakfast-menu

card and hang it on the back of her hotel-room door before 2 a.m. if she's to get breakfast in her room,' he says.

I return to the hotel, crestfallen.

Am I never to meet the gravel-voiced Welsh songbird again?

January 30th

Forgot to annotate my breakfast-in-room menu card before 2 a.m, and although I did receive my complimentary copy of the *Independent*, no food was forthcoming and I was forced to trawl the corridor looking for leftovers on trays. I managed to get together half a croissant and a sausage. Inserting the sausage into the half croissant I invented what I call my French sausage roll – every cloud has a silver lining. I dash off a letter of explanation to Delia Smith – it's just the sort of thing she might go for.

Rather a miserable journey back. Sat next to that same bloke who was sick on me on the way up so couldn't really relax, particularly in tunnels. I resorted to sitting with a torch, and every time we went into a tunnel I turned it on and shone it at his mouth.

Get a text from Duffy saying 'Sorry to have missed you, had a nice breakfast in bed. Great show – Lenny was super but Kermit seemed a bit stiff and hardly moved his arms at all! LOL. Duffy.'

So she seems cool about it. I'll call her in the week and see if I can arrange a meeting nearer to home.

Wogan's people call and say that they don't know anything about any tin jazz frogs and suggest I back off. Their tone is aggressive and out of all proportion to a kindly request for information about a misplaced gift. It's like they're hiding something. I resolve to take a trip out to Wogan's estate at some point.

When I get home I notice that the baby has got very big since we took him on. I suppose it's because I've been away. I check on the bottle of brown sauce and realise we've been feeding it double portions. We can't halve them now because it screams at us and rattles its high chair.

Large chocolate-chip cookie and instant coffee for lunch, maxi pack of crisps for pudding.

January 31st

Much excitement in da house as Simon Cowell calls and asks me whether I'd be interested in being a judge on the new season of the *X Factor*. I say of course I would, and he asks me to come in for an audition.

'An audition?' I say.

He says, 'Yes, I've asked five different people to audition as a judge in front of 150,000 singers of variable ability and mental agility. If they judge that your judgements are fair, you will be made an *X Factor* judge.'

This doesn't sound quite right to me, but heck, he's Simon Cowell! You do what he wants because he can break you in America.

Hot dogs and fries main course, banana split for pudding – big portions like they do in America to get me used to it.

February

The O₂ Arena

February 1st

Wake up in a warm glow, thrilled at Simon Cowell's interest in me, but before I can get too excited I have a little unfinished business down in Maidenhead . . .

I head down to Wogan's prime Buckinghamshire waterfront estate. I park the car half a mile or so away, cover it in brushwood to camouflage it and make my way by red canoe down the Thames. The current is so strong that I am swept out to sea and end up renting a flat in Panama for six years under a different name! Only kidding! I scull quietly, hugging the riverbank, with just the occasional plop of an oar hitting the water until I yell at a couple of kids to 'Quit throwing oars at me!'

Hugging the reed bed for cover and using one of the hurled oars I paddle silently up towards his jetty. Suddenly I hear the loud roar of an outboard motor and turn to see hooded security guards armed with automatic weapons head out into open water on high-speed hovercraft!

'Damn those oar-throwing kids,' I think. 'They must work for Wogan!' Is there no one in Maidenhead that isn't on Wogan's payroll?

I scuttle the canoe and release Mum's disability scooter from the hold. The river is just deep enough for me to ride along the river bed and be completely submerged except for the last inch of my snorkel. I travel underwater enjoying the cooling breeze on the distal end of my exposed pipe.

I'm thirty yards from Wogan's jetty when I hear the guards – they have discovered my canoe. A siren wails and helicopters take to the air – that tin-frog jazz band is obviously pretty important to the Irish émigré and one-time voice of Eurovision!

The water starts to get shallow and I trundle up the softly sloping shoreline. As my head, then shoulders appear above the water I stow my snorkel and do up the zip that houses it and dive into the long reeds that fringe the shoreline, then up and away across the carefully manicured lawn – with a shamrock mowed into it that's only visible from the air. Suddenly the helicopters spot me and swoop down in pursuit, firing rocket grenades and high-explosive air-to-disability-scooter missiles. I weave in and out of the fancy garden furniture dodging the onslaught. Wump! A grenade hits a beautifully appointed gazebo! Bang! There goes the swing seat! Gerbump! A free-standing hammock gets it in the neck. Kaboom! A set of six patio chairs up in smoke. I jump from my craft, allowing it to spin out of control and into an ornamental pond. I roll with the fall and end up under a laburnum bush, and it is there that I wait until morning.

While I'm under there I phone Mum up and ask her to tape *Emmerdale*.

Laburnum-leaf salad for dinner, gobstopper for pud.

As darkness encompasses the huge estate of Britain's most popular breakfast entertainer I crawl from my bush and switch my glasses to night vision and read the paper.

I am woken with a jolt and find myself looking down the end of a .22-gauge walking stick.

'Begorrah, if 'tis not your man Harry Hill!' For it is Mr Terry Wogan himself.

'Drop the cod-Irish accent, Tel,' I say, feeling the brass point of his stick pressing into my nasal septum. 'Where's my tin-frog jazz band?'

'Well, now there's a wee tale for the telling!' he says, lowering his walking aid and offering me his hand. 'Fancy a snorker or two? Lady Helen's firing up the griddle.'

'That's more like it!' I say, and pull on his arm in an attempt to help myself up. Without his stick to balance him the great Celt topples on top of me with a grunt. The two of us writhe around under that laburnum bush for a good three or four minutes until a shadow falls across us.

'So this is what you get up to when me back's turned!' says Lady Helen, proffering a tray of plump Lincolnshire sausies. 'Come! Feast your faces!'

The two of us follow her into the mansion, giggling like two young schoolboys who have just been caught teasing a squirrel.

The next few minutes are a blur of juicy pork stuffed in intestinal casings, ketchup, mustard and, yes, several rounds of toast.

Eventually Terry sits back in his high wicker chair, quaffs a mug of tea, burps and then tells me his story.

'I was born the son of a grocery-store manager in Limerick . . .'

'Not that story, Tel,' I say. 'Just get to the whereabouts of the frogs!'

'Oh! Sorry, yes, of course, those. I gave them back to Jools,' he says. 'They gave me nothing but trouble.'

'Likewise, mate, likewise,' I join in. 'But tell me, Tel, why the secrecy?'

'Come,' he says, and takes me by the hand and leads me through a long passageway hewn from the rock that his house is built on.

'You were wise to build your house on such a rock, Terry,' I say.

'Yes, but it has meant that we're not on main drainage here and so have to use those awful macerator blade things in all the loos.'

We travel down, deep within the bowels of the earth, until eventually we come upon a vast hangar. There in the centre of this high-domed cavern, his body supported by pipes, wires and wheels, is the familiar figure of Jimmy Young.

'You mean . . .'

'Yes, I get all the ideas for my show from Jim here. When he retired I knew that although his body was crumbling, his mind was still incredibly active. I got the idea from watching Davros on *Dr Who*,' says Terry. 'But not a word to anyone. No, Jools has what you seek, but be careful – he will stop at nothing to secure its bounty.'

'Bounty? You mean the jazz frogs contain something precious?'

'Yes,' says the great broadcaster. 'They contain something which will give the holder unlimited appeal to viewers . . . they contain – agh!'

There is the hiss of a blowpipe and the bulky Celt falls forward – dead! Without a moment's thought I kiss him upon his neck and run for my life from the house up the drive and to a waiting disability scooter.

'Quick, Mum, twist your wrist and let's go!'

She smiles grimly.

'I thought there might be trouble with this one,' she says, and with a flash of her copper arthritis bangle we are away.*

February 2nd

Baby spoke its first word today: 'More!' Mum had just finished feeding it, and as she was putting its bowl into the dishwasher he shouted across the room from his high chair. A conventional high chair isn't big enough – it's an armchair raised up on a pile of six wooden pallets, with gaffer tape wrapped round it to keep him in place.

We're trying not to encourage any more words from him as we're worried that once he starts speaking whole sentences he'll spill the beans and land us in pokey.

It turns out that the bird's entrails spoke the truth: the baby's mother has won the lottery with the very ticket she was filling out on the day of the kidnap and has resolved to divert 'as much as it takes' of her winnings into finding 'the evil bastards' that have 'nicked me kid'. We need to be extra careful, but it's difficult with Baby being so big now.

My instinct is to cut our losses and dump the baby with a couple of bottles of sauce on its mum's doorstep late at night, but Mum says no.

Mum has the idea to dress the baby up to look like a man

* Now obviously I've taken a bit of poetic licence with the above description of my trip to Wogan Towers. The facts are less exciting. I went round there and was denied entry. Talking to Sir Terry down the video-entry-phone system he admitted that he'd been given the tin-frog jazz band, and while he'd quite liked them Lady W hadn't and had pressed him to auction them for Children in Need. They are online now, and bidding is due to open in twenty-four hours.

again, but an old one so pushing it around in a buggy wouldn't appear so strange. I put him in a corduroy suit, flasher mac and flat cap, and affix a moustache under his nose while she draws lines on his face with an eye-liner pencil. He looks like he's had his face carved up by Mad Frankie Fraser, so we wipe it off and start again, but the baby grabs the pencil and stuffs it into its mouth and won't let go of it. Mum has read somewhere that you can age someone up by applying Copydex to their face. Picture the scene – the giant baby writhing around with a pencil in his gob, as Mum tries to pin him to the floor so she can daub his face with Copydex. She tries to placate him with a rusk, which crumbles into the glue and makes him look like a great big piece of Kentucky Fried Chicken.

It's no longer cotton wool on a stick either; it's a giant Betterware sponge on the end of a mop. Yuk!

We set out for Asda with the baby disguised as an old man, but its mother has placed roadblocks on all the main arterial routes leading in and out of Bexhill (the A259 and the A269), so we beat a hasty retreat back home.

I get the dolphin that I met at the swimming baths' show-reel in the post, and to be honest it's pretty disappointing. What he does is less acting and more attention-seeking: big smiles, look at me – it's just the sort of crowd-pleasing stuff that you get taught at stage school – but at the end of the tape there's a really compelling scene between him and a woman. The woman is seated so you just see the back of her head, and the dolphin, in a motorised scooter, parades up and down in front of her, berating her for not doing her 'homework' in a series of high-pitched whistles and squeaks. The woman walks over to the dolphin and caresses his chin, then realises the camera is on and leaves the room. I only got the briefest glimpse of her face but I could have sworn it was Susan Hampshire.

Blue-fin tuna steaks for dinner – naughty but nice!

February 3rd

I can't believe it's February already and still no sign of the Betterware salesman! I find myself in desperate need of an ironing-board cover and shammy leather! Normally when he turns up I have no need for any of his wares (and let's face it, most of them aren't 'Better' at all).

Up to London's O2 Arena for the *X Factor* judge audition. It's between me, Lord Sebastian Coe, Steve Ovett, Dame Kiri Te Kanawa and Nick Clegg's wife Miriam González Durántez. We're all really nervous – Seb is sick twice in the joint dressing-room basin and Dame Kiri has the squits. We can hear the mob of 15,000 hardcore ITV1 hopefuls in the arena itself, but knowing that there are a further 135,000 in pubs around the country receiving a live video link, with fingers poised over the handsets of their mobile phones ready to vote, would make even the most experienced performer a trifle nervous.

We hear a roar as Simon takes the stage. They start chanting 'Simon! Simon! . . .' and clapping their hands. The updraft makes the roof of the O2 billow up and strain at its moorings.

'I'm Simon Cowell!' he cries. 'How are you all doing?'

Another huge roar.

'Let's hear it for our armed forces!' he shouts.

An even bigger roar.

'Let's hear it for the fire and ambulance services!'

An even bigger roar.

'Let's hear it for the nurses, especially those that tend to the needs of sick kids!'

Massive roar and the roof of the O2 becomes taught and shiny.

'Let's hear it for those special surgeons that are able to separate conjoined twins!' bellows Simon.

Silence, then cries of 'What did he say? What kind of twins?'

'Sorry, let me rephrase that. Let's hear it for those special surgeons that are able to separate *Siamese* twins!'

This time a massive roar, accompanied by a creaking and a splintering. As the ground beneath us starts to shake, Dame Kiri looks at me as if to say 'What's going on?' Miriam González Durántez reaches for my hand, a look of terror in her eyes. Seb cradles Steve in his arms as we all watch the roof of the O2, swollen with proud-clap updraft, lift clean off and flap into the Thames river, where it quickly sinks beneath the foaming waters.

'I always fancied a convertible!' cracks Simon, being fed the line through an earpiece. Big laugh. 'Ladies and gentlemen,' he continues, 'please welcome Miriam González Durántez!'

More cries of 'Who?' and 'What did he say?' as Miriam shuffled onto the stage and started telling the audience about herself and about life at home with Liberal Democrat leader Nick Clegg. It seemed to go well at first, then someone at the back shouted something about the Liberal Democrat manifesto being a bit thin on substance, and then another joined in with a heckle about increasing the income-tax threshold to those earning £10,000. Miriam, desperate to protect her fellah, overreacted, firing off a tirade of four-letter words. Then the booing started. She simply lifted her hand, gave them the bird, turned on her heel and marched off, head held high, to grudging applause.

Next up was little Seb Coe. He got a good cheer as he went on and kept their interest for a good ten minutes with tales of his early years, of training for the 1980 Olympics with high-protein drinks and runs along canal towpaths. Then, just as the crowd started to get restless, he produced his gold medals to huge cheers and applause. He had them back. Then, after a further four or five minutes, you could see their interest waning again. 'Do a bit of running!' someone shouted from the back.

'OK, mate!' said the pint-sized 2012 Olympic chairman, and he stripped down to his boxer shorts and started to run circuits of the stage. Well, the audience were up on their feet. I was standing next to Steve Ovett in the wings and I could see the panic in his eyes. Then I heard him say under his breath, 'Why do you always do this to me?'

Steve was up next but he'd been out of the limelight a little too long and very few people recognised him.

'Can I have my first slide please,' he announced, rather pompously.

'Show us your medals!' came a shout from the front row.

'Um, I'm sorry, I haven't got them with me, guys,' said Steve. 'But they are on slide fifty-seven, if you'll bear with me.'

Big mistake. The slow handclap started up again – every

performer's nightmare and very difficult to deal with because you can't be heard over the clapping, plus from the audience's point of view it's really good fun and gives you an overwhelming sense of power.

Poor Steve was forced to condense a twenty-minute PowerPoint presentation into about three and a half. The images were flickering so fast on the screen that someone near the front had a fit and had to be stretchered off by the St John's. Steve rushed straight past me, through the stage door and to a waiting car, muttering, 'That presentation killed at the Society of Amalgamated Patisserie Workers awards last week.'

Now it was my turn, and judging from the look in the audience's eyes I knew these Neanderthals were in no fit state to appreciate snappy one-liners and clever wordplay, such as the similarity between the words 'widow' and 'weirdo'. No, there was nothing for it but eccentric dancing! I quickly hitched my trousers up high so that the waistband now resided under my armpits, grabbed Dame Kiri's black fur muffler that she was using to keep her hands warm and arranged it on top of my head just in time to hear Simon announce me on.

'Ladies and gents, it's the floppy-collared loon himself – Harry Hill!'

On I went, gurning, kicking my legs up, bum out, neck at an acute angle, tongue lolling from a mouth with top lip pulled back to reveal my gnashers. Then I said, 'Evening all, I'm Simon Cowell!'

Well, the audience were rolling around convulsed with laughter! I had pulled it off! They were up on their feet applauding as I left.

'Gotta hand it to you, big guy,' said Seb as I passed him in the corridor. 'You da man!'

I didn't bother hanging around for Dame Kiri's performance. I was straight in the car and heading for the A259.

February 4th

Nan phones complaining that someone threw a stone at her. I point out that that is one of the pitfalls of committing adultery in a predominantly Muslim country.

A stone

She bought a holiday home in the Shia Muslim hot spot of Najaf, Iraq, as part of the Channel 4 programme *A Place in the Sun*. She reckoned it could turn out to be a canny investment opportunity – a bit like the Caribbean was in the seventies – but she'd had difficulty getting any rentals in. As she points out, the buy-to-let market has suffered as the credit crunch has bitten down, so she went over to stay there by herself.

She had bought 'off plan' and was disappointed when she first saw her villa on the Dick Cheney Najaf Freedom Resort and Retirement Complex.

'The tiles in the bathroom don't abut closely enough to the bath surround,' she complained to me down the phone from an armoured car.

Trying to be upbeat I suggested that a little bathroom

sealant should solve that particular niggle, but I could tell she was having second thoughts. 'It's over 600 miles to the nearest post office, too,' she said. 'And the entire route is booby-trapped.' I could see that this would make it difficult for her to pick up her pension. 'And you can't use your bus pass on the buses here, either!'

'Never mind,' I said. 'At least you've got the golf course.'

'They work on a different gauge and my balls are too big for their holes,' she said, a note of desperation creeping into her voice.

A weaker person would have written the whole thing off, turned tail and got on the first plane home, but not Nan. No, I had to admire her gumption. She was determined to stick it out.

To be fair, she had tried to integrate with the locals. For the first few months she wore a full burka (named after BBC news anchorman Michael Buerk, who many of the ladies are saving themselves for), and she'd even had bifocal lenses fitted in the slit for her eyes. It didn't suit her. She complained that her tongue kept drying out, as every time she spoke it would flap against the black cloth and towel it down. Her mouth was as dry as a bone by lunchtime, and then she couldn't digest her lunch properly. Also she said that she couldn't see people coming up behind her, and when she fitted wing mir-rors she got a stiff letter from the local mullah.

She'd compounded her problems in my view by falling in love with her milkman, a married man whose wife was the chairman of the Najaf neighbourhood-watch scheme. One morning Nan was trying to water her hanging baskets outside her chalet when Abdul the milkman offered to lift her up, and in doing so caught a whiff of her Yardley sandalwood body spray and naturally fell head over heels in love with her. Glad of the interest, she fell for him too. Unfortunately Abdul's wife was on duty for the neighbourhood watch scheme and spotted the entire thing.

'I can't help who I fall in love with,' said Nan down the phone, and then 'Ouch!' as another stone hit her on the head.

'Are you OK?' I asked, getting concerned – she is, after all, in her nineties.

'Oh yes, they're only small stones,' she said. 'They've run out of the big ones at B&Q. Besides, I just throw them back. They're not used to that here, strong women.'

'Atta girl!' I said.

I hope she's all right, but like a lot of people with elderly relatives I can't be bothered to go and visit her. Well, it's such a long way.

Simon Cowell calls to say that although I was very popular with the crowd at the O2, it hadn't translated into hard votes from the public.

'It may have been something to do with a lack of a convincing sad back story,' he says, explaining that Dame Kiri had won. Apparently she'd opened by telling a story that she described as 'a brush with death' but which was in fact a borderline blood test that wasn't even hers but was due to a mix-up at the hospital. (Who'd have thought there'd be two Kiri Te Kanawas in the borough of Hammersmith?)

Simon went on to explain that I wouldn't be 'coming to London'. I point out that every now and then I will need to come to London for other business, but he says that I am not allowed into London for the duration of the *X Factor* and that if I try and enter the city I will be prevented from doing so by that big minder he has on the show sometimes.

'That's impossible to enforce!' I say. I mean, how can that big minder cover all main routes into London?

'Well,' says Simon, 'we use face-recognition technology, like they do on *The Bill*, which then alerts the minder via his sat nav, which directs him to cut you off and block your path.'

Although Simon doesn't want me as an *X Factor* judge, which is a bit disappointing, the good news is there's a sort of a runner's-up prize. He wants me to be a judge on an 'exciting new show called *Britain's Got Teeth*', in which people of all ages from all over the country who think that they have got bad teeth are paraded in front of three specialist judges: Mica Paris, previous *X Factor* winner Paul Potts (who after his win famously had his front teeth turned round so they were facing the front) and prominent plastic surgeon and part-time tooth expert Dr Jan Stanek. He wants me to take the same role as Ant and Dec have on *Britain's Got Talent* – in other words, gently take the mickey out of the contestants, unless the audience really like them, in which case I'm to be 'all over them like a rash'.

There is also a tooth-fairy character played by Christopher Biggins, who has an as yet undefined role.

The whole thing is voted for by the public at the end of every episode and the results are placed on a noticeboard in all the major town centres.

'Remember, we're not just looking for bad teeth,' says Simon. 'The human story is important too. I mean, some-one with really bad teeth who is happily married and healthy would not be as strong a candidate as someone who had mod-

62

erately poor teeth but had, say, a mum who was disabled and needed constant care. Do you get where I'm coming from?'

The prize is ten thousand pounds' worth of dental work, and the winner's new teeth will be unveiled by the Queen at the state opening of Parliament. They also win a photo shoot in *What Teeth?* magazine.

While I can see that it's great exposure for me, I tell Si that I will have to sleep on it.

February 5th

Having slept on Simon Cowell's *Britain's Got Teeth* idea, I realise that it is hopelessly exploitative of the general public, particularly those who are desperate, unhappy and possibly borderline mentally ill. I sign up for thirty-eight episodes, starting in December, the day after *X Factor* finishes, and plugging the gap before the start of *Britain's Got Talent*.

Simon managed to assuage some of my worries about the format by saying that he had booked out The Priory for all of April to deal with the potential fall-out, which shows a caring side to him that is all too often hidden behind the swaggering money-obsessed bravado and high-heeled booties.

Simon suggests that he, I, Christopher Biggins and the other three judges meet up for lunch next week so we can get to know each other.

Still no sign of the Betterware salesman. If he has not turned up by the end of the week I'm going to have to go down to the town and buy an ironing-board cover and shammy.

The dog, reeking of Lynx body spray, approached me this evening with a folder of papers and said, 'What's this?'

He had found the designs for the God Bed. Also some Polaroids of a baby in a bowler hat curled up in his bed, asleep. So I had to make up a little white lie about how me and Mum had had a baby.

'What do you mean?' he asked. 'What do you mean you and Mum had a baby?'

'Well, when a man and a woman . . . um,' I started, then realised where that was leading. 'Um, do you know where babies come from?' I said, changing tack.

'The stork, right?' he replied.

'Yes, that's right, the stork! The stork dropped one off. We found it behind the bush.'

'We haven't got any bushes.'

'The shrub, I mean.'

'Oh, OK, it works for shrubs too?'

'Yes.'

'OK, what do you want me to do?'

'Nothing, just cut the baby a little slack.'

He shrugged and padded off to the kitchen to fetch himself a can of food.

I'd forgotten how sheltered an upbringing the dog has had. Having been separated from his parents so early on and being largely home-educated, we'd never got round to the facts of life.

Melon balls and Parma ham for dinner.

February 6th

No reply from Richard Branson's office re. financial backing for the God Bed. I'm thinking maybe I should just go straight to hoover specialist James Dyson.

Phone call from Delia Smith re. French sausage roll. She says she loves the idea and could she include it in her next TV show. She asked me how I manage to get the sausage in the croissant, and I say, 'Come round and I'll show you.' I admit I was being deliberately flirtatious, but with huge sales of her books and DVDs she's loaded! Just the sort of backer I need for the God Bed innovation. I figure if I can get her round here on the pretence of showing her how to stuff a sausage into a croissant and ply her with booze, I might be able to get her to sign a contract. It's worth a try. Delia says she'll pop round tomorrow evening.

That doesn't give me long to:

(1) Get a contract drawn up.

(2) Get some sausages.

(3) Buy some wine.

But darn it, I'll try!

Sausages in a white-wine sauce for dinner.

February 7th

Up first thing to get the stuff ready for Delia's visit. I've told Mum to take the baby to see a film in the evening, and the dog is working a late shift at the airport. I need to iron a shirt, but still no flaming ironing-board cover! Damn that Betterware salesman!

Went to the shops to get the necessary provisions for tonight and an ironing-board cover. There are only two suitable shops near by: the Londis, run by Dominic, and an ironmonger's run by my cousin Dennis. As you can imagine, there is some crossover in what they stock.

Popped into Dennis's first.

I was surprised at the wide array of ironing-board covers on offer. Dennis had covers of all different sizes, hues and varieties, from plain, one-colour ironing-board covers to covers depicting scenes from the life of Dannii Minogue.

'Had Sir thought of a personalised ironing-board cover?' said Dennis, the shopkeeper – and also, as it happens, my cousin.

'Personalised? How so, Dennis?'

He explained that if I were to bring in a photo he could have it printed onto an ironing-board cover, drawing my attention to the six-week lead-in. This was very exciting news. I agreed straight away, paid the deposit on the cover, bought a set of two shammies and headed straight home to tell Mum.

OK, it means I won't have the cover for tonight, but I can get a reasonable result using a towel on top of the ironing board, like I did that time that I met Jan Leeming for tapas.

As I got home the Betterware salesman was walking up the path.

As he produced his holdall crammed with household items I explained that I'd just bought two shammies and had a personalised ironing-board cover on order from Dennis the ironmonger (who coincidentally is also my cousin). He went white and had to sit down as I explained to him what a personalised ironing-board cover is.

Mum fetched the smelling salts.

'How about a pack of clothes pegs?' he kept saying as he came to.

'Nothing today, mate,' I say breezily, attempting to make light of the slight. They don't like to hear that, the Betterware salespeople!

'How about some tea towels?'

'No . . .'

'How about a big sponge that will soak up a litre of water?'

'No, I've been had with that before. They're as hard as a brick when dry and you have to wet it and ring it out before you can get it to absorb anything.'

'I'll pre-wet it!' he says, a note of desperation in his voice.

'No!' I say firmly. 'Not today, not this month.'

Giving up he asks me for his catalogue back. I go inside to have a root around but I can't find it.

When I return empty-handed, he hits the roof, swearing at me and explaining how he was Betterware's top salesman in 1996 and had remained there for four years on the trot until James Quimby came on the scene – who with his dusky good looks and manual dexterity had usurped him – how he'd then lost confidence and had a mid-life crisis. For a whole month no catalogues were distributed. They just lay in their polythene bags in a pile in his hall. Somehow he'd summoned an inner strength and had managed to pick himself up and start again, working his way back up the Betterware league table, not back to his former glory but holding his own somewhere in the middle.

'How would you feel?' he says. 'I can accept that you don't wish to buy anything on this occasion, but to lose the catalogue shows complete and utter disregard for what I have achieved both personally and professionally.'

So I bought another ironing-board cover. Well, it will hold me over until the personalised one arrives, and at least I'm assured of a decent result for Delia tonight.

I also bought an extra-large shammy, with the thought that

I might be able to open it out and use it on one of my God Beds, and also one of those big hard sponges that can absorb a litre of water when wetted and some clothes pegs.

Mum and I stop for coffee and go through some of our family photographs, looking for one that would suit an ironing-board cover.

Then I realise that with all the to-do with the Betterware salesman I have forgotten to put the sausages in the fridge and they are quite warm, having been sat on the worktop under the Velux window with the sun streaming through onto them.

'Those are a health hazard,' says Mum. 'You serve those up to Delia Smith tonight and you'll be up before the beak on a murder charge.'

'Yes, and I'll ask them to take in one other case of baby kidnapping as well,' I say ruefully. 'And where are the croissants?' I add, sorting through the carrier bag. I look over and see the sharp end of a flaky-pastry, crescent-shaped roll disappearing into the baby's gob.

'Mum, he's not supposed to start on solids for another six months!'

'You try telling him that!' she shouts, running over with a crooked spoon and trying to prise his jaws apart. I look at the clock and realise it's half past five – nearly another whole day gone and nothing much achieved!

'Where am I going to get fresh sausies and croissants in Bexhill at half past five in the afternoon?' I exclaim.

'Change of plan,' I say to Delia as she hoists herself up onto a high stool at the breakfast bar. 'Not sausage rolls and croissants but burgers and Rich Tea biscuits!'

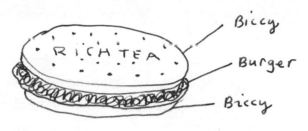

Biccy

Burger

Biccy

The Biccy-Burger

'Even better for my target audience,' she squeals, knocking back a glug of Zinfandel white. Looks like I might have got away with it.

I fry the burgers up and press them between two Rich Tea biscuits and serve them with a few salad leaves and a pickled cornichon. I have to say they were quite delicious! The sweet granular texture of the biscuits complemented the greasy meat perfectly. Delia ate three, talking into a hand-held tape recorder as she went.

'What do you call them?' she asks.

'Biccy burgers,' I say, thinking quickly (I surprise myself sometimes).

'Biccy burgers! Yes!' she repeats. 'I'll get that typed up. Got any other ideas for me or is that it?'

'Hot dogs between two sponge fingers?' I say.

'Go on . . .'

'I call it a sponge dog,' I say, free-thinking as if my life depended on it.

'How do you stop the frank from slipping out?'

'Elastic band.'

'Not sure. Boil one up and let's try.'

We had a great night, trying all sorts of different combinations of biscuits and meat. All the while I kept refilling her glass with the powerful fermented juice of the grape, known as wine.

I could sense the wine was taking effect, as her judgement was starting to get impaired. She gave me a thumbs up to a custard cream–squashed meatball combo that I christened 'the custball meam'.

I saw my chance to get her backing for the God Bed and went for it.

'Ever wondered why dogs sleep so well?' I said. Then, not waiting for her reply, I waded in with my hard sell on the God Bed.

'It's perfect!' she gushed. 'I'll finance the whole thing from the bottom up, and on top of that after every one of my TV shows I will retire to a God Bed, curl up in it, say "Night night" and pretend to go to sleep! It's a great way to end the show, plus it'll send sales through the roof – look what I did for cranberries! Where's the paperwork? I'll sign up now!'

I thrusted the paperwork under her nose, along with a Polaroid of my Chinese baby in the bowler hat.

'Hang on,' she said. 'Isn't that the baby that went missing?'

'Baby? No, you are mistaken. It is an elderly man who lives round the corner and who did a bit of modelling for us.'

'You sure? Looks a lot like that Chinese baby.'

'There is a similarity, I suppose, but no, that's old Lee Pong, the elderly local man who helps me out occasionally with modelling work.'

I snatched the papers back from her and told her that I'd had a rethink and that the deal was off, and ushered her from the house. I gave her a lift down to the station on the back of the mobility scooter.

Mum arrived back with the baby shortly after eleven, anxious to know how the important business meeting had gone. I explained just how close I'd got to securing full financial backing and prime-time TV endorsements, and she was as gutted as I was. We both stared at the baby sleeping in a papoose on her back, and although we didn't say it we both realised what a big mistake we'd made in nicking it.

The dog got in late, thankfully in a mellower mood than of late, and suggested that we use 'that photo we had taken of the three of us on the felled tree after the great storm of 1987' for the ironing-board cover.

He's quite right, of course. The shape of the photograph is long and thin, an aspect ratio perfect for an ironing board.

'That's settled then,' says Mum, cheering slightly. 'Break open the bubbly. This calls for a celebration!'

I duly open a new bottle of bubble bath and the three of us share a bath.

What a day it's been!

As I'm drifting off to sleep I can't help thinking of the poor Betterware salesman, one catalogue short, confidence in shreds. Then I remember that I bought more items from him than ever before and realise I have been tricked again. I picture Delia on the train home to the Big Smoke, her lips still wet from hot-dog grease and cornichons, and our cupboard empty of all biscuits. In my mind's eye I see the warm sausages under the Velux, and the three thoughts make my body contort with anger as sleep's sweet healer o'er takes me.

Assorted biscuits and processed-meat products for dinner.

There's a big article in the paper today about the BBC's new Saturday-night show for the spring. It's another one of those find-a-star-for-a-musical shows like *How Do You Solve a Problem Like Maria?*, *Any Dream Will Do* and *I'll Do Anyone*, only this time they're trying to find a man and woman to star in *Hair*, the sixties hippy musical famous for songs like 'Aquarius' and 'I Got Life', but also of course for the fact that most of it is performed in the nude.

Controversially, the BBC have decided to hold nude auditions before a naked panel of celebrity judges. The whole thing is fronted by Graham Norton, dressed only in a posing pouch. The judges are Andrew Lloyd Webber, who has managed to secure a dispensation to wear a patch, hoofer John Barrowman, respected actress Sheila Hancock, fashion makeover king Gok Wan and (bit of a curveball this one) page-three model Linsey Dawn McKenzie, who used to go out with Beppe off *EastEnders*. Although the judges and audience are completely naked, their embarrassments are covered by strategically placed props – plant pots, a lamp stand and, in the case of Linsey Dawn, two space hoppers. The auditionees are exposed but their naughty bits are pixellated out as the show airs, so no one at home should see anything more than the odd stray pubic hair.

They've called it *Are You Hairy?* and there's been a lot of press attention and build-up to it. The winners get to play nude roles in the musical when it opens in London's West End. ITV are seeing it as such a threat that they have brought forward a specially extended version of *Animals Do the*

Funniest Things and are following it back-to-back with *The Best of Kids Do the Funniest Things 2*. No one at ITV seems to realise that they can't both do the funniest things, although when I phone the duty log to complain I am told that kids are technically animals so it's OK.

Over breakfast Dog says he's seen a four-poster moulded-plastic dog bed in the Betterware catalogue that he would like. I have a go at him for keeping the catalogue when it should have been returned and explain that someone could lose their job over it. 'Very unlikely,' he says.

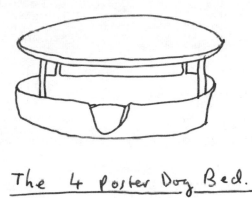

The 4 poster Dog Bed.

'If a butterfly flaps its wings in Bexhill, there is a tidal wave in Bangkok,' I say.

'What you saying then? Kill all the butterflies?' he says.

'That would be a start, yes. If we're to stop tidal waves, that would appear to be the only answer,' I say, feeling a little like I've been outwitted.

'I killed one the other week, so I've done my bit,' says Mum.

Dog says he wants to borrow some money to buy this new-fangled bed. I ask him why he needs to borrow the money when he's on a perfectly good salary, and he says that there was a 'problem at the bank'. When he went to the cashpoint to withdraw some money, the account had been cleaned out. He claims he has been the victim of identity fraud.

This is a big problem for dogs because they do look alike. He says he's stony broke until the bank sort it out and he fancies this bed. I suggest he waits until his account has been reimbursed, but he says that he's fallen in love and wants to impress the bitch with a fancy bed. What can I do? I don't want to stand in the way of romance and so I advance him the money.

Mum says that if the dog is courting, one of us had better talk to him about the facts of life, the birds and the bees – sex basically. I'm not sure it's part of our remit. I mean, you wouldn't take any other lodger to one side and talk to him about contraception, would you? OK, once, but never again. He, Malik, was bringing a lot of girls back, and a pregnancy-testing stick had got caught in the macerator blade in the loo, so I thought it only right to tackle him on the subject. In fact, he ended up having some sort of hormone-injection therapy in a top-security prison wing on the Isle of White. But in the normal run of events your lodger's sex life is his or her own affair, provided it is not interfering with the flow of sewage.

Mum takes the opposite view. She says that the dog is more than a lodger, that we are its guardians. It's true that we are the main beneficiaries in its will and are named as next of kin on its passport, but the whole business is rather hazy from a legal point of view.

We decide to leave a family-planning leaflet in the dog's bed, along with a copy of Desmond Morris's book *Manwatching*. If he wants to consult it, then fine.

I figure that most people learn the facts of life as I did – from an over-amorous auntie.

I'm wondering whether this four-poster dog bed affects my God Bed idea. To reassure myself I spend the rest of the day making a scale model of the God Bed from plasticine. I do eight prototypes but leave them too close to the radiator and they coalesce into one big flat piece of plasticine. What a waste of a day! But I haven't heard anything from James Dyson, so there's no real hurry.

Delia phones at about tea time saying that she'd fallen asleep on the train and had woken up in Bournemouth.

Dog gets home reeking of Lynx body spray and with lipstick on his collar. It's quite clear he's courting.

Mum and I watch through a crack in the living-room door as he pores over the family-planning leaflet.

Pork sausage in anchovy sauce for dinner.

February 9th

Set off for London for the *Britain's Got Teeth* meeting with Simon Cowell, Christopher Biggins, Jan Stanek, Paul Potts and Mica Paris.

I am stopped on the Edgware Road by Tony the bouncer off *X Factor*, who says he has been given instructions by Simon Cowell that on no account am I to come to London. I explain to him about the new show and how I am to meet Simon, but he won't budge and tries to force me back into my taxi.

I say I need to go to the loo. He lets me go into Debenhams, and I manage to give him the slip by Ladies' Accessories.

I phone Simon up, who explains that the London ban he applied after I failed my *X Factor* judge audition should no longer apply as I'm doing his teeth show, and that he'll stand Tony down.

'Stay there and I'll pick you up,' he says. 'I'm taking you to The Ivy.'

'Wow! He's got some money!' I thought. The Ivy! London's premier celebrity haunt, the chosen scram hole of such greats as Posh Spice, Geri Halliwell and Emma Bunton, not to mention Melanie Brown when she's over on business. Members of Westlife, Take That and Boyzone are known to have their dinner there too.

Simon pulled up in a huge stretch Transit van at the front of Charing Cross station. 'Hop in, Hazza!' he said. 'We're going to the drive-thru section of The Ivy.'

Drive-thru section? I parted the double doors at the back of the van and hopped in. There, reclining on plush banquettes, were my fellow judges Mica Paris, Paul Potts and prominent plastic surgeon Jan Stanek, while Christopher Biggins perched on a stool at the rear.

There was, however, a rather frosty atmosphere.

'Come on, everybody!' said Simon, trying to raise spirits. 'Let's have a sing-a-long! "London's Burning"'s a good one – Mica, you start.'

'No, Paul can start,' said Mica.

'No, Mica, I want you to start,' said Simon.

Mica shrugged and opened her throat to sing 'London's burning, London's burning, fetch the engine, fetch the engine . . .'

'Fire, fire!' sang Paul Potts.

'No, no, no!' jumped in Simon, clearly irritated. 'You have to start with "London's burning", Paul. It's a round. Start again, Mica.'

'London's burning, London's burning . . .'

'Now you, Paul,' said Simon, pointing at the snaggle-toothed wunderkind.

'Fetch the engine, fetch . . .'

'No, no, no, Paul! You start with "London's burning"!!!' Simon's face was red now and we all felt rather uncomfortable.

'NOW SING IT PROPERLY!!!' he bellowed.

The atmosphere never really picked up. We swung round through the new drive-in section of The Ivy. Simon had the roasted poulet des Landes, Mica the herb-crusted Blytheburgh pork cutlet, Biggins the Bannockburn rib steak and Jan the veal T-bone chop. I opted for the pan-fried calf's liver, but Paul said he wasn't hungry.

'Oh, have something, Paul,' said Simon.

'No, really, Simon, I'm not hungry.'

'Have something!' Simon snapped.

'Agh! OK, I'll have the celeriac and apple soup and a bread roll,' said Paul.

'We won't have puddings,' said Simon. 'I'll pop into the station and grab us some choc ices.'

On the train back to Bexhill I got a text from Dog. His texts are a little difficult to read, because his paws are not really designed for the tiny phone keyboard, so they are sometimes confusing – particularly when he has predictive texting on. The text read: 'Canny Imam Bing Crosby gurning how tomato nippers?'

Which, using predictive texting on my phone and working

backwards, I think means: 'Can I bring my girlfriend home tomorrow night?'

This is good news for Dog, and I text back 'Yeast.'

Bad news: Baby has learnt to say 'Help! I've been kidnapped!' It's all Mum's fault and I'm absolutely furious about it.

Pan-fried calf's liver and part of Paul Pott's bread roll for dinner, Magnum Ecuador for pud.

February 10th

Delia Smith phoned saying she's stuck in Bournemouth due to engineering works on a bridge between two of her upper molars. She explains that she is due to do *The One Show* on BBC1 this evening and asks me whether I could cover. She says all I'll need to do is go along with whatever they ask me to do and try to mention her new book *Delia's Pound Shop Puddings* as often as I can. She says she'll fax me personality profiles of the two main presenters, Adrian Chiles and Christine Bleakley, plus some key facts about the book.

'What's in it for me?' I ask her.

'It's good exposure, it gives people a chance to get to know the real you and will allow your personality space to breathe. If you can get into a position where the public like your personality, then you can get away with not having to produce any content, which makes life a whole lot easier.'

'You mean like Fearne Cotton?'

'Exactly!' she said. 'Anyway, I'll fax through those weakness/strength profiles of the big two, and don't forget, I'll be watching at eight o'clock tonight or whatever time it's on, so make it good.'

The baby is very restless, so Mum takes it to the Chinese takeaway to see if something sweet and sour will calm it down.

I get Delia's fax through at about elevenses. I was just noshing down an iced bun when the phone rang, and I heard the familiar tweets and whistles of the language that fax machines speak. About three years ago I went on an evening class to learn fax, so I'm now pretty fluent.

'Pip peeep pog pop peee peeep pippop screeeee!' I say down the phone once I've jotted down all the information. Literally translated, that means 'Thanks for the fax.' It's just polite.

'Screee pipop wheeeee peeep pipp peeep wheeescreee,' says the fax machine back (literally, 'Not at all, thanks for taking the time to learn my language. It makes me feel much better about myself').

I feel sorry for a lot of the old fax machines. With the rise of emails many of them are dying out. It was not so long ago that every post office had one and a huge queue of people eager to fax urgent documents would form. Not now. Fax machines lie idle, their rolls of expensive light-sensitive paper redundant. It's sad to say, but most of our young people don't even know how to fax a simple one-page document and top sheet, and soon there will be no speakers of this lost language, apart from the Welsh, of course. I'm kidding! A bit of a cheap shot I know, but this is supposed to be a comedy book!*

I leaf through Delia's personality-profile notes on the two *One Show* presenters. She's got down three headings: general personality points, strengths and weaknesses.

* I love the beautiful countryside of Wales and the Welsh - they're a really bright and talented bunch, plus you never hear of a Welsh serial killer or psychopath, do you? So they must be doing something right.

Adrian Chiles

General: don't let the Brummie accent fool you, this guy is a smooth operator and will try anything to achieve Top Dog status. Look out for sudden changes of subject, last-minute requests to perform genuinely dangerous stunts, questions that are liable to land you in hot water with the press, such as "'Ave you ever attended a political rally or been dogging?' (he asked this of Sir Roger Moore).

Strengths: the common touch, puts you at ease, safe pair of hands should a video link fail to materialise or animal guest misbehave.

Weaknesses: women.

Christine Bleakley

General: don't let the broad Belfast accent fool you, this is one tough cookie who will do anything within her power to gain Top Dog status. Watch out for sudden hand movements that will throw you off kilter and a bewitching smile that will ensnare you and lead you into a love triangle and ensuing expensive public humiliation.

Strengths: smart forensic ability to match shoes with a top or handbag, broad knowledge of current affairs, specialising in Benjamin Disraeli and his role in the protectionist wing of the Conservative Party of 1844 – if that subject comes up, don't even bother trying to compete.

Weaknesses: Cadbury's chocolate fingers – useful to have a few on you.

I rock up to the *One Show* studios at about half seven in the evening.

'Where's Delia?' says an ashen-faced celebrity booker.

'Didn't she tell you? She's on a dental. I'm covering for her,' I say.

'What a *****!' he says. 'What a *******ing ******* ****!' turning the air blue with his old-school BBC profanities.

He shows me through to Delia's dressing room, where a low table is piled high with items that she has requested – her rider. Here's the rather odd mix of stuff that Delia insists on:

1 tray rollmops, 1 jar Gentleman's Relish, 1 sack Babybels (the tiny Edam cheese balls), 12-pack Frazzles, litre bottle Thunderbird wine, litre bottle Bulls Blood wine, box Zinfandel white, 1 Kit Kat Chunky, handful of fresh coriander, three sachets Uncle Ben's 2-minute rice, *Good Pub Guide*, family pack of wet wipes, small bottle of Charlie perfume, season three of *Sex and the City* on DVD, *The Best of Anton Du Beke* on CD and a Magic Marker.

Before I know it I'm being hustled onto the set of *The One Show* to the quasi-familiar strains of its theme tune. It's real seat-of-your-pants stuff as we're live. No item lasts longer than a minute and a half, the idea being that we've moved on before anyone can take any offence or read too much into an off-the-cuff comment. First up is a story about a cow that is deaf and has been fitted with a hearing aid and is now able to hear itself moo. The farmer joins us on the couch and we have a live link to the cow, which, for health and safety reasons, is in the car park. When the cow won't moo for us, Christine handles the whole thing beautifully and launches into a whole load of farmyard-animal impressions. 'What farmyard animal can you do, Harry?' she says, throwing to me.

My mind freezes for a split second. I can't for the life of me think of a single farmyard animal.

'The peacock!' I say. Chrissie and Adrian look at me as if I've gone mad, and I launch into my peacock impression. It goes on for over a minute before Adrian playfully puts a hand over my mouth and announces the next item.

'Should we be treating people who are suffering from smoking-related diseases?' he says. 'This special report from Lawrence McGinty.'

During the recorded item Adrian takes me aside.

'A word of advice, mate: people don't like aloofness. You saying "peacock" there made you look like you were completely out of touch with the common man. Wise up.

'We are joined by Sid, who has a serious smoking-related lung disease,' says Adrian, changing gear perfectly. 'Wotcha, Sid, what did you think of Lawrence's little report there?'

Sid starts coughing and continues for a full minute and a half, by which time it is time to move on to the next item, in which Una Stubbs returns to Swanage to visit the home she grew up in, except when she gets there it has been turned into a centre for children with behavioural problems.

Then it's back to the studio, and Una is on the couch with us, reminiscing about Cliff and the Shadows, Swanage social services and a positive Mantoux test that left a scar on her upper arm that is still clearly visible today.

'I suppose if it had happened today I could have got a payout for it,' says Una, pushing the top of her arm towards the camera.

An item on a new feminine-freshness product that is being fronted by Camilla Parker Bowles, with all proceeds going to the Prince's Trust, follows, then a gent whose homing pigeon is an agoraphobic. Finally it's my turn.

'And, Harry, you're going to do a demonstration of a recipe from Delia's new book *Pound Shop Puddings*!'

I heard myself saying, 'Yes, that's right, Christine,' and I was ushered over to a worktop with various utensils and a selection of ingredients on it. I emptied all the ingredients – six eggs, Kit Kat, litre of milk, extra-strong mints, instant coffee and a tin of tuna – into the food mixer, whizzed it up, stuck two straws in it and offered it to Adar and Chrissie, who were duty-bound to take a slurp. Chrissie gagged, but Adrian threw up all over the worktop and then staggered over to the couch and threw up all over the dairy farmer, Una Stubbs and the man with the chest complaint. Then, as he bent over with his hands on his knees, a jet of sick hit an electric cable on the floor and an arc of electricity travelled up the sick bridge into his face and knocked him flying across the room.

'That's all from us at *The One Show*, see you tomorrow,' said Christine, ever the pro.

I take Una back to my dressing room and clean her up as best I can with Delia's wet wipes, then quietly slip from the building.

Let's hope it did the trick and Delia sells shedloads of books.

Baby kept waking up all night because it was thirsty. Mum reckons it must have been that Chinese takeaway.

Beef jerky and green beans for dinner, packet of Frazzles for afters.

February 11th

Door-to-door calls by a private detective asking whether there's a baby in the house, and if so can he take a DNA sample. I denied it, of course. I asked his name, and he said 'Herod', which was his joke. Then he heard the cry of 'Rusk!' coming from inside and pushed past me into the front room. Fortunately Mum had time to Copydex a moustache onto Baby's face.

Herod looked at Baby long and hard, then broke his stare with 'Sorry to trouble you, old timer', then turned heel and left. I wish we'd never nicked that baby, and to be honest I can't remember why on earth we did.

In the evening the dog brought back a female friend to meet us, Deborah, a collie cross whom he works with at the airport. She seemed perfectly presentable, if a bit dull. They sat around looking into each other's eyes, then sat on the sofa with us and watched *Coronation Street*. I noticed that she growled every time Liz McDonald came on the screen, which seems a bit harsh. I like Liz, the brassy blonde. She's been a good mum to Steve and has a heart of gold in there, although her fiery temper – particularly if anyone seems about to hurt her Steve – has made her some enemies. She's a one-off, a rough diamond, and it's a shame how she's been let down so many times by men.

I drove the collie home afterwards and gently probed as to what her problem was with Liz, but she wouldn't tell me. It's obviously going to take time to earn her respect, but I'll find out eventually.

Mum phones me in the car to say the baby has worked out how to open the fridge.

Braised hearts for dinner, lollipops for pud.

February 12th

Woke up this morning with another brain wave re. the God Bed. I will start it initially by marketing *children's* God Beds, which are essentially just standard dog beds that you can buy from any pet shop. All I have to do is brand them with an appropriate sticker. Now, for promotional purposes, I wish the baby was smaller and less like a man.

Get a call from Dennis at the ironmonger's (who is coincidentally also my cousin). He says that the personalised ironing-board cover is ready, so I hot-foot it straight down there.

I had given Dennis the strip of negatives that the photo of Mum, me and the dog lined up on a fallen tree in the aftermath of the Great Storm of 1987 was on, explaining that it was 'second from the right'.

Unfortunately he's counted in from the left and thus the ironing-board cover sports a photo of Mum topless on the beach at Eastbourne, shortly before she was told by the police to cover up (you can just see the tip of the policeman's helmet over her right shoulder). The place where you rest the iron coincides with her bikini pants. Worse than that, he's got it in the shop window.

'What do you think you're doing, Dennis?' I ask.

'Just a bit of fun,' says Dennis. 'She looks pretty good for her age.'

'She's your auntie, Dennis.'

'Is she?' he says, his face colouring up.

'Yes. You're my cousin, so she's your auntie.'

'Oh, sorry. I'll get a bag for you.'

I get home to find the baby has barricaded itself in the kitchen and is refusing to come out. It has jammed the door shut with a chair, and every time we go near it roars like a lion and rattles the carving knife in a bucket. It's quite frightening. We are stuck slightly because we can't call the fuzz as they'll ask questions about where the baby came from. If we give in to the baby's demands – which are not clear but I'm guessing involve more food – we'll be spoiling the child and will be making a rod for our own backs should we decide to hang onto it.

'Let's kill it!' shouts Mum. I must say I was surprised at her. I mean, she's never been what you might call a great mum but this, even for her, is going a little far. I respond with indignation.

'I beg your pardon?!' I say.

'Sorry, not kill, I mean drug it, drug it with Night Nurse!' she says, looking sheepish.

'You can't do that either,' I say. Then I come up with a plan. 'Lullabies!' I blurt. 'We'll play lullabies to it at high volume until it gets sleepy, then we leave a trail of rusks out from the kitchen door and into a sleeping bag. When the baby is safely in the bag we tie a knot in the end . . .'

'And kill it!' cries Mum.

'No! Not kill it! We get it in the car and we release it into the front garden of its mother.'

Well, we'd both had enough of it by now. We'd got our

86

photos. Come to think of it, I don't know why we've been hanging on to it for this long.

'Coolio!' says Mum, and selecting 'Rockabye Baby' on the karaoke machine she starts to sing.

It took an hour and a half of intensive lullaby action to get the child sufficiently groggy to allow us to wedge open the kitchen door to expose the rusk trail. Sure enough, the baby crawled down the line munching the expanded-crumb biscuits. When it got to the mouth of the sleeping bag it hesitated somewhat before carrying on in and down the quilted tunnel. Quick as a flash I was up from behind the sofa and had the end tied with my belt. The baby thrashed about inside, emitting a high-pitched squealing noise, then with Mum's help we got it into the front basket of her mobility scooter. The whole process was, of course, made harder by the fact that I had to have one hand on my trousers to stop them falling down.

We set off for its millionaire mum's mansion, Mum driving, me on my roller skates hanging onto the back with one hand, the other firmly planted on the waistband of my trousers.

As we approached her house we donned novelty masks to conceal our identity – I Saddam Hussein and she Osama bin Laden. As Mum gunned the engine of the motor scooter I ran up the drive of the house with the sleeping bag, turned it out onto the front step and rang the doorbell. The baby, blinking in the sunlight, took a huge gasp of breath and proceeded to scream at the top of its voice. As it saw me run off it lifted the hand with the knife in and sent it hurtling towards me.

'Duck!' shouted Mum as the knife flew over my head and embedded itself in a passing mallard with a sickly thud.

'Step on it, Mum!' I cried, and we were off.

The early-evening news was full of the story of the return of the baby, accompanied by CCTV footage of what appeared to be Saddam Hussein and a cross-dressing Osama bin Laden on a mobility scooter.

Apparently vets were working 'round the clock' to save the duck.

PC Baxter in charge of the case said that his plan was to wait 'a couple of years for the child to start speaking and then hopefully it will tell us what happened'.

By the time Mum and I got back to the house we were absolutely bushed, so we put the lullaby tape on and slept the sleep of the dead/guest of the Dignitas centre in Switzerland.

A bag of Frazzles each and leftover rusks for tea, tangerines for pudding followed by a Quality Street each – well, we all felt we'd earnt it.

February 13th

It's the first night of the BBC's new audition show *Are You Hairy?* Mum and me spend a little time preparing the front room. We pull the sofa and two armchairs in closer to the TV. I make sure the necessary remote controls are positioned correctly. Mum puts some nibbles in bowls. I chill the box of Zinfandel white.

At 7.30 Mum and me, the dog and his girlfriend Deborah all sit down with our tea on trays to watch it.

It starts really well. Graham Norton has a lot of fun with the fact that everyone's nude, making jokes about 'cracks' and 'bum holes'. It's perfect territory for him and he doesn't miss a trick. Soon Mum, me and Dog are rolling around laughing.

Then we are introduced to the first bunch of contestants. There's the usual mix: a rather large girl with a great voice but no confidence whose auntie has got emphysema; another who's been on the wrong side of the law and had five kids by six different men but who now wants to 'put her life back on track'; there's a slightly effeminate man who lives with his mum, who was bullied at school and who wants to 'prove it to them bullies that I can be somebody'; a man with no ears who can only hear by looking at Ceefax; an older Irish lady who up until *Are You Hairy?* has been in a convent and not spoken a word since she was eighteen and who 'wants to emit a whole lot of sound to make up for lost time'; plus about twenty stage-school wannabes who can't be bothered to put the hours in and get roles by the conventional route.

So it started great. The pixellated nude bits were only slightly distracting, and once you got used to it you didn't really notice it and even stopped trying to work out . . . well, you get the idea.

Then about halfway through the show the pixellation machine became overloaded and started to malfunction, allowing free views of the contestants' genitalia but perversely pixellating out Andrew Lloyd Webber's face. I could see

Andrew Lloyd Webber

straight away that the show was going to get the BBC in very hot water indeed.

I got straight onto the internet and started monitoring the ratings, which were going through the roof – higher even than Morecambe and Wise's Christmas special in 1978 and *The K Factor Not Live Final*. As soon as the show finished I got a call from Peter Fincham. To be honest I was expecting it.

'Need to get more full-frontal nudity on prime time, H. Got any ideas?'

'Leave it with me,' I said and spent the rest of the evening brainstorming with Mum.

The two dogs retired to his bed and Mum and me line up at the crack in the living-room door for a shufti, but the canny canine has had the crack filled with bathroom sealant, so bang goes our evening's entertainment.

Packet of Frazzles starter, Sainsbury's Taste the Difference bangers and swede for mains, half a pack of Starburst each for pud.

February 14th

We are woken by the sound of the dog weeping. It seems his new lady friend Debbie the collie cross from the airport chucked him and left in the early hours. No other dog is involved. She just said that she didn't feel they were compatible. He's in bits about it. On Valentine's Day too. It does seem cruel, but I can see her point – why waste money on a card and stamp if she's not really that into him?

Mum got two cards, one in the distinctive scrawl of Uncle Bob. 'Loving You Always, Forgetting You Never' it says, then he's crossed out the next two lines that complete the poem and put 'Bob likes lady's [*sic*] bottoms' in crayon. Bless!

It's not clear who the other card is from but the handwriting looks vaguely familiar – I think it's Dennis from the ironmonger's.

'Your eyes like two fried eggs, your mouth like two lovely rashers of bacon, don't worry I can provide the sausage!' it says.

She's got no idea as to its author either.

'André Previn?' she says.

'Why do you say him?' I ask.

'Well, he's no longer with Mia Farrow,' she says, giving me a knowing look.

'He's married to someone else, you old fool!'

'Yes, but he was married to Mia Farrow too, and look how that ended.'

When she's in this mood it's not even worth trying to reason with her.

I received two Valentine's cards. One is, I'm afraid, from me – returned to sender. I won't tell you the name of the popular brunette who helps to present a factual show on a digital channel that I sent it to, but she clearly moved or that internet website where I got her contact details is deliberately misleading gents like me who merely want to get in touch with their idols and, who knows, maybe more. The other card is from Uncle Bob. I would recognise his handwriting anywhere, plus he's signed it 'Uncle XXX'.

There's a huge furore in the papers about last night's *Are You Hairy?* show on BBC1. The *Daily Mail* is calling for director general Mark Thompson to resign, and the Conservatives say that if they win the next election they will impose a profanity tax on the BBC whereby their grant will be reduced by a pound for every swear word or unclean thought that they broadcast. Labour peer Peter Mandelson backs the BBC and appears on the one o'clock news topless in support. Everyone agrees that he looks great for a man of his age. For their part the BBC say that the show will continue and that there will be a back-up pixellator machine on standby for next week's show.

Beccy Wade from the *Sun* phones me for a comment and I shoot off a quick *Hair*-related nudity gag. 'The moon certainly was in the southern sky last night! I can't wait till next week's pubic, I mean public vote!'

'Gold dust! Thanks, H!' she says, slamming down the phone and filing her copy.

Peter Fincham phones. 'You seen this nude thing?' he asks.

'Yes, yes, Peter, it's not bad.'

'We're planning a whole season of nude shows for the autumn, fronted by that woman off the Bisto ad. I'm asking all our big stars to do their shows as normal, only nude, and just so you know I will be turning up to the office nude for that period too.'

'Sorry, Peter,' I say. 'That's not something I could consider.'

'That's what everyone says!' he cries. 'What's wrong with people? Don't they want to be famous? You sit behind a desk, Harry! They wouldn't even see your trombone and bells!'

I'm sorry to say I hung up on him – well, there are limits.

Toad in the hole for dinner, melon balls for pudding.

I suggest to Mum that we go through the list of ideas we came up with on the back of *Are You Hairy?*, prime time-style ideas with a nude bent – but not too graphic – that Peter F might buy into.

The strongest of them is *Strip Mastermind*, in which various academics are grilled on a specialist subject, followed by a general-knowledge round. If they get their question right they get a point; if they get it wrong they have to remove an item of clothing. The only real sticking point I can see is getting the rights to *Mastermind* from the BBC, because a lot of those academic types are longing to let their hair down and show that they're up for a laugh. I phone up Peter F and outline the concept. He sees the copyright element as being a real issue.

'What else you got?'

'To be honest, the other ideas aren't really fully formed.'

'Don't worry,' he says, 'we're friends. Shoot!'

'Um, OK,' I say, fumbling around. Then I hear myself say, '*Bumcrack*?'

'Catchy title, how's it play out?'

'OK . . .' I blather, making it up as I go along. 'Joe Pasquale . . . um . . .'

'Like Joe a lot, got a lot of time for Mr P.'

'Joe goes around the country in a specially adapted van . . .'

'Yes?'

'. . . measuring people's bum cracks and entering the data into a computer, which then does a prize draw.'

'What's the prize?'

'John Lewis vouchers.'

'Not sure,' says Peter. 'Sounds more like something we'd do with Steve Penk. Can you write it up and get it over to me? Anything else?'

'How about the *Ten O'Clock Nudes*, the day's news presented by naked newsreaders?'

'Don't think so. What if you had a tragic story like an earthquake or a children's nursery bombing? Do you think people really want to hear about that kind of stuff from people with no clothes on? I'm surprised at you, Harry. Love the bumcrack idea though. Might put in a call to Steve Penk's people to check availability. We can move fast on this – let me have a detailed breakdown as soon as you can. Cheery bye!'

I wish I'd never opened my mouth!

Mum's very disappointed when I tell her that Peter reckons there'll be a problem with *Strip Mastermind*. Then I tell her about *Bumcrack*, and she is quite disgusted.

'You should be ashamed of yourself!' she says. 'A man of your age! It's lowest-common-denominator mass entertainment at its worst. You'd better call up The Finch right now and tell him you're pulling it!'

She's right, of course. I don't know what I was thinking! I phone The Finch up straight away.

'I'm pulling my *Bumcrack*, Pete,' I say.

'What you do in your spare time is entirely up to you!' he says, laughing. 'Ha ha! Couldn't resist it, sorry, H. I found out that Penk's on a sabbatical at the moment anyway, so I can't see it working with anyone else, except maybe Paddy McGuinness, and he's not interested. Shame, because it could have been a real tea-pot moment. The good news is John

Humphries is on board for *Strip Mastermind*. We're just waiting on legal.'

When I tell Mum, she's thrilled.

'Ha ha! We're going to be rich!' she screams, and we dance a jig round the front room.

We celebrate with the last of Delia Smith's freebie Frazzles.

February 16th

I am presenting Mum's case to the Royal College of Psychiatrists tomorrow, so spend the day practising in front of the mirror.

I've billed it as a rare case of cuckoo complex and goldilocks syndrome. I am a little nervous, I must admit. I have padded out the presentation with information about the life cycle of the cuckoo and a telling of the complete Goldilocks story, which I'm doing with hand puppets. I figure with this and a Q&A at the end the forty minutes should pass pretty quickly, without me having to go into too much detail about my hypothesis.

If I'm honest I don't think there really is such a thing as a cuckoo complex or Goldilocks syndrome, and even if there is I don't think Mum's got either of them. Let's hope the audience is friendly.

Nan calls to say that she's having difficulties making ends meet due to the difficulties getting to the post office to pick up her pension. She says that just last week an IUD exploded moments after she'd gone to pick up a parcel.

'I think you mean IED. An IUD is an intra-uterine device, a form of contraception.'

'No,' she says sharply, 'IUD. It was a rogue batch.'

I didn't press the point. It's a waste of time when she's in that mood.

So, to supplement her pension, Nan, like a lot of elderly people, has successfully applied for a job at the Najaf branch of B&Q. One of the perks of the job is that she is able to get to any deliveries of large rocks before the mullahs.

She says that they've just had a new delivery of large stones which have been personally endorsed by Iran's spiritual leader, Ayatollah Khamenei.

'Perfect for applying Sharia law,' says the legend on the side of the bags.

I tell her there's nothing she can do but order all the large stones for herself, to keep the shortage going. She points out that if she pays for all the stones it will cost her more than she's earning and she will be left with a whole load of stones she doesn't need.

I email her a diagram of an elaborate rockery.

Sent what I've done of the diary so far through to Stephen Page at Faber, who says he'd like a few more short entries. I point out that the length of the entry is purely dependent on the amount of incident I encounter. If I'm doing a lot in the day, then the entry will be long, and if I'm doing less, the entry will be short. He suggests I do less during the day to keep the entries short or I edit the entries down. I said I'd give it a try.

February 17th

Went to the post office.

February 18th

Saw two magpies fighting over an Eccles cake.

February 19th

Marinated some pork.

February 20th

It's no use. These short entries aren't working for me. I feel like I'm holding back too much information. I feel like you, the reader, and me have built up a relationship over these past few weeks and that me withholding information is a bit like me being unfaithful to you. I suppose all the great diarists felt the same. Where would we be if Samuel Pepys had kept his entries short just to please his publisher: 'September 2nd 1666 – big fire in London. September 3rd 1666 – saw Nell Gwyn.'

No. I am fully aware that one day this book will be considered a hugely important historical document, so I'm going to go over those last three days in more detail.

Marinated pork medallions, broccoli and tinned sweetcorn for mains, chocolate mousse for pud.

February 17th

Went to the post office. Presented Mum's case to the Royal Society of Psychiatrists.

Badly heckled all through the life cycle of the cuckoo. Apparently there is no larval stage – I'll kill that Wikipedia. The Goldilocks tableaux got cheers, particularly when Baby Bear realised his chair had been broken. Grown psychiatrists wept openly into their briefcases. There was a short wine and cheese afterwards and most were friendly. Ate far too much cheese – a big chunk of mature Cheddar and a whole truckle of red Leicester. I put Mum on the train home. She had responded surprisingly well to the necessary nudity involved in the presentation. Two of the psychiatrists recognised her from the ironing-board cover's brief stint in the window of Dennis's hardware store.

I stay up waiting for the reviews to come out.

Chocolate liqueur for dinner, with a small bit of cheese and a bag of Frazzles.

February 18th

Terrible nightmare last night! God, that cheese wreaks havoc on my dream centre! Dreamt that Debbie Meaden had acquired 75 per cent of my God Bed business for two grand. Never again!

The good news is that there's a five-star review of my presentation in the *British Journal of Psychiatry*, singling Daddy Bear out for special praise; a very positive review in the *Handbook of Modern Psychiatry*; but Alain de Botton in the *Journal of Clinical Psychiatry* has slated it under the heading 'Cuckoo Presentation *Bearly* Scientific in Its Approach'. I wouldn't mind but the review is quite personal, larded with cheap bird puns and jibes about my lack of hair, describing me as 'that baldy-bonced *nuthatch* from Croydon' and claiming that 'the *jay*-walking *magpie* with his *pigeon* English made the same mistakes time and *ptarmigan*'. I rush off a letter explaining that while my mother is from Croydon, I am from Kent.

A swarm of psychiatrists have gathered outside the house asking for a comment and photo, and so I elect to lie low in the house.

Peter the Finch Fincham phones saying that John Humphries has changed his mind about *Strip Mastermind* – something about catching a glimpse of himself in the bathroom mirror. He asks me what I think about nude *Dancing on Ice*, but I can see a lot of problems there – mainly for the guys. I tell him he needs to keep working on it. He sounds very down.

'I wish I'd never reversed that footage of the Queen now,' he says ruefully. 'I'd still be at the BBC and probably in line for a major honour.'

'Don't worry, *Primeval*'s back in the autumn,' I say, trying to cheer him up.

'Yes, yes, you're right,' he says, the old fighting spirit returning. '*Dr Who*?! I've shit 'em!'

I go out and allow the psychiatry press pack their photos and soundbites. It's mental, but when these shrinks go for something they go for it in a big way.

Saw two magpies fighting over an Eccles cake.

Isotonic energy drink for breakfast, dinner and tea.

February 19th

Letter from Alain De Botton explaining how being from Croydon is passed down through the maternal line like Jewishness. Then at about half past ten Richard Branson arrives completely unexpectedly in his helicopter on the front lawn.

I welcome him into the house and introduce him to Mum.

'Hello, gorgeous!' he bellows, grabbing her, giving her a big kiss and turning her upside down – his usual greeting for a lady. He's a right handful but his playfulness is infectious, and before long we're all a little hyped up.

It turns out he's really keen on the God Bed idea, but interestingly he's thinking that they might be the solution to the lack of sleep on long-haul flights. He's seeing a plane of the future in which there are no seats at all, just an empty space with white plastic garden furniture handed out from a stack. Then, when it gets dark, the chairs are collected back up and God Beds (which also stack) handed out if you want a bit of shut eye.

'The whole thing would operate on a ticket system, like deck chairs on a beach,' he says.

'What about safety?' I ask.

'Complete waste of time, all that life-jacket-under-your-seat, safety-belt crap. Listen, if you're in a plane and it crashes the only thing that's gonna save you is if you've been good and you're on God's list. Besides, these God Beds float, don't they?'

'I guess . . .' I say.

'There you are then, you've got your own bed and lifeboat all in one, and if you want a belt use your own bloody belt! The God Bed is the best idea since man filled a bag with feathers and called it a pillow. It's pure genius and I want in – fifty grand plus 30 per cent of the business.'

'Five per cent,' I counter.

'Listen, I've been in the leisure industry in the south-west for over thirty years . . .' he says.

'Hang on!' I thought, that voice sounded familiar, softer, more feminine than I remembered, and his upper chest area is fuller than that of a man in his sixties. Studying him now I clock plump arms leading to small hands and feet. I try to grab a look at his Adam's apple but he zips up his fleece . . .

'Deborah? Deborah Meaden . . .?' I say, grabbing Branson's beard. It snaps off in my hand.

'Hey!' he says, nursing the stump. 'What the hell are you . . .'

'Sorry, for a moment I thought . . .'

Clearly hurt, with tears welling in his eyes, he admitted that he'd been using far too much gel on his beard. Then he confessed to using his mum's hormone-replacement patch.

'How does that leave the deal?' I ask, and he says he wants to go away and think about it. He gets back in his helicopter and he's away, up into the clear blue sky over Bexhill.

Damn! Looks like my curiosity has killed another brilliant business cat – and my ticket out of here. What rotten luck!

And I dismantled Amanda Holden's trampet before February too, so it can't be that.

Mum and I are hooked on Frazzles now, so I had to go down to the Londis and get a couple of packs for lunch, followed by half a Kit Kat each.

Peter F phones and asks whether the *Strip Mastermind* idea would work with *Who Wants to Be a Millionaire?*

'Probably,' I say but I know that once Tarrant gets his hands on it I won't be seeing any of the back end.

Marinated some pork.

February 20th

Feel better about redoing the last three days' entries.

A new Betterware salesman came round today and I found myself buying a tube of Miracle Metal Cream, a fridge and freezer defroster, a bottle of sink-outlet slime remover, a four-piece spout-brush set, a worktop bin, an anti-bacterial tea towel, a sponge caddy with three free sponges, twenty-five disposable aprons, a pack of two metallic scourers, a chenille mitt and static duster set, a bra washbag and a retractable clothes line when I hadn't planned to buy anything at all!

'What happened to the last bloke?' I ask, writing out a cheque for two hundred and eighty-two quid.

'Went off the deep end, I'm afraid.'

'Dead?'

'No, laid off due to a catalogue shortfall. Shame, he was a good man once. I've taken over his patch.'

'Sorry, I didn't catch your name,' I say.

'Oh, sorry . . . James . . . James Quimby.'

With every band of brothers there will always be rivals.

Marinated pork medallions, broccoli and tinned sweetcorn for mains, chocolate mousse for pud.

February 21st

Had a rather odd meeting with Trevor Nunn. We met at a little Italian restaurant in Hastings, La Mini Roundabout, and after we'd both sat down and ordered our food he said, 'Now tell me about this exciting new project of yours.'

'My exciting new project?' I said. 'It's your exciting new project that we are here to discuss.'

'Is it?' he said, opening his diary. I peered over his shoulder and could see he had written my name and next to it the letters 'E', 'N' and 'P'. 'Oh, I thought it was your exciting new project.'

'No, no,' I said.

There followed a long silence of about forty minutes. I tried for the life of me to think of things to say and I sensed he was doing the same, but nothing came. Finally he said, 'Shall we go Dutch?'

We paid up and left.

It's been three months since I heard anything from the builders who are working on my house and I'm due to move in next weekend, so I give them a ring to make sure they're on target. I suppose as a project manager I have been a little laid back, but I trusted them and trust goes a long way in this business.

As I mentioned earlier I'm doing the project as part of the Channel 4 programme *Grand Designs*, presented by Kevin McCloud, and am converting a windmill in Kent into a

A Windmill

wind-powered railway station. Ultimately I intend to lay track from my new station to connect up with the Channel tunnel link at Dover. I've already applied for a Cuppa Cino cafe licence and intend to make my money back on the croissants and giant chocolate-chip cookies so loved by rail passengers countrywide. I'll use the flour that I've ground up in the eight months that it's a windmill to make the dough. In showbusiness, as my agent used to say before he went off on his gap year, it's good to have something to fall back on.

I'm not letting the rail network know about my plan, but I once saw a programme on Channel 4 explaining how if you keep something a secret for I think it was seven years, then it automatically becomes legal, so I'll convert the windmill into the station, lay the track and connect it up in seven years' time and the local authority won't have a leg to stand on. Then I sell the station and cafe as a going concern and retire on the proceeds. Cushtie! Pukka! Nice one!

I tried several times to get hold of the builders today on the phone and then I tried Kevin McCloud, but there was no response. I'll try again tomorrow.

Removed slime from sink with product brought from the Betterware salesman and did the drying up with the anti-bacterial tea towel.

Spaghetti carbonara for dinner, tiramisu for pud.

February 22nd

With no way of contacting the builders, or indeed Kevin McCloud, I decide to go down to the site of my new windmill conversion, where I find that no work has been done to convert the windmill *at all*, apart from a toilet complete with macerator unit. On top of that Kevin McCloud appears to be living in the windmill and subletting a couple of the rooms to the builders. I must admit I lost my rag with him a bit but am wary of the cameras rolling and don't want to blow all the goodwill I've built up with the viewers over the years.

'Now listen here, Kevin!' I rage. 'This is my non-functioning windmill accommodation and you have no right to be living here!'

'I've been here for over seven months undetected I'm afraid, Harry,' he says in that thin-lipped sardonic tone of his and which as a fan of *Grand Designs* drew me to the show in the first place, '. . . and so I'm afraid it's legal.'

'It's seven *years*, you muppet!' I bark back at him.

'Eh?' he says, the cool exterior dropping for a moment.

'It's seven years, not seven months.'

'Yeah, I heard seven years,' says the cameraman, and one of the builders says it rings a bell with him too.

Kevin retires to his bedroom with his mobile phone and re-emerges some forty minutes later with two Samsonite suit cases and a man bag.

'Sorry about that, Harry,' he says with a sheepish grin, handing me the key to a padlock. 'It's going to look great when it's finished, if you can just match the sweeping majesty of the building to its place in the landscape. Also those macerator toilets can be a nightmare.'

With that he climbs through the sunroof of his Nissan Figaro, fires up the mighty 800cc engine and is away.

You can't help admiring the guy's nerve!

Then he remembers that he's still involved with the project as presenter of *Grand Designs*, and has to reverse back up the drive. He then hovers about in the background as I shout at the builders to get a move on.

Cheese on toast for dinner, Fruit and Nut bar for pudding.

The drainage from the sink is definitely improved after yesterday's slime-removal session and there are no bacterial infections among Mum, me or the dog, so the tea towel's working its magic too.

February 23rd

Get a phone call from the British high commissioner for Iraq, who tells me that Nan has been arrested for snogging an ice-cream man on the beach at Basra. All she went in for was a 99. While it's wonderful that she is still searching for Mr Right at her age, it's also a little worrying as she faces a lengthy prison sentence if convicted. Also, what happened to Abdul the milkman? The high commissioner suggests I fly out immediately, but I don't fancy it to be honest. It's such a long way, plus there's the heat and the flies. I say I'll give her a poke on Facebook.

Received the new Torville and Dean dollies through the post from Peter F. ITV marketing have brought out a new pair every year since their resurgence on *Dancing on Ice* four years ago. When you squeeze their bare midriffs they say a phrase from the show – variously 'Great skating, Duncan from Blue!' or 'Try to skate out more, Gareth!' or 'No, Dr Hilary, your arm lines are all wrong.' This year there's been some sort of cock-up. It seems that in the editing process they've included the out-takes from the Torville and Dean doll voice sessions. When you squeeze these new dolls they sound grumpy, surly and not at all like the friendly bespangled middle-aged athletes that we have grown fond of again.

'Where's my car?!' Jane is heard to bark.

'Can we just get on with this please?' a testy Chris grumbles.

'You've got ten minutes with us. If you can't record it in that time you can go **** yourself!' says Jane.

This can't be good for their profile.

Made a large batch of chicken tetrazzini and froze half, pineapple chiffon flan for pud.

February 24th

I notice Nan's Facebook status was altered yesterday to 'No longer single', but since then nothing. This is a worry.

The tabloids are all over Nan's ice-cream-man snog folly. The *Daily Mail* leads with 'Harry's Nan Licks More Than Her Lolly!' The *Mirror* goes with 'You've Been Shamed! Harry's Nan in Ice Shocker', the *Sun* with 'Harry's *Nan's* TV Slurp!', while the *Finsbury Park Gazette* leads with 'Ancient Infidel Strumpet Brings Debauchery to Our Beaches! Kill Her! Kill! Kill! Kill!'

There are a number of reporters and paparazzi outside the house waiting to get photos and a comment from me, so Mum and me decide to stick it out and order a Chinese takeaway from Bexhill's premier Chinese restaurant, the Wing Wah.

The Chinese man who delivers it is clearly being bothered by the news hounds. 'You'd better come in,' I say. He steps in, I pay him, then I notice him picking at the skin around his eyes. Before I know it he's pulled off his Far Eastern characteristics and black wig to reveal none other than editor of the *Sun* Rebekah 'Beccy' Wade. I have to admire her resourcefulness.

'For that little stunt, Rebekah, you've earned your interview!' I harrumph, ushering her into the kitchen and laying an extra place. 'But we don't use forks!' I say, handing her a pair of chopsticks.

Well, you should have seen her trying to pick up the sweet-and-sour pork balls! There was sauce and pork everywhere except in her gob! It was quite hilarious. Mum and me were rolling around on the floor laughing. In the end I got my camcorder and taped a whole load of it. It would be perfect if we ever do a Chinese-food section on *You've Been Framed*.

All the time she's pushing that ball around her plate she's probing me for answers about Nan – personal stuff about her previous love life, how many partners she's had, what her favourite ice cream is. I don't suppose she had more than a mouthful of pork in batter in all, despite Mum and me pigging out on the salty sweet Asian fodder. In the end I had to make her a pork-ball sandwich with the leftovers for her to take home.

She then got back into her Chinese-man make-up, and as she left the house she got cornered by a *Sunday People* journalist, who paid her for her story – so a nice day's work for Beccy.

Set meal A for dinner.

February 25th

The fuss over Nan's blasphemous kiss won't die down. Plus they've tracked down Abdul the milkman, who is photographed with a sad expression on his face in front of his float, along with his wife and sixteen kids. He says that Nan used him, that he gave her discounted milk and, more damning, claims she never paid her Christmas club money despite taking delivery of a Bernard Mohammed turkey crown and a Sara Lee white chocolate gateau in the shape of the Dome of the Rock. He is also rather disparaging about her hanging baskets.

Nan's defence team are claiming that she wasn't kissing the ice-cream man but was merely licking a pledget of ice cream that had become lodged on his face due to a faulty ice-cream dispenser. There's a big double-page spread in the *Sun* of my interview with Rebekah. Meanwhile, Nan's old milkman, Graham, has sold his story to the *Sunday Mirror*.

I phone the producer of *You've Been Framed* and suggest a Chinese-food special, but he is suspicious of my motives, so I drop it.

Asparagus rolls and smoked-salmon pinwheels for tea, gateau marguerite for pud.

February 26th

Disappointed this morning to see that the dog has sold his story to the *News of the World*, under the headline 'She Groomed Me'.

He goes into all sorts of stuff that by itself is quite harmless and yet with the tabloid interpretation looks pretty sordid.

He details how 'Nan tickled my tummy and got me to roll over on to my back,' and how 'She made me sit and beg for a biscuit.' Even something as harmless as a trip to the vet's sounds appalling when handled by the tabloid press: 'She got a man to stick his finger up my anus, and he gave me a piece of ham.'

I know he's depressed at the moment about the break-up with Debbie the collie cross, but ratting out your family is pretty low.

'I'm not family, I'm merely a lodger here,' he says. At least now we know where we stand, and I walk straight over to his bed and remove my copy of *Manwatching* by Desmond Morris.

Later on I get a text from Dog: 'Harry sock abnormal ears just needle tip to get hearse toggle.'

Which, using my own phone on predictive texting and working back, I am able to decode as: 'Harry sorry about earlier just need time to get head together.'

February 27th

I've had an enquiry from Piers Morgan's chat show *Piers Morgan's Life Stories*: they'd like me to take the chair and be interviewed in depth, with a view to making me cry.

'This could be great for you, Harry, a real tea-pot moment!' says the producer. 'Being seen crying on TV is brilliant for your profile because it makes people see that you're human, flesh and blood, just like them. It allows them to see the side that they never get to see normally on shows where you are being professional and not crying. It could also open up a number of new revenue streams for you: for instance, adverts for more female-friendly products, such as wipes and sanitary stuff, as well as maybe being asked to do a documentary on a subject close to your heart such as – and I'm guessing here – donkeys that are being mistreated, or maybe a documentary about someone you admire and who you maybe think hasn't got the credit he deserved, like, say, Rod Hull, and maybe you could retrace Rod's steps and interview people who knew him . . . something like that?'

This threw me rather. I mean, I'm happy to talk about myself on TV but wasn't really sure about the crying bit or indeed the Rod Hull documentary.

'What if I don't feel upset enough to cry?' I ask.

'Oh, don't worry, Piers knows exactly what buttons to press. He knows where your cry buttons are!' she laughs.

'But what if I don't cry on the show?'

'Um . . . well, that's never happened before, so I don't know.'

'Would I still get paid?'

'I'd have to check that with accounts, but don't worry, you will be crying on the day.'

'What if they're tears of joy, like if I was remembering something happy from my past?'

'Obviously we prefer sad tears,' she says. 'I'm sure that tears of joy still count but I'll check with the producer.'

'OK then, yes, I'd love to go on the show.'

This has now become a challenge for me – to appear on *Piers Morgan's Life Stories* without crying.

Really enjoying reading *Manwatching* by Desmond Morris again.

Two lamb chops and two scoops of mash for mains, tinned peaches for pud.

February 28th

Abu, the Iraqi ice-cream man who snogged my Nan, has recorded his own version of Benny Hill's classic 'Ernie', calling it 'Abu, the Cheekiest Ice-Cream Man in the Middle East'. It has entered the Iraqi pop charts at number 12, just behind 'Modern Girl' by Sheena Easton.

March

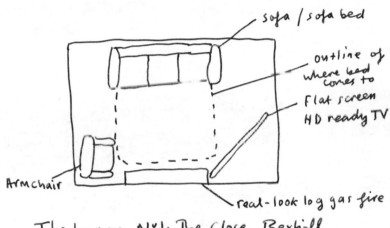

sofa / sofa bed

outline of where bed comes to

Flat screen HD ready TV

Armchair

real-look log gas fire

The lounge Nº 4 The Close, Bexhill

March 1st

Got a massive electricity bill addressed to Mr K. McCloud this morning. When I tackle him about it he says that it was very hot in the windmill and so he had turned 'the fan' on. He means, of course, the blades of the windmill, which he connected up to a huge electric motor, thus pretty much cancelling out all the good work that the wind farm down the road has been doing. What a dummy! Still, he has a certain vulnerability about him that ladies like.

The good news is we *are* doing a *You've Been Framed* Chinese-food special, and I've submitted the footage I have of *Sun* editor Rebekah Wade trying to eat some sweet-and-sour pork balls with chopsticks under an assumed name.

The other half of the chicken tetrazzini for dinner.

March 2nd

Peter Fincham at ITV phoned, saying that someone in the office had noticed that my teeth are not quite up to the standard they expect on prime time – particularly the lower ones at the front, where I must admit a gap has opened up between the two incisors. These are the teeth I use for cutting food before chewing it and getting it ready to be digested by my stomach.

He says I need to get the teeth looked at before he will approve my role on *Britain's Got Teeth*, the new dentistry-based reality-TV talent show.

'It's not just for the show, Harry,' he says. 'Your smile is your fortune.'

'Not really, Peter,' I reply, 'as I get a good rental income from my buy-to-let flat in Eastbourne, which is proving very popular with French exchange students.'

'Get the teeth fixed,' he growls, showing a steely side, adding that it's a condition of my contract because I'm letting the side down. 'Look at the money that Simon's spent on his teeth, and just look at the rewards he has reaped from them,' he says. 'That could be you with a flat in Provence, a mansion in Hollywood, elderly parents in St John's Wood and eighties singing sensation Sinitta on your arm for premieres at a moment's notice.'

I point out that Sinitta only really had one hit and couldn't really be described as an eighties singing sensation.

'She was on *Dancing on Ice*.'

'True, but she was the first to be voted off.'

'Get the gap fixed and make them whiter,' he snaps back.

I look at a photo of Simon Cowell. Peter's right, of course – he does look more professional than me.

Soft stuff for dinner – Cornish pasty and Dairylea cheese triangles. No crackers – I daren't risk it.

March 3rd

Big fuss in the town today: a UFO sighting over the De La Warr Pavilion. Apparently Dominic, the manager of Londis, was walking his two-year-old cocker spaniel up past the green when a disc-shaped object descended, then moved and hovered over the Wing Wah Chinese takeaway. It then emitted a series of smoke signals (which one local wag reckons was an attempt to order a meal!), before flying off in the direction of Eastbourne. There is no apparent explanation, but I suspect the hand of Richard Branson or the *Top Gear* team. Dominic failed to get a photo of the thing, and since he was the only person to see it (Mr Yip of the Wing Wah says he saw and heard nothing out of the ordinary but was inside at the time, and the windows on the restaurant are of that frosted, toughened glass that you can't see out of) we must wait to see if it turns up again. I hope so because something like the world's first contact with extra-terrestrials could really put Bexhill on the map.

I think I might have M.E. It's just that I've noticed I get really tired, especially after drinking one of my wine boxes. I phone the doctor's surgery and try to make an appointment.

'Doctor's very busy I'm afraid,' says the rather fierce receptionist. 'I've got nothing for six weeks.'

'Six weeks!' I exclaim. I mean, I knew things were bad, but not this bad. 'I could be dead in six weeks!'

'I doubt that very much,' she says sarcastically. 'And if you are dead can you let us know so we can reallocate your appointment?'

I reluctantly accept the appointment in six weeks' time.

Dinner: steamed cod fillet main course, Haliborange Vitamin C tablet for afters, washed down with a can of Red Bull.

March 4th

Bumped into Robbie Williams in Londis. He said he'd heard about the Bexhill UFO and had come down himself to investigate it. He was wearing a sort of silver full-body suit with a hoover on his back, a bit like on *Ghostbusters*. 'I'll use the hoover to take air samples, then I'll analyse them when I get back to my van. Wanna come?' he asked.

I walked with him back to the Londis car park, and sure enough, there was a motor caravan with the letters R.W.M.S.I.U.

'Robbie Williams's Mobile Supernatural Investigation Unit,' he explained. 'I travel round investigating things that can't be explained by the laws of science. I've got night-vision goggles, tiny video cameras, motion sensors and other stuff that I got from the Maplin catalogue. It's got a phone in it and everything, and a computer' – indicating a laptop – 'and this digital watch is also a camera. I've made a name for myself in music, yes, but I think my main contribution to humanity will be sussing out exactly what is going on in far-off galaxies. And I also hope to locate exactly where heaven is, so we can access all the old stars of yesterday, like Elvis, Frank Sinatra and Tupac. We hear a lot about heaven in songs and that, but no one has really ever tried to locate it properly.'

'Have you tried Google Earth?' I ask, smiling.

'No, but that's a good idea,' he says, producing his iPhone and tapping in the word 'heaven' into the powerful search engine.

'It reckons it's located in a nightclub in Charing Cross, London!' he blurted, his eyes wide like when he sang on the *X Factor*. 'I'd better get going.'

With that he ushered me from the cabin, started up the engine and was off.

I hope he's onto something.

Toasted marshmallows for tea.

March 5th

I saw my dentist today and explained the situation vis-à-vis the tooth situation with ITV. He launched into a very persuasive PowerPoint presentation on the benefits of tooth veneers, with before and after photos of Cher and Gordon Brown. I explained that I didn't want to spend that sort of money. He suggested filling the gaps between the teeth with ordinary bathroom sealant, explaining that it was something I could do at home myself and was relatively cheap, and while it doesn't quite give the finish of veneers — especially close up — it would probably look OK on camera. So I let him get on with it. I am effectively left with just two horseshoe-shaped

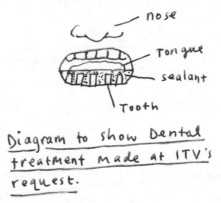

Diagram to show Dental treatment made at ITV's request.

teeth, one on the top and one on the bottom, and it feels good. It looks really good from a distance of about 25 feet, although any closer and it just looks like severe tartar and plaque build up, or like I've had a big plate of tofu and not flossed. I can live with that, but can Peter F? He's asked for a glossy 10″ by 8″ photo of me smiling before he'll sign on the dotted. So fingers crossed.

Mum proudly tells me that every day this week she's managed to keep to her five a day of fruit or vegetables – 'Just like Jamie says. Look!'

She hands me her diary to show me what she's written.

'Five grapes a day doesn't count.'

'Why not?!' she says, all hurt. 'That's five bits of fruit, and on one of the days I had six and on another I had a kumquat!'

I can't be bothered to explain it to her so I pretend to spot a heron through the window.

'Look, Mum!'

'Where?!'

'By the pond. Oh, you missed it.'

Steak-and-kidney pud for dinner, caramel custard for pud.

March 6th

Appeared on *Piers Morgan's Life Stories* today, my first engagement with my new teeth. It all went fine toothwise until I guffawed with laughter and spat a pledjet of sealant at the hapless talent-show judge.

I was determined not to cry and was doing really well. I'd managed to put on a brave face as PM asked me all about the time I got my foot caught in a cattle grid and had to use cow saliva to free it, about the time my dad nearly died during the Second World War when he had an allergic reaction to his make-up, and about the time I got my thumb pushed right back and thought maybe I'd broken it, but hadn't. I'll admit right now I came close to blubbing, but I managed to keep those tears safely locked up in their ducts, like I'd put a padlock on my lachrymal glands.

Then Piers started showing me photos of people who had been injured in road accidents and began bombarding me with facts and figures regarding infant cot death, and before I knew it I was bawling like a baby.

'Thanks for talking to me tonight, Harry,' he said, signing off. 'I am the cry master, goodnight.'

I had to hand it to him. It's as if he has a pull-chain directly attached to your heart strings. Great to see a professional at work. In the green room after the show he congratulated me on my stoicism.

'Thought I wasn't going to get you there for a moment, H,' he said with a grin.

'What would you have done if the sad pics and facts had failed?' I asked.

'Electric shocks,' he replied. 'That chair is wired directly into the national grid. It took eight individual shocks of two thousand volts each to get Brown to blub!'

I couldn't help but admire the lantern-jawed journo turned full-time celeb.

'Thanks, Piers,' I said, shaking him by the hand.

'Just doing my job,' he replied, and grabbing me by the wrist he proceeded to give me a full Chinese burn that made me cry in agony.

He pulled me in close and I felt his breath, hot from the canapés, on my tear-stained cheeks.

'I am the cry master, now get out there and spread the word,' he said, pushing me back into a table of miniature Yorkshire puddings.

I cried twice more that night, once on the way home and once in the bath.

Smoked-salmon pinwheels for dinner.

March 7th

Cried again this morning, then again at elevenses. It happens when I think of Piers Morgan or see his name in print or hear his voice on the radio. It is a powerful spell he has placed on me.

Stephen Page from Faber, the publishers, phones.

'Where is it?' he says. 'We were supposed to have the diary a month ago.'

I point out that if it is to be a diary of a year of my life, then it will take at the very least a year.

'Well, we never had this problem with T. S. Eliot,' he says.

'Well,' I explain patiently, 'TSE wrote poems, didn't he?'

'Did he? Well, can't you pad it out with some drawings or something?'

Thank God for that, I thought he'd never ask.

Taramasalata and freshly made moussaka for dinner.

March 8th

Went to the witch doctor today in an attempt to get Piers 'The Tears' Morgan's spell lifted.

'Him make powerful ju-ju,' said the witch doctor, whose real name is Tim and who is not, I suspect, a real witch doctor, but he was the only entry under 'Witch Doctor' in the *Thompson Directory*. 'You eat pack of wet wipes backwards, and the curse is lifted, twenty-five pounds please,' he said.

After the session he asked me into the garden and wondered whether I fancied a spot of lunch. He shook out a blanket on the damp grass, opened up a large hamper and produced a magnum of champagne. As the wine flowed he loosened up, and I asked him how he'd got into the witch-doctor game.

'Happy mistake,' he said, dropping the Nigerian accent completely. 'I worked for *Which?* Magazine, and we did a special on doctors. We got a number of enquiries from people looking for witch doctors, and I saw a gap in the market and filled it. I did my training under world-renowned witch doctor Anassi Mewgrobes, over in Lagos. Most of that time was spent perfecting the accent. When I got back I put the advert in the *Thompson Directory*. That advert has paid for itself four times over and I'm building up a nice little client base.'

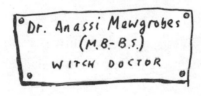

Name plate of
Dr. Anassi Mewgrobes,
witch Doctor of Lagos.

'This is just the sort of specialist we could do with up at Arley Street,'* I thought, and offered him a job on the spot – three sessions a week, increasing if he pulls in the punters.

Bought a pack of wet wipes and ate them on the train home from the bottom of the pack, washed down with the last

* The Penge-based medical centre which I founded, specialising in showbiz-related diseases.

drops of the champagne that Tim had put in a Tupperware container for me to ease my journey.

Watched Piers on *Britain's Got Talent* and didn't cry once. It worked! Thanks, Tim.

March 9th

Peter Fincham phoned to say that he saw me on *Piers Morgan's Life Stories* and that 'The teeth look great!' but is now suggesting I get my eyes lasered. 'Glasses are so two thousand and late,' he says.

'Is it a deal-breaker?' I ask.

'No, but would you do it as a favour to me?'

I couldn't help but be affected by the passion in his voice, so albeit reluctantly I booked an appointment with a bloke called Dr Herbert Datta, who apparently is fairly quick and, most importantly, cheap.

Talking to Dominic at the Londis this afternoon I inadvertently spat a small piece of bathroom sealant at him too. It hit his glasses and slid down the lens on a trail of saliva. Well, I made my excuses and left. I told Mum, and she had a good look in my gob and came to the opinion that it was probably just a stray bit of leftover sealant and described it as a 'teething problem'. Well, we both had a good laugh about that!

I hope she's right. I need to feel secure about this new smile.

March 10th

The sad news has broken in the papers today that Cheryl Cole's hair has been seeing someone else. Apparently after she takes the big piece of hair off at night it has been sneaking off for secret assignations with other women and has been sending suggestive texts to Lindsey Dawn McKenzie when she's right in the middle of presenting *Are You Hairy?* and putting her off her voting.

There are photos in the *News of the World* of Cheryl's hair in bed on the head of Victoria Beckham's nanny Osterley Van Der Bruges, and some grainy pictures of the hair coming out of Spearmint Rhino on the back of personal-fitness instructor Chelsea Sponge. Accompanying the story are photos of Cheryl in the back of her four-by-four forklift truck.

Nan phoned, very upset. Apparently Abu the fastest ice-cream man in the Middle East hasn't returned any of her calls and it seems he has dropped her like a . . . well, like a *stone*.

March 11th

Went to the opening night of Andrew Lloyd Webber's new musical tonight. It's a prequel to the *Phantom of the Opera* and is called *Toddler on the Roof,* which charts the early life of the notorious phantom. It details how he lived in the waste-disposal system of a French kindergarten in downtown Paris, and explains how he gained his love of opera and of underground living in general. It tells too of how he acquired the unsightly blemish on his face that required covering up with a white plastic mask. The story suggests that it was merely a very strong reaction to a BCG jab. On top of that the young phantom kept picking the scab and it got infected by some of the stray strands of waste swishing about in the disposal system, and in the end his entire right cheek became denuded of skin, exposing a seething mass of sinew, veins and semidecayed muscle – so there's a moral to the story too (i.e. don't pick scabs). I went with a dermatologist friend of mine, who reckoned that although unlikely, it could have happened.

The lyrics have been written from beyond the grave by Bob Monkhouse, via star psychic Derek Acorah, and the music is, of course, by none other than our own Andy Webber.

I was enjoying the show immensely. The sets are fantastic, using back projection of rotting food to conjure up life in the Parisian waste-disposal system and a revolving stage which the actors march round to imply distance travelled. And the songs weren't bad either – I particularly liked 'The Scab Song': 'Pick it! Pick the scab! Go on, give it a grab! Now eat it!' etc. But they lost me completely in the bit where the young phantom takes tap-dancing lessons and then tries to get on *Who Wants to Be a Millionaire?* There's a nice bit of business when the phantom reaches puberty and becomes obsessed with Carla Bruni, culminating in an episode of frottage on the Metro. Carla herself was in the audience two seats away from me, and her face broke into a broad grin at this point (no mean feat when you consider the amount of plastic surgery she's supposed to have had).

Saw Andy at the after-show party, which was held on the stage, but couldn't get close enough to chat as he was surrounded by all the various West End faces – Cameron Mackintosh, Sevvy Ballesteros, Lord Rix, James Herriot actor Peter Davison and Jamelia.

Then suddenly there was an almighty crash and a high-pitched scream. We all looked up, and there swinging down towards us on a rope from up in the gods was the figure of Andy's ex – Sarah Brightman. In her hand she held a souvenir programme that was on fire and she was heading straight for Andy, clearly intent on causing him harm. I dashed forward, grabbed the composer and rolled with him onto the floor, only to look up and see Sarah's knickers and legs flying overhead. She smashed into the wall at the far end of the stage and fell unconscious to the floor.

'Lumine! That was close!' said the mighty tunesmith, kissing me squarely on the chin. 'I told her there wasn't a part for her, but she just won't take no for an answer!'

He was quickly up on his feet and at the bar ordering champagne all round, but the atmosphere was completely destroyed and gradually the guests made their excuses and left.

Crisps, nuts and picnic eggs for tea.

March 12th

Rave review for Andy's phantom show from Fearne Cotton on Radio 1, plus apparently Holly Willoughby is going to mention it on *This Morning* tomorrow, so Andy will be well chuffed. Rupert Christiansen had a bit of a go at it in the *Telegraph*, describing it as 'a bit shitty', which to be honest is probably fair.

Andy phones to thank me for saving his life last night and tells me he is now incorporating the bit where Sarah Brightman swings in with a lighted programme and brains herself on the back wall into the actual show. He's calling it the 'chandelier moment that the show lacked'.

'Any goss from the after-show?' I ask.

'Not really, except that Carla Bruni spent the night cosying up to Matt from Blue and they left together!'

'Anything else?'

'Well, Joy from the Beverley Sisters was seen doing shadow puppetry on the door of the ladies' loos for a mystery man whom we think might have been Marty Pellow.'

'Anything else?'

'James Hewitt seen leaving with Simon Cowell, Mezhgan Hussainy and Justine Frischman from Elastica with a four-pack of Stella Artois tucked under his jumper?'

'That'll do,' I said. 'Good luck with the show, Andy, I think it will run and run,' I said, 'cos yeah, OK, I felt sorry for him. Is that a crime?

Pie for dinner, pie for pudding.

March 13th

Got the appointment through from Dr Datta, the laser eye specialist, accompanied by a brochure. On page three there is a big picture of former home secretary David Blunkett and Lennie Peters from singing combo Peters and Lee, and I'm afraid I phoned the surgery straight back and cancelled my appointment. Sorry, Finchy, but there are limits.

Mum said that if I was to go blind, 'Think of the money you'd save on wallpaper,' but no, being bald and gap-toothed is disability enough for this entertainer. Besides that, I like woodchip wallpaper, which can of course be appreciated by blind people too.

March 14th

Mum says she wants to convert the loft into a 'hydroponic marijuana-growing area'. She says it's for her M.S. I said, 'You don't have M.S.' She said, 'Exactly, it's working.' I explain to her the huge electricity bills we'd be getting with all those fluorescent lights going twenty-four hours a day, and she agrees to drop the plan. I wouldn't mind but it's only eighteen months since she converted the loft back into a loft. Previously it had been a bedroom with en-suite bathroom. The idea was to convert it back into a loft to reduce the value of the house, which in turn would bring down the cost of the mortgage repayments. Apparently it was the idea of local entrepreneur Dave, and she'd put down a large deposit before I could intervene.

Dog's been behaving very strangely, very grumpy and occasionally tearful. I wonder if he's got a problem at work?

Phoned Peter F about the eye-surgery problem, and he's agreed to let me keep on working if I drop the glasses and wear two monocles. It's a workable compromise.

Phone the optician and get him to make up two monocles to my prescription.

Prawn and cod bisque, followed by veal escalopes with sauce aurore for dinner, brandy snaps for pud.

March 15th

Got down for breakfast early just as Dog was leaving. When I asked him where he was going, he said, 'For a walk.'

'Mind if I come?' I said. I thought maybe he'd open up to me on the walk, just the two of us, walking.

'What's going on, Dog?' I asked.

'What do you mean?'

'Well, all this aggression, the mood swings, the odd hours you're keeping.'

It was then that he confessed to me that he'd killed and eaten a mouse.

'I never meant to kill it!' he said, choking back tears. 'It ran across the front room and I ran after it – I didn't even think I'd catch it, but I suppose it was instinct kicking in – and before I knew it, it was in my paws, squeaking at me. I was just going to toy with it for a bit, but that squeaking! That bloody squeaking! I tried to get it to stop, but it just went on and on until . . .' He tailed off.

'Hey, come on, it was just a mouse.'

'But I ate it!' he cried.

'OK, so you ate a mouse, get over it.'

'You don't get it, do you?' he shouted.

'Get what?'

'That's what cats do!' he bawled, and collapsed in a heap.

I left him to his grieving. When I went back half an hour later he was asleep. What has upset me most about his situation is the way he kept it to himself for all that time. It saddens me to think of the dog carrying around that burden, that awful feeling of guilt.

March 16th

Dog seems much brighter today. A problem aired is a problem shared, I suppose.

He texted me from work: 'Thatched foreskin yeast dagger.'

Which I took to mean: 'Thanks for yesterday.'

Phoned Nan, and Ross Kemp answered. He explained that he's in the area filming for a new series on Sky TV about how dangerous Najaf is called *Ross Kemp in Najaf*. He'd booked

Mr Ross Kemp & Nan in Najaf

into the George Bush Intercontinental Hotel, but when he and his crew arrived it was still pretty much a bomb crater, albeit with tea- and coffee-making facilities, shaving point and twelve Corby trouser presses. He'd needed somewhere to stay and had answered an advert Nan had placed in the Najaf post-office window looking for lodgers.

'How are the two of you getting on, Grant?' I say, accidentally calling him by the name of his *EastEnders* character. 'I mean, Ross?'

'Er, not that well, H, to be honest,' he said, going on to explain that he has injured his foot – not as a result of Sunni rebels or Iraqi insurgents, but he'd got up in the middle of the night to go to the loo and hadn't seen Nan approaching on her Stannah. She ran over his foot. It would have been worse if the points hadn't changed at the last minute.

He puts Nan on the line, and she says that Ross is very nice and that she has been changing the dressing on his foot twice a day and that he can't do any filming while his foot is injured. It sounds a bit like *Misery*, with Nan in the Kathy Bates role.

Nan goes on to say that she is worried that if Ross's show

goes out, it is going to drag house prices in the area even further down.

'I won't be able to give it away at this rate,' she says. 'He spends ages in the bathroom in the morning too.'

She puts Ross back on, and when I suggest to him that he be a little more considerate in the mornings, he says, 'It's my moisturising regime, mate: light cleansing with a Clarins lotion, followed by a gentle facial peeling, followed by the Iris toner for normal to oily skin, followed by Yonka number 15.'

'How do you get Yonka 15 out in Najaf?' I ask, surprised.

'I get it mail order from Linda Meredith of Knightsbridge.'

'Cool! Anyways, try and shave a little time off, or maybe get up a bit earlier.'

'Well, I don't know why she's complaining,' he says, 'because Nan's doing it for me in the mornings anyway.'

'Yeah?' I say, a little surprised that he's calling her Nan.

'Yeah, after my bed bath.'

'OK, look, your arrangements are really none of my business. Give her a kiss from me.'

'Yuk! No ta!' he says, and hangs up.

I hope he knows what he's let himself in for. I don't blame him, though. I've had one of Nan's bed baths and they are really good fun.

Pilchards in tomato sauce on toast for tea.

March 17th

Up for a voice-over job. They want me to audition for the voice of the 'fluffy ball'. They can't tell me any more about the project. Apparently it's top secret and very exciting.

Thought about various voices that I could do for the fluffy ball. In the end went for a Midlands accent. Fingers crossed.

March 18th

Simon Cowell phones to say there has been a double booking at The Priory for the month when he wanted it to deal with the fallout from *Britain's Got Teeth*. Channel 4 have it on hold for the final series of *Big Brother*. He says it shouldn't be a problem as he is to build his own purpose-built mental institution – the SyCo Centre – and by charging the cost of booking it out back to his own company he will make a nice bit of dough on the side.

I'm having second thoughts about the whole *Britain's Got Teeth* thing anyway. I didn't really like the other judges and over the last three weeks I've lost a lot of the sealant from between my teeth, so my dental confidence is at an all-time low. I tell Simon I'm thinking of pulling out.

'If you do, you're dead,' he snaps back.

Well, I figure you've got to die of something, whether it be cancer, heart attack, stroke or on the end of a bullet fired by an assassin hired by Simon Cowell. I know which I prefer (it's the heart attack – well, it's quick and you're guaranteed the insurance money).

Chicory and orange salad with French dressing for dinner, gateau marguerite for pud.

March 19th

Jools Holland came clean with me today: he has buried the tin-frog jazz band and has placed clues as to their whereabouts in his music, a bit like Kit Williams did with that golden hare in the book *Masquerade*. 'It's a marketing ploy,' he explains over the phone. 'Now people have got two reasons to come to my shows.'

'Two?' says I.

'Yes, (1) to listen to the boogie-woogie and, (2) to get the clues to where the tin jazz frogs are buried.'

'There's also the opportunity to have a few drinks in the interval.'

'Yes, sorry, three good reasons to come and see my show.'

March 20th

Heard back about the voice of the fluffy ball today. They've gone with Mariella Frostrup. Fair enough, I suppose – it's probably who I'd cast in this situation.

My new monocles arrived this morning. Practised all morning with them in each eye, and now my eyebrows ache and I've had to rub Bonjela into them (the eyebrows, not the monocles). They'll take some getting used to.

Cumberland sausage for dinner, Swedish tea ring for pud.

March 21st

Thought I'd better pop up to London to see how my clinic is doing. I run it as a sideline, as something to fall back on if the entertainment business ever turns its back on me. I had the idea after doing the Royal Variety Show one year. Sitting round in the dressing room with my fellow stars after the show, one by one they asked me about a variety of medical complaints that are pretty much exclusive to the showbiz industry. Naturally I can't name names, but one well-known actress of middling height and blonde hair asked me about how she could feel more secure about her slight Midlands accent; another household name with coarse lank hair and a fondness for scarves asked about feelings of self-doubt when confronted with her audience figures; a young broad comic from up north who has been married three times and has curly hair confessed to me that he was obsessed with the number of column inches devoted to him in *Heat* magazine. Others queued up to tell me of their anxieties and neuroses, as well as minor ailments and obsessions about their height, weight and lip thickness. All had conditions that you would never encounter outside of the entertainment world.

I realised that here was a business opportunity ripe for the taking.

I formulated in my mind a centre devoted purely to show-business-related conditions and immediately started looking for premises. I was not prepared to pay the sort of prices required to secure a Harley Street address and so went for a cheaper alternative. I secured premises in Arley Street, in Penge, which when said quickly over the phone sounds pretty much like Harley Street. It's only when the celebs got the letter that it dawned on them it was in south-east London, but by then there was a cancellation fee involved.

I rented a space under the arches down on Arley Street, put a quick coat of white paint on it to make it look sterile, bought a couple of desks, a filing cabinet, one of those light boxes for showing X-rays, a couch and a skeleton and put a small ad in *The Stage*, the Bible of showbiz types. Thus the Harry Hill Showbusiness Disease Centre was born.

That was two years ago, and it has grown and grown ever since.

For the first year I'd get down there as often as I could – perhaps three or four times a week – but as my other commitments took off I simply hired Harry Hill lookalikes from an agency. I'd be perfectly open about it: if a celebrity came in for a session and I wasn't there, the nurse would be primed to say, 'I'm afraid Dr Hill is not in today, would you mind being seen by a lookalike?'

Nine times out of ten they concurred. Well, Penge is a bugger to get to, and by the time you're there you might as well have the session. Plus, of course, the monstrous cancellation fee exerted a little pressure too.

Pretty soon I found that a lot of the celebs preferred seeing the lookalikes to me, and I was able to scale down my commitment even further. I gave the lookalikes prefixes according to their areas of expertise. There was Empathy Harry, Stern Harry, Listening Harry, Camp Harry and Mrs Harry, a woman dressed as me and wearing a bald cap for those lady celebs who prefer to see a lady lookalike.

One of the Harry Hill lookalikes

As I say, that was a couple of years ago, and we now have a waiting list of six months. The beauty of such a long waiting list is that by the time the appointment comes round, a lot of the clients are feeling much better, so they don't bother coming in. They still, of course, incur the crippling cancellation fee, which I have increased to the point where it is now higher than the fee for actually making the appointment.

Saw a couple of patients. Obviously I can't go into details (believe me, I'd love to, but it would kill the business), but suffice to say I saw a member of a prominent boy band with a nasty Strepsil habit (it wasn't so much how many he was taking as where he was putting them), a famous TV judge who finds that he is now unable to meet new people without scoring them out of ten with a numbered paddle, and the lovely Jan Leeming popped in for a chat about where it all went wrong with hubby number five. (It's OK, I checked with Jan about mentioning her name and she's cool with it.)

March 22nd

The big story today is the ash cloud. It seems David Hockney finally got round to clearing out his ashtrays, a gust of wind took hold of the ash and now there is a huge cloud of the stuff hanging over his place. As a result all flights in and out of Bridlington have been cancelled.

Spaghetti carbonara for dinner, raspberry-cream ring for pud.

March 23rd

Got tickets to see Jools Holland's Big Band. Previously I'd

seen him in the early days playing small theatres; then, as his brand of big band boogie-woogie became more popular, he moved to larger venues; then one could only see him in the grounds of stately homes; until he has now reached a point where no venue is big enough to house the huge numbers of people who want a piece of Jools's special thing. Frustratingly, all the usual venues are limited by just how many people you can cram in. His promoter Harvey Goldsmith has had the brilliant idea this year of booking a venue with no boundaries, one that would actually have a limitless audience capacity. Jools explained the plan over the phone as I waited patiently for him to confirm my freebies.

'He's booked me to play the sea,' he said.

'The sea? How's that going to work?'

'Well, me and the band are mounted on a floating pontoon in international waters off the coast of Dover. The punters watch the show from a flotilla of boats and lilos or simply tread water.'

'How do you collect the dough?'

'Well, Harvey's booked a whole bunch of gondoliers, flown over specially from Venice, with ticket machines like they used to have on the old double-decker buses. These gondoliers patrol the seas issuing tickets and selling merchandise – Jools Holland's Big Band water wings, swimsuits, rubber ducks that look like Lulu . . . that kind of thing.'

The logistics will be a nightmare, and what of the acoustics? I hope he hasn't bitten off more than he can chew.

Crab-stick salad for dinner, Müller Fruit Corner for pud.

Uncle Bob's been stealing knickers off washing lines again A couple of Mum's friends at the WI had discreetly confided to her that their smalls had gone missing, and naturally we both figured it might be him. When we checked the CCTV footage from the back garden you could clearly see him climbing over the garden wall at 23.30 and returning at 2.18 with his pockets stuffed full and a pair of open-crotch tights on his head.

A pair of lady's knickers

Mum and me bang on his door, but he refuses to come out.

'We know what you've been up to!' shouts Mum through the keyhole. 'Stop it now or you're going to be in big trouble!'

'That's a rather non-specific threat, Mum,' I say.

'What do you mean?'

'Well, better if you say what the sanction will be should he reoffend.'

'Oh, OK,' she says. 'Bob? If you carry on I will apply for a chemical castration!'

'Much better!' I say. 'Right, let's get ourselves a cup of coffee and a Rich Tea biscuit.'

Later that day the toilet wouldn't flush, and when we went to try and unblock it there was a huge bolus of screwed-up pants in the U-bend. Clearly Uncle Bob was trying to dispose of the evidence. I took the lot down to the launderette for a service wash.

Thatched haddock for dinner, Malakoff cake for pud.

March 25th

This morning at 7.30 there was a knock at the door, and when I opened it a stern-looking PC Firminger asked whether he could come in.

'Do you recognise these, Mr Hill?' he said, producing a pile of neatly pressed ladies' underwear.

'Yes . . . I mean, no! I mean, hang on a second here, Brian.'

'Harry Roy Hill, I am arresting you on suspicion of committing the offence of stealing pants. You have the right to remain silent . . .'

'No, Brian, wait! I can explain!' I protested as he handcuffed me and bundled me onto the back of his bike.

Well, I was down at the station for four hours protesting my innocence, and it was only when I got Mum to bring down the CCTV tapes that they decided to let me go.

'Sorry, H,' said Brian, as he rode me back up the hill to The Close. 'But you must admit you do look a bit like a perv.'

Charming, but I know what he means. Maybe I should get a stylist?

Despite protestations from me, Brian says he has no plans to prosecute Uncle Bob. 'I don't want him stinking out my cells,' he says. 'He's your problem.'

Flaked haddock for dinner, tinned tangerine segments for pud.

March 26th

Brief trip up to Penge once again to pop into my Showbusiness Disease Centre.

On the train up to London I'm not sure when to start my packed lunch. Starting it at the right time will help break up the journey. Start it too soon and I'll be hungry again by the time we get in; start it too late and I'll be left with some to eat.

I start it at Rainham and finish it by Gillingham. I make a mental note that I could easily have started it at Rochester, or even Chatham.

In the clinic I see a popular entertainer who wears a wig atop a ruddy face and who was married to a society beauty and who was complaining of an itchy rash on his knees. It took me a while to work it out, but on closer questioning I ascertained that he had the night before been insulating his loft in just his pants. As he kneeled on the huge roll of loft insulation the glass fibre from which it is made irritated his knees.

I prescribed a steroid gel for the knees and some more sellotape for his wig.

Hot cross bun for elevenses, chicken dupiaza for tea.

March 27th

Nan's in trouble again for public nudity in Najaf, the Shia Muslim hot spot which she has made her home and which is coincidentally twinned with Leamington Spa.

She claims in her defence that while on a camping trip to one of the local bomb craters there was a particularly long walk from the shower block back to the tent and a freak gust of wind claimed her towel. I don't doubt the wind element of her story but I must say I find the rest a little far-fetched. Anyway, she's being held in the nudist wing of Najaf jail. She asks me to come over to see her, but to be honest I can't really be bothered. It's not as if she's being threatened with a stoning. No, under Sharia law the punishment for brief nudity in a public place is apparently to have your pants pulled down and your bottom smacked in front of the whole village. While I can see that this would be embarrassing for Nan, she should really have done her homework on the laws in her new country of choice. I send her a towelling jacket as a present to cheer her up and promise to contact Gordon Brown next time I see him.

March 28th

I get a note from Stephen Page at Faber, who says he's really enjoying the diary so far but is a little worried about the possibility of being sued for libel. He says that most of it is fine but urges me to change any references I have made to Jeffrey Archer to 'someone nice who won't be offended – like Rob Brydon'.

I'm called into Channel 4 and asked to front a one-off TV special, *Britain's Top 100 Trees*. I love this type of run-down show where subjects are covered in a superficial way by listing them in order of popularity, but I can't in all conscience agree with the rankings they have given the trees. I mean the oak number four? Come on! And the eucalyptus shouldn't even be on the list. I have said I'll think about it.

In the evening I went down to Dover to see Jools Holland live from the English Channel.

Jools arrived by stretch boat (or 'barge') to cheers from a water-winged mosh pit ten miles off the coast of Dover. All went well until in the middle of the gig, with Ruby Turner about to let rip, the pontoon they were playing on was hit by a Sealink ferry. Jools and the band were scattered into the water and had to be picked up by the coastguard. Fortunately no one was hurt, apart from Ruby, who was nipped on the elbow by a crab.

Sadly the audience fared rather worse. During the first twenty minutes of the concert four hundred people developed cramp and had to be rescued by the lifeboat service, eight were sick, twelve were eaten by sharks, eighty stung by jellyfish and thirty were not happy with the running order.

Harvey had to shell out compensation left, right and centre, leaving himself out of pocket and Jools with a fraction of his usual pay packet and a tide mark on his velvet trousers that even his mum couldn't shift.

'We need to wait for the technology to catch up,' said an unbowed Harvey Goldsmith at the after-show. 'Then we do it again.'

It had apparently also become clear during the preparations for the concert that neither Jools nor Harvey could swim.

Harvey still says he's planning to invoice an oil rig which he says got into the gig for free.

Hot dog and fries for dinner.

March 29th

Channel 4 call to say that if I agree to do *Britain's Top 100 Trees*, they will change the order of the trees to suit my own preferences. This is just the sort of dishonesty that has led to the public's complete loss of faith in broadcasting, but it would be nice to see the conker at number one. So I'm torn. My mind races with the possibilities – I could put the conker first, then the oak, then perhaps the beech, and I could ban the evil eucalyptus altogether. I suppose this is how Hitler felt when he was handed the keys to the Reichstag.

I talk to Mum about it, and she says that there's no real harm in adjusting the order of the trees and that any publicity for trees in these days of deforestation is good news. Also she said she would like to put in a word for the silver birch, which she says has contributed its sap to the making of all sorts of different medical treatments (as it contains salicylic acid – or aspirin), not to mention that when it is fermented it makes a very palatable beverage, the beauty of which is that no matter how much you drink you don't get a hangover because of the aspirin in it.

This thought stirs her to go in search of a silver birch to tap and make some of her sap wine.

I phone Channel 4 and agree to present *Britain's Top 100 Trees*, and immediately start working on the list.

Pork parcels for tea, bag of Haribos for pud.

March 30th

Another trip up to my Arley Street Showbusiness Disease Centre in Penge again today. It was a very slow train and the man operating the buffet trolley was extremely cunning. He went so fast on his first pass he was gone before I could say, 'Have you got any Jaffa Cakes?' Then on the second pass we all knew that we had to be a bit sharper, and so he had to change his game. He wore a false beard and sou'wester and partially hid the trolley under his coat, leaning forward over it as if it were some sort of mobility device. I only suspected something was afoot when I heard the unmistakable sound of the rustle of a Twix wrapper. Due to engineering works on the line we had to take a connecting bus service from Lewes to Three Bridges. I managed to corner the buffet trolley as he tried to manhandle it up the stairs to the top deck.

I wouldn't mind, but all I wanted was a Kit Kat Chunky.

At the S.D.C. I had an interesting morning. I saw a new patient, the aging front man of a well-known sixties rock band who was complaining that his 'hair hurts' and wanted a local anaesthetic injection as he was going to have his hair cut; a renowned children's author complaining of itchy teeth; one of the *Loose Women* team complaining of an ingrowing iPod; and a prominent matador complaining of a blocked penis.

Asparagus spears and hollandaise sauce for lunch, raspberry-cream ring for pud.

March 31st

Wake up to the sad news that the successful partnership of Kate Winslet and Sam Mendes has broken up. Such a shame because this was a good mix of genes for we in this country to be breeding from if Britain is to be great again. Fortunately they have already bred, but only once. Ideally we need great, successful and attractive people like this to have three or four children to restock the UK gene pool, so I have taken the liberty of dropping them a line encouraging them to attempt to conceive a child for the common good. With a good nanny it needn't be a big commitment, and who knows, they may restoke their friendship in the process. Now that Ashley and Cheryl Cole have split we need couples like this to look up to.

4 The Close
Bexhill
East Sussex
March 31st

Dear Kate and Sam,

Just a note to say how sad I am to hear that the two of you are to split up. Particularly as I see from Wikipedia the online encyclopedia that you have produced just the one offspring, thus not even replacing yourselves! I'm sure that you agree that in these times of recession, with high unemployment, poor literacy in schools and hordes of what the popular press describe as 'chavs and drongos' roaming the streets in their hooded T-shirts, what we really need if this country is ever to stand a chance of getting back on its feet is more motivated kids with a pedigree genome and parents with an address book that gives them a head start in life. That's where you come in! Although I know your relationship has broken down, would you not consider mating again? Just one last time for the good of the nation?

I enclose a 'predictor kit' and pregnancy-test stick gratis, for your convenience.

All best wishes,

Harry Hill

April

The De La Warr
Pavilion

April 1st

Visited my accountant James Horn today in his flat in Piccadilly.

The last bit of financial advice he gave me was to 'Do as I did, invest in shows at the Windmill Theatre'. The Windmill Theatre is, of course, Soho's primary nude revue destination. 'Sex sells, Harry,' he says.

James informs me that having looked through the accounts of the Harry Hill Showbusiness Disease Centre in Penge, he's realised that I'm making 90 per cent of my money from the cancellation fees and that the most cost-effective action is to close the centre completely and only offer appointments to those customers who are likely to cancel. He points out that should someone decide to keep an appointment, I could fulfil the commitment in a hotel or coffee house.

Sadly this would mean laying off all the lookalikes, but as he says, business is business.

Trout meunière and profiteroles for lunch.

April 2nd

I call a meeting of all the Harry lookalikes who work for me down at the Arley Street Showbusiness Disease Centre in Penge to tell them that I'm laying them off. It's hard because these guys have been loyal and hard-working and have helped me build the business.

'I'll get straight to the point,' I said. 'You're all fired.'

149

Thinking about it now, I probably could have broken it to them more gently – worked up to it maybe, explained my reasons – but it's done now.

Empathy Harry took it really well. 'I understand completely where you're coming from,' he said. 'I'd probably do the same thing in your position.'

Stern Harry didn't take it at all well. 'This is unacceptable!' he said, sternly.

Listening Harry didn't say anything at all, just nodded.

Camp Harry hit the roof, but in a kind of over-the-top sort of way that didn't quite ring true, and Mrs Harry accused me of sex discrimination in the workplace.

It was a tough decision to make, particularly so close to Easter, but I'm glad it's over.

April 3rd

Easter is a special time for our family because although we're not strictly Christians, we all do really like chocolate.

Don't get me wrong, I do believe in God and Jesus, but I'm just not sure they were that close. I think that what God did with His son Jesus started off as a good idea – when He went round solving mysteries and healing the sick – but if you're someone like God who's got a million other things to organise and keep an eye on – and I know this from being a busy entertainer – you're bound to take your eye off the ball. It is my belief that God lost interest in the project, or maybe Jesus wanted to take it in one direction, God another, because He was His son and wasn't like a robot that God had made.

Maybe Jesus was a bit of a handful in his teenage years and

fell out with God a bit. I don't know, maybe they fell out due to artistic differences, or maybe when Jesus got His girlfriend Mary Magdalene that upset the apple cart – a bit like when John met Yoko, which then led to the break-up of the Beatles. Maybe Mary wanted to come along to some of the miracles or wanted to perform some herself, and God said no and so Jesus said He didn't want to work with God any more but agreed to do one last big miracle on a hill to kind of go out on a high. I don't know, I'm just riffing here. All I know is that God hasn't had a new book out since He went solo.

I do still believe in the Easter Bunny. What I mean is, I don't believe that it is a giant bunny that hands out chocolate eggs to children all round the world. No. I think that it is a myth that has grown up around a rabbit, perhaps larger than average, with a kind streak.

What about the egg element? Well, as the guys on *Springwatch* will tell you, rabbits' droppings consist of only partly digested food and so the rabbits often re-eat them. These droppings are small and round – much as eggs are. Also human faeces is often referred to by children as chocolate, so I'm suggesting that the whole Easter Bunny thing grew up out of a larger than average rabbit with a kind streak who shared out its droppings with the other rabbits. Thus the myth of the Easter Bunny was born. It's just a suggestion based on my knowledge of nature and I have no real proof, but I think it holds together.

On the Saturday we always have an Easter egg hunt for the local children. Sadly this year Mum had forgotten all about it, and by the time she went down to Martin's the newsagent's all the Easter eggs had sold out apart from the very big and expensive Milk Tray one. We went ahead with the hunt regardless – well, we couldn't disappoint the kids.

Me and Mum stood and watched guiltily as thirty children poured all over the front and back garden looking for choccy eggs which were not there. Most left after about forty minutes, but one determined little bugger stayed until it started to get dark. Eventually he left, only to return twenty minutes later with a torch. In the end I gave him a fiver and told him I was locking the front gate.

Got a call mid-afternoon from an insider at the *News of the World*, who tells me that Camp Harry from the Harry Hill Showbusiness Disease Centre, Penge, has gone to the papers exposing my system of cancellation-fee payments, and what is more has promised 'big revelations at the weekend' about some of my top-name clients. This could ruin me. I go about planning a damage-limitation scheme: basically I get myself down Santander and withdraw as much money as I can from the cashpoint, then head off on the ring road to the Asda in Hastings, get a week's shopping in and ask for fifty quid cashback.

We will have to wait and see just how bad it is at the weekend, but at least now I've sured up my position.

Coquilles St Jacques for dinner, Lindt chocolate rabbit for pud.

April 4th

Put clocks forward an hour – well, there's no point in trying to hold out any longer – and successfully missed church.

The *News of the World* headline today is 'You've Been

Shamed – Harry Fame Centre Is a Sham', with 'World Exclusive' splashed over a picture of Camp Harry from my Disease Centre.

My face reddens as I delve into the so-called revelations. The article details how the Penge railway arch was billed as a state-of-the-art treatment centre good enough to treat graffiti artist Banksy himself, but then Camp Harry explains that it didn't even have broadband and all calls were made from a pay phone in the pub round the corner. It explains how proper hygiene procedures were not followed and paints a pretty grim picture of me as a tight-fisted egomaniac bent only on making a profit. Which of course I am, but you don't necessarily want to read about it in the papers.

They describe one client, a famous author, a lord of the realm with a conviction for perjury, being treated for People Not Liking Me Enough syndrome, who is quite clearly Rob Brydon.

Today we had our own traditional Easter egg hunt, just Mum and me. Mum found mine pretty quickly – I'd put it behind the telly. It took me most of the day to find Mum's. She refused to give me any clues. She'd rather stupidly hidden it behind the radiator, so when I did find it it was pretty runny. It was the big Milk Tray one from Martin's that she'd managed to get a reduction on. I ran with it to the fridge and left it in there for an hour or so. Unfortunately the bag of chocolates within the egg had melted into one solid lump, which in turn had become encased in the molten chocolate of the egg, which itself was embedded within the folds of the foil wrapper. I winced as I tried to eat it, the bits of the foil wrapper playing havoc with my fillings.

April 5th

It's not just Easter at this time of year, of course. It's also the time when our thoughts turn to tax returns. In fact, Mum suggested this morning that the whole crucifixion thing could have been some sort of tax dodge. She's right, it does seem odd that Jesus should choose to disappear right at the time when you're supposed to be filing your tax returns.

The *Sunday Times* ran an item yesterday attempting to combine the two subjects, in which Richard Dawkins, the prominent God-denying scientist, talks about his atheism and his approach to personal finance. In the article he admits that he hasn't declared any of his earnings from his atheism for the last three years and has only declared the money he's got from his science work. He went on to say that he's now making more money from atheism than he is from his science work. He also admits that he has made a number of large donations to the Church of England to bolster it in these recessional times. He realises that if it goes under, there'll be very little opposition to his theories and all his atheism work will dry up.

I sometimes think that God is making things deliberately hard for Himself.

I know it's a bank holiday but there's no rest for the wicked – and they don't come much more wicked than Channel 4! I start work on their one-off special celebrating Britain's trees, *Britain's Top 100 Trees*. By three in the afternoon I've got to twenty and can't think of any more, and to be honest one of the trees I've included is really a bush. At this rate I may have to include the eucalyptus after all.

In the afternoon I wander round the country lanes looking

for trees that I might not have in the list, but in the end I get Channel 4 to send me their list so I can cheat some off that.

Nuts and berries gathered from the thicket for lunch, washed down with Mum's birch-sap wine.

April 6th

Channel 4 biked round their list of trees but there are only twenty-eight trees on it. By my reckoning three are really bushes and one is a climbing plant. When I tackle them about this they say that it is my responsibility to come up with the full complement of trees and that it was in the contract, and if the list comes up short, I won't get paid. What a headache this is turning out to be!

I phone Kew Gardens, and the lady there gives me a long list of trees, most of which I've never heard of, so I sling them down on the list willy-nilly. There are only thirty-six types of tree in Britain, unless you start going for fancy ones in private collections.

I pass this on to Channel 4, who are adamant that they need a hundred and so ask me to include bushes and some plants with a thick stem.

I do feel now that with this list I've let myself down and also the world of trees, but at the same time I can't be bothered to get to know the trees that are new to me.

I realise that this is exactly how corruption starts. You alter something small like a list of trees, then the next thing you know you've invaded Poland.

I send my list in to Channel 4, but I'm only really confident about the first twenty:

1. Conker
2. Oak
3. Sycamore
4. Silver birch (for Mum)
5. Ash
6. Beech

21. Alder buckthorn
22. Purging buckthorn
23. Walnut
24. Acacia
25. Conifer
26. Cypress

A Conker
(Author's collection)

7. Willow
8. Yew
9. Poplar (not as popular as the yew!)
10. London plane
11. Douglas fir
12. Lime
13. Cedar
14. Norway spruce
15. Stone pine
16. Scots pine
17. Sweet chestnut
18. English elm
19. Bay tree
20. Hawthorn (is it really a bush?)

27. Dogwood
28. Dutch elm
29. Huntingdon's elm
30. Silver fir
31. Hazel
32. Holly
33. Hornbeam
34. Juniper
35. Larch
36. Locust tree
37. Magnolia
38. Maple
39. Medlar
40. Mountain ash
41. Lombardy poplar
42. Balsam poplar

43. Rowan
44. Eucalyptus
45. Sloe
46. Pussy willow
47. Whitebeam
48. Wayfaring tree
49. Worcester Pearmain apple tree
50. Cox's Pippin apple tree
51. Bramley apple tree
52. Granny Smith apple tree
53. French Golden Delicious apple tree
54. Egremont Russet apple tree
55. Allington Pippin apple tree
56. Crimson King apple tree
57. Crab apple
58. Pear tree
59. Damson
60. Peach
61. Nectarine
62. Cherry
63. Elder
64. Rhododendron
65. Lilac
66. Box
67. Bullace
68. Rose bush
69. Aspidistra
70. Rubber plant
71. Tulip tree
72. Burning bush
73. Hydrangea
74. Dogwood
75. Witch hazel
76. Privet
77. Cactus
78. Fern
79. Yucca
80. Sunflower
81. Clematis
82. Honeysuckle
83. Red hot poker
84. Bamboo
85. Hollyhocks
86. Hyacinth
87. Lupin
88. Tomato
89. Potato
90. Carrot
91. Parsnip
92. Pea
93. Bean
94. Cabbage
95. Peanut
96. Banana
97. Aubergine
98. Grass
99. Bean sprout
100. Cress

Although the eucalyptus is on the list, at least it hasn't made the top thirty.

April 7th

I get a call from Channel 4 asking me what the difference is between the alder buckthorn and the purging buckthorn, and of course I am unable to answer. I have to explain that I never set myself up as an expert on trees; I was merely hired to present the show and perhaps give it a lighter touch. Besides, that's the least of their worries, as far as I can see.

The Queen's Saturday tea-time show aired last night on ITV1, but she was very wooden. The high point, I suppose, was when she introduced the chief rabbi of Gibraltar, who sang 'Build Me Up Buttercup' – which gives you some idea of the standard of the rest of the show. I can't see it getting recommissioned.

April 8th

I feel a bit sorry for the Pope today. He's become embroiled in a scandal involving child abuse in the Catholic Church.

Yes, it's true the Pope was in the Nazi Youth as a child, and yes, he did cover up the odd bit of child abuse at various times in his life, but that doesn't make him a bad person, does it? Well, yes it does, I suppose, particularly at the time he did those bad things, but if you think how much praying he's done since, how many man-hours he has put into that, then surely the two must balance out? I say give the guy a break. He's old, he's probably not got that long left, let him enjoy all the nice luxuries that come with the job – servants, great Italian meals, first-class travel abroad and a hotline to the Creator.

Atheism is, of course, really popular in comedy at the moment and is a rich vein for some of our young comedians to draw laughs from. I just hope that God has got a sense of humour because if He hasn't, those comics are really going to get it in the neck when they get up to heaven. Their lives are literally not going to be worth living.

Angel-hair noodles for dinner, Angel Delight for pud.

April 9th

My list of the top 100 trees has been leaked to the press and there is a big furore about it in all the papers. The headline in the *Sun* is 'Log Off Baldy!' and in the *Mirror* 'He's Conkers!'

Of course, everyone has their own idea about which tree they would like to see at the top of the list. I think I underestimated how emotive a subject this would be.

April 10th

I get a call from the SNP leader Alex Salmond asking whether he can take me out for dinner to talk about the position of the Scots pine in my list of trees, bushes and plants with thick stems.

April 11th

Dizzee Rascal has joined in the whole conker debate by re-releasing his number-one hit 'Bonkers' as 'Conkers', with new lyrics incorporating references to trees and one or two derogatory comments about my appearance. With the chorus:

> Harry likes his conkers,
> They grow on a tree.
> I reckon it's 'cos they look like him,
> The big-collared baldeee.

Not very nice, is it? Particularly as we worked together on the Queen's Speech. I think extending the word 'baldy' so that it rhymes with 'tree' is very poor penmanship.

In my ire I immediately sit down and try to rewrite the 'Bonkers' song, having a pop at Dizzy. I get as far as:

> I say Dizzee's a plonker
> 'Cos he don't like my list of trees.
> I think he's talking out of his ass
> In that voice that is funneeee.

Then I realise I'm doing exactly what he did – extending the word 'funny' to rhyme with 'tree', except it's supposed to rhyme with the plural of 'tree', 'trees', so it doesn't even work properly.

The chances are he won't give permission for me to change the lyrics of his own song to bad-mouth him, so I tear up my attempt and put it in the bin. Another morning lost.

Forcemeat balls and Instant Whip for tea.

April 12th

On the lunchtime news today on BBC1 with the excellent Sophie Raworth the Pope is seen apologising for all the child abuse, and has asked for twelve counts of shining a laser pen at an aircraft to be taken into consideration too.

I receive a threatening phone call from someone claiming to represent the Australian Forestry Commission, telling me if I don't move the eucalyptus further up the list an accident might befall my mum.

'I can live with that,' I said.

Of course, I don't mean it. Like most guys I love my mum, but at the same time it would be nice to get my hands on the house so I could customise it more to my needs.

April 13th

Lunch with Alec Salmond. If you don't know him, he's the head of the Scottish National Party and looks a bit like Muttley the dog off *Wacky Races*.

A lec Salmond
leader of the S.N.P.

When he said he would take me out for lunch, I naturally assumed it would be to a restaurant or to the House of Commons canteen, but no, he met me outside the Houses of Parliament, then walked with me to St James's Park and handed me a tin-foil package which contained a round of jam sandwiches, a bag of Hula Hoops and a Club biscuit.

'Now listen, wee Harry,' he said. 'I ken that ye ha' a prooblem wid yon Scoots pain?'

'Pardon?' I said.

'Sorry,' he said, removing two Hula Hoops from his cheek pouches. 'I said, you seem to have a problem with the Scots pine.'

I explained that it wasn't a personal list and that it had been compiled by experts within the tree industry, not by me at all.

'Oh!' said Alex. 'So you won't know anything about this then, bonnie lad.' He produced a transcript of phone calls that had taken place between me and the head of Channel 4, in which I am clearly heard haggling over which trees should go where, and worse than that, using a string of four-letter words to describe the genus *Eucalyptus*.

'Unless ye nae tarry a nadge . . .'

'Eh?'

'Sorry,' he said, removing a piece of Club biscuit from his gob. 'Unless you revise your list before broadcast, with favourable results for Scotland, I will take this to the press.'

'The Club biscuit?'

'No, the transcript, a-hee-hee-hee-hee-heee,' he tittered.

It turns out he also laughs like Muttley off *Wacky Races*.

Just like Hitler, I am now fighting a war on two fronts.

April 14th

Susan Boyle came over for elevenses.

Being the world's most famous singer she really can't go anywhere without being recognised, so she's taken to wearing a heavy disguise. When she came round today she was dressed as one of the Black and White Minstrels – blacked-up face, spangly top hat, big bow tie, sequinned waistcoat and white gloves. I wasn't sure about the disguise and I expressed my concerns about people possibly thinking it was racist. 'Ach! Awa wid ye!' she said, tucking into a Cadbury's Mini Roll.

Alan Bennett turned up about half an hour later. He'd heard she was a friend via a Morrissey website and had contacted me.

'I'm such a big fan of Suzie!' he said. 'Would it be possible for me to perhaps meet her?'

I thought it would be fascinating to watch Britain's finest Oxford-educated playwright hook up with Scotland's most famous singer, and so I agreed. He came laden with SuBo memorabilia: copies of her CD, a couple of magazine articles and his *Britain's Got Talent* final ticket, which he wanted her to sign.

They got on like a house on fire, Alan probing her to find out details of life backstage at the talent show, what Simon is really like, who chooses Amanda's dresses, whether Piers Morgan had continued to stay in touch – that sort of thing. For her part she was very patient with the Yorkshire sage, trotting out the story of her early life in Scotland when she was a roadie for the Bay City Rollers, and how she helped build two giant oil tankers at the Clydesdale shipyard. They seemed to be getting on so well I decided to leave them to it, and went up to my office to complete my entry form for Bexhill's fruit and veg competition.

When I went back to check whether either of them would

fancy a hot-beverage refill, I was shocked to find them locked in an embrace on the sofa. Alan looked up, his face smeared with black and white paint. 'She's gorgeous, H,' he said. 'And so talented!'

SuBo giggled recklessly and pulled him in for another gruelling kissing session.

Well, I made my excuses and left.

I suppose about eight hours went by before I dared enter again. The two cultural leviathans were sat back on the sofa, he smoking, she singing the Stones's 'Wild Horses' at the top of her voice.

'Refill?' I said.

'Sorry about this, Harry,' said Alan. 'Oh, is that the time? I'm supposed to be picking up my cat from the vet.'

With that he straightened his cap in the hall mirror and, blowing a kiss to the supine SuBo, was off, wobbling down the path on his bike.

'Not a word to anyone!' he shouted back. 'You never saw me!'

Well, I certainly hadn't expected that!

Leftover pork for dinner, jelly for pud, with a generous portion of Chantilly sauce.

April 15th

Dizzee Rascal's 'Conkers' song has entered the download chart at number one.

I phone Dizzee up several times throughout the morning but go through to voicemail. He's obviously avoiding my calls.

It's the first live televised election debate between the three main party leaders, chaired by evening-news anchorman and convicted drink-driver Alastair Stewart. Mum and me pulled the sofa and armchairs in, got the nesting tables out and spread a little buffet in readiness.

Well, it was very exciting! You'd think that three stiffs in suits banging on about law and order and VAT would be dull but it wasn't – far from it! It was utterly gripping.

Cameron, his forehead freshly painted with putty, was keen to give us the impression that he is a man of the people and dropped in smart little anecdotes clearly designed to prove that he lives like the common people and does whatever it is that common people do.

'I met a black bloke once and he had a job and was really cool,' he said. Then later: 'You know, I was down at the ironmonger's the other day buying a can of WD40 when a young single mother with a pitbull terrier asked me what she could do to mend this broken Britain.' Then later still: 'Just the other day I was rapping in the hip-hop style of Tinchy Stryder when I noticed a pensioner trying to grab my attention. "Please help us, Mr Cameron," she said, "not just for me but for my grandchildren."'

It was pretty powerful stuff, and so of course the other two were quick to jump on the street-anecdote bandwagon.

Gordon seemed slightly confused when attempting his story. Something was wrong. You could see in his face that he was fumbling to remember the details of it.

'You know, I once knew a little girl whose grandmother was ill,' he said in his deep Scots brogue, 'so the little girl decided, off her own bat, to take her grandmother some

165

biscuits. The route to her granny's was through the woods, and so Little Red Riding Hood took her basket of cookies and set off. Then all of a sudden out jumped a wolf and . . . er . . . hang on, I think I might have got that wrong.'

A look of blind panic settled on his face.

'David Cameron!' barked Alastair Stewart, moving the spotlight back onto the dashing Tory leader.

'Listen, guys, my granny used to say to me here's two hundred quid, go and buy yourself and a couple of your mates something nice to eat from Fortnum's,' says Dave.

'Gordon Brown!' barked Alastair.

'I met a young lad, a big boy, in fact he was an egg and he managed to climb up onto a wall. A very risky thing to do, I'm sure you'll all agree. There was no surprise then when he fell down, and due to Tory cutbacks all the king's horses and all . . . oh, hang on, that's not right . . .'

'Nick Clegg!'

'Listen to me, I am young, I am virile, I have a thick head of hair. Feel that arm muscle,' says the leader of the Liberal Democrats, pouting at the camera, slipping his shirt and jacket off to reveal a well-toned, muscular torso, wing collar and bow tie. He flexes the biceps muscle for the camera, licks his finger and pokes it in and out of his belly button.

'Vote Liberal Democrat and all this will be yours,' he purrs.

I look over at Mum, and she's transfixed.

'Grn!' she grunts.

'Right, that's enough! Bed!' I snap at Mum, and turn the TV off at the wall.

April 16th

The whole nation is abuzz with talk of Liberal Democrat leader Nick Clegg. It's like that film with Robin Williams where he treats those zombies and they wake up from a long sleep.

The papers are saying that he was 'mind-blowingly brilliant'. Suzanne Moore in the *Daily Mail* describes him 'looking straight down the camera and making love to me, winking, pouting and rubbing his crotch as he outlined how he often went up to Sheffield and how things had improved up there as a direct result of their policy on crime'.

I'm glad I turned it off when I did.

Nan phones from Najaf to say that she's bought Dizzee Rascal's record on her iPhone and thinks it's great, and sings the chorus down the phone to me.

Nice, isn't it, when your own relatives turn against you?

Pork and ham galantine for dinner, Müller Light for pud.

April 17th

The press have got wind of Alan Bennett and Susan Boyle's relationship. They were spotted at the Marble Arch branch of Kentucky Fried Chicken drinking one milkshake from two straws and sharing a pudding, he feeding her and then vice versa. Admittedly she was disguised as a Confederate soldier from the American civil war, but someone saw through it and tipped off the *Sun*. By the time they were ready to go there were hordes of reporters and photographers outside, and they had to leave via the rear exit in two wheelie bins. Unfortunately, due to a mix-up they both ended up at different depots – something to do with the KFC being on the boundary between Westminster and Kensington and Chelsea councils.

They do look so happy in the photos, him gently fingering the peak of her Confederate cap and she sinking her teeth into one of the Colonel's chicken pieces.

I had begged him to be discreet, and now this.

Frikadeller with home-made barbecue sauce for dinner, Activia yoghurt for pud.

April 18th

Someone's turned up a photo of Alan and SuBo holding hands on the log flume at Legoland. She's dressed as Adam Ant, but you can easily tell it's her.

Alan phoned me in a right bate.

'Has anyone been in touch with you?'

'No, not so far. Besides, my lips are sealed.'

'Bless you, I just don't know what to do!'

'Do you love her?'

'No! Yes! I just don't know!' he spluttered.

I tell him to follow his heart.

April 19th

Bumped into my arch-rival Dizzee Rascal outside the Londis in Bexhill. He's clearly embarrassed, but he can't run off because he's standing hemmed in between a bin and a bike.

'Fancy a game of conkers, Dizzee?' I say, playing it cool.

He looks at his shoes and mutters something about it being business and not personal and 'Maybe we could hang out again some time,' and asks me whether I had seen the Queen thing on ITV with Richie Blackwood and the chief rabbi of Gibraltar.

I must say I did enjoy seeing him squirm.

'What are you doing in Bexhill?' I asked.

He shifted uncomfortably in his giant baggy trousers and designer trainers.

'Um . . . I'm doing some promotional stuff for the single,' he says.

'Oh great,' I thought, 'what a Judas! Right on my own doorstep!'

'I thought we were friends,' I said. 'Why did you diss me, Dizz?'

'Dis wasn't no diss,' he said.

'Dis was a diss, Dizz,' I countered. 'What are the dos and don'ts of a diss, Dizz? Your diss is depressing, you got a dissing disease, Dizzee.'

'Sorry,' he said limply.

He said he was doing a big live gig at the De La Warr Pavilion tonight and did I want to come along? Talk about taking the mick!

'No, no!' he said as I turned to walk off. 'It would be good 'cos people would think you didn't mind laughing at yourself, so it would make people think you is a cool guy.'

'I'll think about it,' I said.

He might have a point.

April 20th

Against my better judgement I went along to the Dizzee

169

Rascal gig at the De La Warr Pavilion last night, and it was full of old people who thought he was some sort of tribute act to Dizzy Gillespie. I haven't seen so much grey hair since we watched Digby the giant dog on DVD. Michael Parkinson was there, Des Lynam, David Dimbleby – all the principal greys, standing round the outside, arms folded. At one point a fight broke out between them and a bunch of ginger-haired kids over an acorn. No, hang on, that was some squirrels I saw on the way to the gig.

Yes, so it was packed to the rafters with elderly jazz fans, but the surprising thing was that they loved it and soon were up out of their seats, clapping along and shouting out the words, which Dizzee had had printed on sheets of A4 paper. He was doing a lot of audience participation as well. He got four old ladies up on stage and got them to take it in turns singing the words to 'Fix Up, Look Sharp'. Yes, it was shaping up into quite a night. That is, until I went on.

When the opening chords of 'Bonkers' started up there was a big cheer from the greys. Suddenly they were all on their feet – even those who had serious illnesses and were on a drip. Then he starts singing the 'Conkers' version. Halfway through Dizzee yells at the top of his voice, 'Ladies and gentlemen, Mr Harry Hill!' – like George Michael does on 'Don't Let the Sun Go Down on Me' when he brings on Elton John.

I walked on from the wings, and to show I'm a really good sport I'd dressed up in a hurriedly made conker outfit and painted my face a rich mahogany colour. Far from cheering madly or appreciating my self-deprecating stance the greys started jeering and pointing. I looked down and saw one elderly man, his face contorted in hate, shouting 'Conker head!' Another shouted 'Baldeeeee!', extending and thus emphasising the end bit.

I looked over at Dizzee, who shrugged in a 'search me' kind of way as if he didn't understand what was happening. Then a bread roll hit me in the face. I staggered back slightly, then someone threw a Ski yoghurt, then another roll, a slice of cake, then, worse than that, when they had run out of food from the packed lunches provided by their care homes they started throwing false teeth. Dizzee immediately killed the music.

There I stood dressed as a conker, my poor boot polish-coated head covered in cake, yoghurt and bread crumbs, amidst the deafening clatter of falling false teeth.

It's at times like that when I wonder why I ever started working in showbusiness.

Giant sausage roll for dinner.

April 21st

Got a call from Dizzee this morning apologising for last night, which was nice. He said that they'd had to spend two hours after the show trying to allocate the false teeth back to their respective owners.

Thinking back, maybe the greys were frightened by my appearance. I mean, a lot of these people had lived through the Second World War – maybe they mistook me for a doodlebug? It's just one hypothesis.

The one good thing to come out of this 'Conkers' song is that it has stoked renewed interest from young people in the game of conkers. A few years ago I was so depressed at the sight of conkers lying undisturbed under the conker tree by the playing fields that I was moved to write a poem called 'Conkers Lie Ungathered', which I reproduce here for your interest.

'Conkers Lie Ungathered' by Harry Hill

A moment of sadness hit me
As I walked in the park.
Conkers lying ungathered
And still there after it got dark.

Conkers lying on the ground
Underneath the swing.
Oh, children, how can you ignore
This potential play thing?

Oh, I know there are Barbie dolls
And toys like that of Tonka.
But none can compare with the fun you'll share
From the swing and crack of a conker.

Take your nose out of your book!
No need for Harry Potter or Willy Wonkas.
String up these nutty brown balls
And whack mine with yours, in conkers.

A moment of sadness hit me
As I walked along today,
Until I played my conker game.
Three cheers, hip hip hooray!

I sent this poem in to John Julius Norwich in the hope that he would include it in his Christmas collection, but he sent it straight back. I then sent it to the poet laureate of the time, Ted Hughes, and he wrote me back a long letter detailing how he thought it could be improved, but I couldn't be bothered to fix it so I sent it to Pam Ayres, who sent me twelve quid for it.

I have a bonfire in the garden with some of the leaves and twigs still left from autumn's charade, and once it gets going I put my makeshift conker outfit on the top. As the flames engulf it I remember that a lot of the padding I used to bulk out the form of the conker was foam rubber from the cushions of the old sofa, and thick yellow smoke starts pouring off it and up into the trees, killing a family of doves that have nested there. It's a weird sensation standing there, watching the big conker burn as birds drop out of the tree to be cooked by its sulphurous flames.

Kentucky Fried Chicken and chips for tea.

April 22nd

Recorded *Britain's 100 Favourite Trees*.

Due to budgetary constraints, it was pretty much me in front of a blue screen operating the camera with a foot pedal. They'll drop in the pictures of the trees in the edit and jazz it up with some lively graphics.

'We're looking for some ideas for music to go with it,' said the producer as I was packing up my make-up. 'You know, songs that have a tree in them.'

'"Tie a Yellow Ribbon"?' I say.

'We've got that one,' he says.

'"Don't Sit Under the Apple Tree with Anyone Else but Me"?'

'Got that one.'

'"Strange Fruit"?'

'Got that.'

'"The Holly and the Ivy"?'

'Got that.'

'"Under the Spreading Chestnut Tree"?'

'Got that.'

'"Lemon Tree"?'

'Got that.'

'"Trail of the Lonesome Pine"?'

'Got that.'

'"Knock on Wood"?'

'Got that.'

'"The Lightning Tree"?'

'Got that.'

'"Wonderful World"?'

'Got that.'

'"Feed the Tree" by Belly?'

'Um . . . let me see . . . yes, got that.'

'How about "Kookaburra Sits in the Old Gum Tree"?'

'No, we haven't got that one, and we were looking for one that helps our item on the eucalyptus. Thanks, Harry!'

Damn! I really should have thought that one through.

It was a bit of a long day.

Stuffed vine leaves with mushy peas for dinner, Müller Fruit Corner for pud.

UPBEAT TITLE SEQUENCE TO INCLUDE SHOTS OF MANY DIFFERENT TREES.

CUT TO:

CHROMA-KEY BACKGROUND OF A FOREST. HARRY HILL STEPS OUT FROM BEHIND A TREE.

HARRY: Hello and welcome to *Britain's Top 100 Trees* with me Harry Hill. The show with branches everywhere!! (*pulls face*) No, seriously, the show that runs down all the country's favourite trees!

And what an arborial treat we've got for you tonight! We'll try not to leaf (*pulls face to side camera*) no stone unturned. Where will your favourite tree come in the list? Find out after the break.

BREAK TRAIL

BILL ODDIE (v/o): Don't forget to send off for your free information pack from Channel 4, 124 Horse Death Road, London, or go to our website Channel 4 forward slash tree show forward slash death to all horses forward slash only kidding dot com.

END OF PART ONE BUMPER.

PART TWO BUMPER.

CHROMA-KEY WOODY OUTCROP. HARRY STEPS OUT FROM BEHIND A BUSH.

HARRY: Hi, I'm Harry Hill. Welcome back to *Britain's Top 100 Trees*, the show that has branches everywhere! (*pulls face*) Before the break I explained how tonight I'll be running down all the country's favourite trees for a real arborial treat. Where will your favourite tree come in the list? Maybe you should place a trunk call to find out! (*pulls face to side camera*) Let's find out now with our first favourite tree. And to kick the night off let's have a look at number 100 in the list of Britain's top 100 trees!

CUT TO:

VT STOCK FOOTAGE OF TREE. SUPERIMPOSE GRAPHIC NUMBER 100 MADE FROM TWIGS.

April 23rd

Bumped into Gordon Brown, out canvassing in the Hastings branch of Asda, by the frozen-food section. He was with a couple of plain-clothes Special Branchers.

Gordon was pushing the trolley but all three were putting stuff in it. Gordon was taking his time, checking the prices on everything and looking for the best bargains. Then one of the policemen put a big bag of chicken nuggets in. 'Hey! We don't need those! Have you seen the price?' shouted Gordon. 'Besides, Jamie says they're bad for us!'

'No, that's not for you, Gordon, that's for me,' said the copper.

'Yes, and that half shoulder of lamb I put in, that's for me, and the Cadbury's Celebrations and the six-pack of crisps,' said the other Special Branch officer.

'But I put in a six-pack of crisps,' said Gordon.

'Yes, but that was two ready salted, two cheese and onion and two salt and vinegar,' said the copper. 'Mine is two prawn cocktail, two roast chicken and two barbecue beef.'

'How will we work out who owes what?'

'We'll add it all up in the car.'

'Yeah, but who gets the reward points . . .'

'Ahem! Gordon!' I interject. 'Can I have a brief word?'

Immediately the Special Branch officers spring into action. One grabbed a cucumber and hit me over the head, the other bundled me into the chest freezer.

'Um, it's me, Harry Hill?' I said meekly, my nose nudging into a bag of frozen peas.

'Oh, it's that fellah off the TV,' said Gordon. 'Better let him up,' and I swung my legs over the freezer and stood in front of him. 'Lovely teeth!' I said. Well, I couldn't help myself. They looked great, a dazzling white, almost translucent at the tips, like the teeth of a young girl. Although looking more closely I could see that they were serrated about their edges.

'Thanks,' he said. 'What is it I can do to help?'

I explained about Nan's Najaf nudity charge.

'A streaker, eh?' he chuckled, looking knowingly at his minders, who laughed back as if there was some shared joke.

'Leave it to me,' he said. 'By the way, I've got all your shows on my iPod.'

'Peter told you to say that, didn't he?' I ask.

'Er . . . no, no. Anyway, see you around, and I'll get back to you about your naughty nan.'

I left the three of them arguing over a tin of anchovy paste.

I know for a fact that Gordon doesn't watch TV or listen to music, and that Lord Mandelson has told him that when he meets someone from showbusiness he should say that he has their shows on his iPod.

Those teeth, though – wow!

Watched *Britain's 100 Favourite Trees* go out with the conker at number one, the Scots pine at number two, and the eucalyptus at number three. I feel like I failed.

April 24th

Audience figures for *Britain's 100 Favourite Trees* are over 8 million, and Channel 4 are cock-a-hoop. They send round a bottle of port and some pâté, and the head of Channel 4 Kevin Lygo calls personally to congratulate me. He asks me whether I'd be interested in hosting *Britain's Top 100 Shrubs*, and I say I'll think about it.

I come off the phone and just start casually jotting down a few of my favourite shrubs, and straight away I realise it's a total minefield. People rightly have really strong opinions about this sort of thing, and if I get involved I'm going to end up being attacked in the press again. I call Kevin back and turn down the shrubs project, wishing him the best of luck.

Get a phone call from Peter Fincham at ITV saying he saw 'the tree thing' and asking whether I'd be interested in hosting a show where celebrities have to climb really tall trees. They've already got Trevor McDonald signed up to climb a big leylandii in the middle of Chessington Zoo, and Cilla Black is getting back to him once she's had her bunions done. I tell him I don't really think it's my sort of thing.

Four cans of Fosters arrive with a thank-you note from the Australian High Commission, followed by a box of Highland shortcake biscuits from Alex Salmond.

Nothing from our own government. Typical!

Pâté for mains, shortcake for pud, all washed down with lager. Delicious!

April 25th

As I walk around the town of Bexhill on an errand, lots of

people come up to me and slap me on the back for the conker winning *Britain's Top 100 Trees* last night, so it wasn't all bad, I suppose.

Simon Cowell has stepped in and called a halt to SuBo and Alan Bennett's relationship, saying that all that kissing might damage her singing voice. In a single stroke he has banned SuBo from ever setting foot in Camden again and withholds her disguise allowance – which knocks further trips to the KFC on the head. He also strong-arms Alan into releasing a statement dismissing the relationship as just 'Whitsun bank holiday madness'.

Later in the day Alan phones me up in pieces. After I'd talked it through with him he started to see that it probably would never have worked out.

'Still,' he said, cheering slightly, 'you never know, I might get a play out of it!'

That's Alan, always working!

As the general-election campaign heats up Gordon Brown has put his foot in it big time. While out canvassing in nearby Eastbourne he was seen on camera talking animatedly to elderly lifelong Labour supporter Jeanette Massingbird, signing off by wishing her well and saying, 'I hope your grandchildren turn out to be strong and attractive like you.' But then as he got in the car, unaware that his microphone was still picking him up, he was overheard describing Mrs Massingbird as being 'a bit masculine-looking'.

He was whisked straight to the Jeremy Vine show on Radio Eastbourne, where Jeremy then played the audio snippet to him straight down some wires and directly into his ears. Gordon was of course mortified and tried to pull the headphones off, but Jeremy rushed round the desk and held them there, shouting, 'Can you hear it, Prime Minister? How do you feel now?!' and repeatedly playing the clip on a loop, adding in a back beat with some bongos strung between his knees.

Meanwhile, the media posse had descended on Jeanette Massingbird's place, rousing the manly octogenarian from her mid-morning nap and playing her the tape.

'I'm certainly thinking about scaling down my Labour-supporting activities,' she said, clearly shocked, adding, 'I will certainly be thinking about perhaps only canvassing for Labour on alternate days from now on!'

Gordon's people acted quickly. Ed Balls slung the shocked PM over his shoulders in a fireman's lift and ran the half mile from the radio studio down Eastbourne High Street to Jeanette's house. She refused to come to the door, so Ed forced Gordon down onto his knees and told him to shout through the letter box, 'I really like your face! If I was thirty years older you'd be just the sort of girl I'd go for!'

Eventually Jeanette opened the door and Gordon fell in, banging his head on the hall table. He was out cold, but that didn't stop Ed taking some photos of him lying half propped up against the stairs with Jeanette.

'Look, they're friends!' he said to the news-hungry press pack, forcing Jeanette to hold Gordon's limp hand. 'It was all a fuss about nothing!'

They're all saying it's over for Labour, but I'm not so sure. I think this latest gaffe makes him appear more human-esque.

'We've all done it, of course', says Mum, turning off the TV. 'Just the other day I was slagging you off behind your back, calling you a fat numb-nut who's hardly got a hair on his head and is a prize wally.'

I laugh along with her but inside I'm hurt and shocked, as I have never, ever bad-mouthed anybody behind their backs or, indeed, in front of their backs either.

The thing is, all us locals know Jeanette used to be a man and had a sex change in the sixties, so it's difficult not to notice her slightly manly appearance.

Nut loaf for dinner.

April 26th

David Cameron has been round to the Eastbourne home of Jeanette Massingbird. He talked to her at length, and then when getting into his car deliberately left his microphone on and was heard saying, 'What a nice lady, and great legs too.'

Not to be outdone, Lib Dem leader Nick Clegg immediately headed to Eastbourne and chatted to Jeanette. As he got back on the coach he allowed himself 'accidentally on purpose' to be overheard via his lapel microphone saying, 'Phwor! She was a bit of all right! Wouldn't mind rubbing some Ralgex into her arthritis any day of the week!'

It's a welcome fillip to Mrs Jeanette Massingbird, whose Facebook profile has been poked senseless ever since.

Finally got the paperwork through for the Duke of Edinburgh Bronze Award. I hadn't realised how much was involved! Surely there must be some sort of fast track for people who are already well known? I phone the organiser, but she's pretty adamant that if I am to get the award I will have to do all the stuff in the brochure – silly stuff like diving for a brick dressed in my pyjamas, diving for an anvil in morning dress, then diving for a baby grand piano dressed as Archbishop Makarios. The most bizarre one, though, was having to work on one of Prince Edward's TV documentaries about the royal family.

Doubts start to creep into my mind as to whether I should embark on this punishing reward regime.

In any situation of doubt I tend to ask myself one question: 'What's in it for me?' How much will passing my Duke of Edinburgh Bronze Award improve my life chances? Looking through the paperwork at the happy, smiling faces of previous recipients as they canoe along rivers, climb down rocks and retrieve bulky objects from the bottom of swimming pools in inappropriate clothes, it's clear to me that the benefits are huge, so I fill out the application form and wander down to the post box to send it off, not wishing to waste a moment.

When I get home I change into my pyjamas and have a shower. Well, it's that sort of groundwork that's going to give me the edge on the day.

Chicken for dinner, meringues chantilly for pud.

April 27th

Had a visit from Major Peter Andrews of the Devolution for Bexhill Party, who was canvassing for votes. He reckons we in Bexhill are being dragged down by what he describes as 'the chavs and drongos' of Hastings. He says that Bexhill, with its more affluent demographic, could be doing much better. Also, he reckons if we were able to harness the power of the sea, Bexhill could be energy self-sufficient by March of next year. Plus, of course, there's the usual policies on keeping the pound and reinstating the bushel as the standard payment for servants. It's pretty persuasive stuff. I agree to take his leaflet and we part friends.

Channel 4 must be desperate – they contacted me today asking me whether I'd be prepared to present *Britain's 100 Favourite Veneers.* Thinking someone was having a pop at my recent dental work, I hung up. They rang straight back and explained that the show was about Britain's favourite w*ood* veneers, not dental veneers, following on from the success of Britain's favourite trees and Britain's favourite bushes. I told them a curt 'no'.

April 28th

In an attempt to get match fit for the Duke of Edinburgh Bronze Award I've decided to go swimming first thing every morning at Bexhill's Vera Lynn Leisure Centre.

I wear verruca socks in the pool, not because I have a verruca, but to prevent me from getting one. I figure that a reasonable proportion of people with verrucas who use the public baths are either unaware that they have them and don't wear verruca socks or they can't be bothered. If I wear two

A verruca sock

verruca socks, then OK, I get the stigma of being a verruca carrier, but I reckon I'm pretty much immune from getting one. Plus people tend to give you a fairly wide berth when you're wearing two socks, so I'm getting a clear path down the practice lanes.

I managed five lengths before I started to feel dizzy, and thought it best if I gradually increase my tolerance.

A woman came up to me as I was getting a well-earned Mars Bar from the vending machine and accused me of giving her son a verruca. I explained that I didn't in fact have any.

'Don't lie! I can see the socks!' she said, pointing at my feet. The verruca socks were clearly visible through my sandals. I had decided that to be on the safe side I would take them off when I got home. I tried to explain to her that the socks were a preventative measure, but she wasn't having any of it. Why must the general public be allowed to all the sessions at the leisure centre? Surely there's a case for some sort of segregation?

Picnic eggs, miniature pork pies and crisps for lunch, Toffee Crisp for pud.

April 29th

Watched *Britain's 100 Favourite Wood Veneers* on Channel 4 last night. They got Julian Clary to host it, but in a clever move by him he didn't ever appear on screen; you just heard his voice, which appeared to come from a piece of mahogany veneer cut out to look like him. In his capable hands what could have been a fairly run-of-the-mill trawl through some of the nation's best-loved surfaces became pretty exciting. Somehow he managed to keep the tension going, with break teasers like 'Will walnut dash past the beech or will it end in ash? Find out after the break' – that sort of thing. Both Mum and I stayed up until three in the morning to find out the result – walnut. A foregone conclusion really.

Domino's pizza for tea.

April 30th

A lot of the reviews in the papers are saying that *Britain's 100 Favourite Wood Veneers* was a better programme than *Britain's 100 Favourite Trees*, but what they fail to see is that I paved the way for the veneers show. I was breaking new ground. Without trees there would be no veneer.

I got a letter from the Vera Lynn Leisure Centre saying that they're introducing 'Verruca Only' sessions at the swimming baths and that my name has appeared on a list of verruca sufferers. That cow who accosted me by the vending machine has clearly grassed me up, even though there's nothing to grass – I don't have a verruca. The letter goes on to say that I will, from now on, only be allowed to swim on Tuesdays between two and four, and only in one of two designated lanes – until 'such time as your viral papilloma has responded to treatment'. Honestly, I'm a pariah in my own leisure centre.

I dash off a letter to Major Peter Andrews of the Devolution for Bexhill Party to try and gain his support.

Chicken curry and raspberry pavlova for dinner.

May

The Nemesis
Rest Home

May 1st

I try to get into my usual morning session at the Vera Lynn
Leisure Centre and am barred from entering by the manager
brandishing a clip board.

'You're on my verruca register, Sir,' he says.

'This is ridiculous,' I say, and take my shoes and socks off
to try and demonstrate my disease-free feet, but he isn't having it and threatens to call security.

May 2nd

Eastbourne's most famous octogenarian, lifelong Labour supporter Jeanette Massingbird, has sold her story to the *Mail on
Sunday*, telling how she used to be a man, was once in a perfume advert and had a fling with Jeremy Thorpe back in the
seventies, and how her first husband fought in the war against
illegal parking – in other words, he was a traffic warden.

'It's a disgrace what Labour get up to when all my Alf
wanted to do was clamp people's cars who hadn't paid for a
parking ticket or who had parked in an area where parking
is prohibited, such as on a double yellow line or red route,'
she is quoted as saying, holding up before and after photos of
someone's car being clamped.

She says she intends to use the money from the sale of the
interview to 'have a bit more bone chipped off my chin'.

Got a nice letter pushed through my door from Major
Peter Andrews of the Devolution for Bexhill Party. It turns

out he's on the same list as me at the local swimming baths as he has 'two great big mothers of verrucas on each foot'. He goes on to blame 'the chavs and drongos of Hastings', and signs off with 'See you at the pool between 2 and 4 p.m.'

What a fat lot of good he's turned out to be. I'm certainly thinking twice about voting for him now.

Baked trout for dinner, vanilla soft scoop for pud.

May 3rd

Actually the guys at the verruca session at the leisure centre are really nice and there's a great camaraderie. Fellow sufferers up against the rest of the world, them and us – although really, as I don't actually have a verruca, I'm technically not one of them, but they're not to know. I slip quietly away from the 'You show me your verruca and I'll show you mine' session in the changing rooms after the swim, but could hear the sounds of admiration as Major Peter Andrews took off his two verruca socks.

May 4th

Uncle Bob's night-time grunting is becoming an increasing problem. God knows what he's doing in that room of his, but neither Mum, me nor the dog are getting a wink of sleep. It starts at about midnight and goes on till two in the morning, when it gives way to another sound – teeth grinding.

'Enough's enough,' said Dog over breakfast. 'Either he goes or I go.'

So later on the three of us go and visit the Nemesis rest home, a warden-controlled flat along the coast in Rottingdean.

It seemed OK, but I must admit I'd never seen armchairs with seatbelts before. We put his name down and he can start on Monday. The problem now will be getting him to agree.

Mum suggests we book a 'man and van' to help get Uncle Bob to go.

Chicken nuggets and chips for dinner, Fruit Pastilles for pud.

May 5th

Nan phones and says she's still in prison and now sharing a bunk with *EastEnders* actor turned gutsy documentary-maker Ross Kemp, who is out there filming death as it goes on its business.

It's a new show he's doing called *Ross Kemp on Pestilence*, in which Ross travels around the Middle East filming people getting ill, while trying not to get shot at by angry *EastEnders* fans who wish he was still in the show.

He was arrested for 'flying low outside a mosque' – that's not flying as in a plane but flying low as in being caught with your flies down. Poor guy, he had been to the loo behind a tree but hadn't checked his zipper. The imam spotted his low flyer from the top of his minaret, and before he knew it he was banged up with Nan in the nudist wing. His camera team are still with him and filming it, and the good news is that the ratings are holding steady. I watched an episode of it last night after she'd called, and it's pacy and suspenseful and I'm pleased to say that Nan comes over really well. The two of them seem to be getting on like a house on fire, and I'm pleased to see that the towelling jacket I sent her fits like a glove.

I write to Nick Clegg asking that should he hold the balance of power in tomorrow's election and then be sent on a morale-boosting trip to Iraq, could he take a parcel for Nan: some Marks and Spencer's vests and pants, a jar of Marmite and some Tesco's finest pork chipolatas – well, she's worth it! The postal system is so unreliable, especially as far as sausages are concerned. If he could take them to Basra or wherever it was he was doing his main morale-boosting, I could get them biked round from there to Nan's jail.

Watercress and chicory salad for dinner, apple puff for pud.

May 6th

The day of the general election. I'm not going to tell you how I voted. That is between me and my ballot box. Oh, OK then, I voted for Major Peter Andrews, standing for the Devolution for Bexhill Party. Well, he's a friend.

Mum insisted that she voted for two different parties, putting a cross in both the Natural Law Party's box and that of the BNP. When I ask her why, she says she 'wants to see more flying Nazis'.

'You've spoilt your ballot paper, you silly mare!' I say.

'Yes, I did that as well.'

'What?'

'Soiled my ballot paper. Well, there was no bog paper in the cubicle.'

Roll on the totalitarian state that Major Peter Andrews dreams of.

Stayed up all night to watch the general-election show. I waited till two in the morning for it to start, then realised I was watching the wrong channel. They weren't covering the election on Babestation for some reason. I quickly turned over to see the BBC's coverage, which was mainly Andrew Neill on a barge in the River Severn along with all the top movers and shakers in the world of politics. Brian Belo from *Big Brother* had some very interesting thoughts on the possibilities of a hung parliament, while Cheryl Baker from Bucks Fizz pointed out the dangers of joining the European Monetary Union.

'If the financial climate is not right,' she said, 'the whole thing could go tits up.' Then she ripped off her skirt to reveal a coloured leotard.

May 7th

None of the main political parties have got a majority – and neither have the Liberals! Sorry, bit of a cheap joke at the expense of Nick Clegg and co., but as Stephen Page at Faber says, 'For God's sake make it funnier, or we'll never shift enough units to break even.'

It's what they're calling a hung parliament. Nick Clegg has responded by meeting David Cameron at the Stork Club, Piccadilly, for talks, drinks and nibbles.

The Natural Law/BNP coalition won the Bexhill seat, and a squadron of flying Nazis did a fly-past along the coast and landed on the roof of the De La Warr Pavilion.

It seems that in my haste to get dressed during my last session at the Vera Lynn Leisure Centre I picked up the wrong verruca socks and now have a verruca. On each foot. Fan-bloody-tastic.

The man (Ian) and van (Transit) arrive first thing to help get Uncle Bob to his warden-controlled flat. To say Bob wasn't keen would probably be the understatement of the century! Mum tried everything to coax the old boy out – promises of money, biscuits pushed under the door, as a last resort a pair of lady's knickers fresh from next door's line – but no, he wouldn't budge.

So Ian and I smashed the door down with an axe. It's never what I'd intended but our patience had been tested to the limit, and I was aware that I was paying Ian by the hour.

Once in the room it took us another twenty minutes to find Uncle Bob amongst the old papers, discarded soup cartons, eBay items and ladies' underwear. I lifted the lid on a cardboard box marked 'Bob's Panic Room Do Not Open', and there he was. He came flying at me, fists flailing, and it took four of us – me, Mum, Ian and the dog – to subdue him. Mum held him still and I poured Night Nurse down

Uncle Bob
Pretending he's
invisible

his throat through a funnel. We then dragged him still kicking and screaming to the van. You could hear his expletive-laden screams as the van disappeared round the corner of the close. Still, he's gone now, that's the main thing, and we will visit him . . . at some point in the future when he's settled in.

I must say that fifty quid for the man and van was the best fifty quid I've ever spent! Couldn't have done it without you, Ian, if you're reading this.

Suckling pig, apple sauce and roasties for dinner, followed by sherry trifle and After Eights – yes, we're celebrating!

May 8th

The warden at the Nemesis rest home, Uncle Bob's new residence, phoned saying he couldn't cope with Bob's behaviour and could he have the number of our man and van? Apparently he managed to escape from his room last night and is 'somewhere in the ventilation system'.

'Sorry, mate, I've got an eighteen-month contract,' I said, hanging up. Well, really! They're very keen to take your money but not so keen to put the work in.

Still no firm news on the hung parliament. Nick Clegg has said that 'I really like David but there are a few other people that I'd like to see first.'

May 9th

Veteran TV presenter Cilla Black has been called in to help Nick Clegg decide whom to lend his support to in the new hung parliament. A room in Whitehall has been set up with a special screen. Nick sits on one side of the screen, David Cameron and Gordon Brown sit on the other side on high stools, and Nick asks them questions as Cilla encourages them to show off and try to woo the buck-toothed hopeful.

'I like a higher level for when people should start to pay tax. Where do you stand on tax?' asks Nick.

'Well, if it's lower taxes you want,' says Dave from behind the screen, 'I would certainly like to carry you over my threshold!'

'Oooh, he's ever so forward, in't he, chuck!' says Cilla, throwing her head back and laughing. 'Number two, your turn.'

'Well, I think it's quite clear where we stand on taxation,' replied Gordon B. 'We in the Labour Party have a commitment to a fairer society, we have increased the threshold already and see no reason to do it again. You know, we face a very difficult time ahead with the global banking crisis, and now is not the time to be reducing revenue and promising tax breaks. I was brought up in Scotland, the son of a Methodist minister, and I know how difficult it can be to make ends meet, but my dad taught me my values and those values are the ones I stand by today.'

'Oooer!' says Cilla. 'Get him! Swallowed a dictionary, chuck?'

Nick chose Dave, and the two of them have gone to see *Les Misérables*, followed by dinner at Garfunkel's and then on to Boujis night club.

The other big news is that *Weakest Link* (Mum calls it 'Leakiest Wink'!) presenter Anne Robinson has landed the lead role in *Billy Elliot* – the first time a woman in her sixties has played the tormented miner's son who eschews the coal mine for the Royal Ballet. She will have to master a few of the simpler dance steps, and for the complicated stuff someone beneath the stage will put their hands up from below into her shoes and take over. Of course, the National Union of Contemporary and Ballet Dancers is up in arms, saying she is depriving a genuine dancer of the role and that in effect she is little more than a glorified puppet. It is threatening strike action.

It's a great show, though, and has had the effect of completely turning youngsters off mining, thus helping to kill off the last vestiges of the mining industry in this country and finishing the work that Maggie Thatcher started.

May 10th

Mum comes home from her WI meeting full of praise for a new lady member, a Mrs Riefenstahl. She describes her as having 'bags of personality and piercing blue eyes that make you feel like you're the only person in the room'. She says that she's very ambitious and plans to drag the Bexhill chapter kicking and screaming into the tweenies.

And for the first time I've heard Mum criticise Mrs Eileen Spencer, the current head of the Bexhill WI.

'But I thought you reckoned Mrs Spencer was doing a good job,' I said.

'I just think she could move faster on those within the organisation who show weakness,' she said, and pointed out that membership is down and that last year's fête was a little poorly run and that Mrs Spencer lost two out of the five categories she had entered in the fruit-and-veg competition and that her Victoria sponge had a sunken look in the middle. 'A leader should lead', she says, 'by example.'

On that note, Gordon Brown has resigned as leader of the Labour Party but says he's going to stay on as prime minister for 'as long as I want', adding that 'I had my fingers crossed when I announced the election anyway, so it doesn't count.'

Meanwhile, Nick Clegg and David Cameron have agreed to a civil partnership and announce that they will be formally married at Wandsworth Town Hall in June, with a short honeymoon in the Maldives. 'It's time to roll our sleeves up or buy a number of short-sleeved shirts,' David Cameron says, fingering a Boden catalogue. 'This is just the sort of difficult decision I will be having to make to provide this country with strong and stable government,' he continues.

In the afternoon Bruce Forsyth phones me, saying he's worried about his chin. He thinks he might have overdone the intra-chin chin juice and asks whether I will go round to see him urgently.

I arrive at his Wentworth mansion, and his lovely wife Winnie answers the door.

'Daktari, come quickly!' she says in a thick Portuguese accent. 'Master very sick!'

She ushers me through the lobby of the splendid eight-bedroom detached property with superb views over the golf course, and into the master bedroom.

There, seated in a club chair, is Britain's most versatile light entertainer, and he looks bad. His chin is swollen out of all proportion to the rest of his body. It reaches down past his waist to the floor, where it rests upon a hot-water bottle.

'Thank Christ you're here!' says the legendary game-show

host. 'I put the drip up as you said, then nodded off. Now look what's happened! I've got *Strictly* in three hours!'

'OK, keep calm,' I whisper, kneeling to examine the giant organ of his fortune. I could see tiny needle marks cleverly hidden between the wrinkles.

'You've been injecting again, haven't you, Sir Bruce?'

'I don't know what you mean!' he replies indignantly.

'Look, I can't help you if you're not honest with me!' I snap. 'Now tell me, have you been injecting the chin juice I gave you for emergencies?'

'It's worse than that,' he says, a look of remorse on his face. 'I've been getting supplies from Anton Du Beke, the big-chinned ballroom dancer.'

'But I deliberately matched you and Jimmy Hill age for age! Injecting gear from a much younger man like Du Beke was always going to be risky, and now look at you.'

'I'm shorry,' he says, the hot-water bottle wobbling as he speaks. 'Pleeesh help me!'

'Perhaps you should shoot him, Daktari, put him out of his misery,' chirps in Winnie. 'That's what we do in Brazil.'

'There'll be no need for any shootings, thank you!' I say, fumbling in my bag for my chin-drainage paraphernalia. 'A slight prick . . .' I say, inserting a needle attached to a tube leading to an Evian bottle.

'Yesh, you are,' says Bruce with all he can muster of a grin.

I smile at him. He's still got it – the amazing quick wit of someone half to two-thirds his age. I sit watching as the straw-coloured fluid slowly leeches out of the mega-chin and into the polythene bottle.

'How do you do it, BF?' I say in admiration.

'Fruit for lunch and the love of a younger woman,' he says, winking.

'Coffee and a Danish?' says Winnie, presenting a big tray of refreshments.

'Yeah, go on then,' I say, and the three of us bonded.

Two hours later, I lugged the last crate of Anton Du Beke chin juice into the boot of the car, and my work was done. Well, almost. The drained chin was now looking like some kind of skin duvet hanging down over his knees.

'Don't worry, I'll put a bit of make-up on it and tuck it under my dickie bow,' says Bruce, slipping on a pair of patent-leather shoes.

He walks me to the front door and takes my hand.

'Thanks, H, I thought I was a gonner back there, career over, and I can't face doing *Have I Got News* again.'

'Never,' I say, presenting him with my bill. 'Chin-chin!'

Oops, a bit tactless, but never mind.

Fruit for lunch – well, one out of two ain't bad!

May 11th

Despite Dave and Nick Cameron-Clegg (as they will be known from mid-June) agreeing to form a coalition government, Gordon Brown is refusing to leave 10 Downing Street and has changed the locks so no one can get in. Technically, David and Nick are not allowed to be pronounced Prime Minister and First Husband respectively until the Queen has been activated, which requires Gordon taking her an Activia yoghurt and a can of Red Bull.

At about half past eight in the evening there is a news flash.

Footage live from Whitehall shows Gordon on the roof of 10 Downing Street holding Ed Milliband by the hair, threatening to throw him off.

'If you people don't back off and let me and Sarah watch *EastEnders*, the little guy gets it!' he bellows, taking his red tie off and tying it round his head like a bandanna. He then pulls open his shirt and beats his chest, shouting, 'Me Gordon! You press!' and throws a brass cigarette case – a gift from the people of Tahiti – at Sky News anchorman Adam Boulton.

About twenty minutes later the phone rings and Mum answers.

'It's Alastair Campbell,' she says, handing me the phone. 'Didn't he used to be the lead singer of UB40?'

'He's asking for you, Harry,' says Ali Campbell, his voice cracking. 'Will you come?'

'S'pose so,' I say, pulling on my pacamac and climbing aboard Mum's disability vehicle.

I ran out of battery power on the outskirts of Hastings and had to call out the RAC, and so arrived in Downing Street on the back of the pick-up truck at about midnight. There were a couple of huge spotlights trained on the roof. By this time Gordon had put Ed Milliband down and was stroking his hair.

I was ushered through Number 10 and up a stepladder, which protruded through a Velux window.

'Careful, Sir,' said Metropolitan Police chief Sir Paul Stephenson, steadying the ladder with one foot and proffering a red and swollen forefinger. 'I tried earlier and he attempted to bite me.'

I took a quick glance at the PM's dental X-rays and I was up and out onto the roof.

'Gordon?' I said, inching along the parapet into the gloom, the wind battering my pacamac like a panel-beater working on a 2CV. Then I saw him, crouched over Milliband, licking the lid of a jar of Marmite.

'Gordon, it's me, Harry,' I said.

'Wuh?' he said, jerking his head round. 'Oh! The man from the supermarket.' His face broke into a broad rictus smile. I felt in my pocket for my secret weapon.

'You must be hungry,' I said, and whipped out a piece of haggis, still warm from the interior of the RAC cab.

'H . . . A . . . GG . . . IS?' said the bulky premier, cocking his head to one side. 'H . . . a . . . ggis!'

'That's right, Gordon, just like Mum used to make when you were wee!' I pulled off the pacamac to reveal the robes of a Methodist minister. As Gordon gorged himself on the savoury minced offal enrobed in a sheep's innards, I gently whispered to Ed Milliband, 'Go! I'm on it now,' and he crept off along a gutter and shinned down a drainpipe to safety. Then, producing a set of bagpipes, I played as if my life depended on it – 'Flower of Scotland', 'Amazing Grace', 'Mull of Kintyre', finishing on the theme from *Animal Hospital*. As I played I backed slowly towards the Velux, and as if in a trance Gordon followed.

'Come on, big man, let's get you into the warm,' I said to Gordon, adopting a Fyffe accent and shoving him down the hinged window and into the arms of Balls and Campbell.

'Thanks, H,' said Campbell, squeezing a twenty-pound note into my hand. 'You're a life-saver.'

'I did it because I care about this country, Ali,' I said, 'and am after a strong and stable government.'

I stayed the night on a Z bed in Number 11, tended to by Alistair Darling's wife.

Warm haggis pieces and Kit Kat Chunky for dinner and pud respectively.

May 12th

I was amongst the gang who welcomed Dave and Nick into Number 10 this morning. I then attended the press conference in the garden. It all ran pretty smoothly until a journalist reminded Dave that before the election he had referred to Nick as 'a buck-toothed wally whom I'd never form a coalition with in a million years'. Nick laughed graciously at the slight, then the same journalist pointed out that just yesterday Nick had called Dave 'a fat prat with a head that looks like a boiled egg with a face drawn on it'. Dave took it in good humour and they walked hand in hand back into the house. Then we all heard a muffled slap and the sound of a man crying.

With the disability scooter now fully charged, I headed back up to Bexhill. Ran out of juice at Bromley and had to rely on my friend at the RAC again to get me home.

The dog came home in the evening in tears, claiming he saw Deborah in the park being 'taken' from behind by an old English sheepdog. When I say, 'How old is old?' he reckons this dog was well into his sixties in dog years. Dog doesn't know how to handle it – whether he should challenge Deborah the collie cross or just turn a blind eye and put it down to experience.

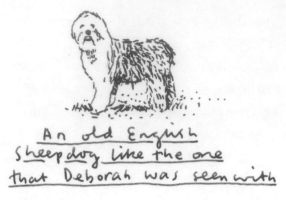

An old English
Sheepdog like the one
that Deborah was seen with

I tell him that turning a blind eye is basically 'just papering over the cracks in their relationship'.

He points out that I papered over the cracks in the spare room just before I sold my flat and got a good price for it – and he's right. In fact, one of the cracks went from my bedroom all the way down into the basement and was six inches deep. But he has inadvertently highlighted the problem with this metaphor.

'There are plenty more fish in the sea,' I say.

As he points out, with modern saturation-fishing techniques fish stocks are probably at an all-time low, so that saying no longer applies either.

I suggest that he call Deborah and arrange to meet up, which he duly does.

'How did she sound?' I ask him when he comes off the phone.

'Breathless,' he says. I feel for the creature, I really do.

Dog has a meeting with Deborah after work and she 'fessed up straight away. She said that it was a one-off with Chico the sheepdog, but she couldn't guarantee that it wouldn't happen again and suggested they have an open relationship.

'What do you think?' asked the dog, putting me on the spot rather.

'I think . . .' I hesitated. Fed up with him bouncing my sayings right back in my face, I keep it deliberately vague. 'Many a mickle makes a muckle,' I say.

Being in a long-distance relationship myself, I speak from experience. I mean, if I phone Lay Dee's room after midnight and a gentleman answers, I have to accept her explanation that it is her brother-in-law who is adjusting the satellite dish so that she can get better reception for *You've Been Framed*; or indeed that the number of empty packets of prophylactics visible on her bedside table on the webcam are the result of a 'water fight at the Christmas party'. That's what you need for a relationship to work – trust.

'I think if I say no, she's gonna leave,' says the dog. 'And if I say yes, I might get a couple more weeks out of it, and I'm expecting that new dog bed any day now and maybe that will keep her.'

'If that's what you think,' I say, but I could see he was desperate.

In view of Dog's problems, as night falls I decide to link up with my own Lay Dee in the Philippines on the webcam, via the Manila Envelopes website. It's so frustrating! The picture is so indistinct I could be talking to a completely different girl each time! And so difficult to control the joystick and attempt to get a meaningful conversation going.

I log off and have a restless night.

May 13th

David and Ed Milliband have declared their candidature for the Labour leadership.

'They are an amazing family,' says Mum. 'My favourite was Glenn Milliband, the American jazz musician. I had all his records – 'In the Mood', 'Moonlight Serenade', 'Tuxedo Junction'. Tragic the way his plane went down over the English Channel during the Second World War. His body was never recovered, you know.'

It's really not worth me trying to explain to her that she's got the wrong end of the stick, so instead I join in.

'Yes, Mum, what about Steve Milliband as well,' I say, 'who had that hit with "The Joker" back in the seventies?'

'Yes,' she says with a sigh. 'Happy days.'

I noticed that Mum's chin looks a bit bigger than usual today. When I check the Evian bottles from Brucie's place, there's one missing.

Bumped into that cow from the leisure centre and her potato-headed son at the chiropodist today. She tutted when she saw me and muttered 'No verruca, indeed' under her breath. I feel like a right prat.

Went to see Anne Robinson in *Billy Elliot* in the evening. For much of it you could clearly see someone's hands clamped round Anne's ankles from below, but it didn't really detract from its important message:

Dancing = good, Mining = bad

Stuffed-olive pinwheels and smoked salmon and cheese pinwheels for dinner, Swiss roll for pud.

May 14th

The National Union of Contemporary and Ballet Dancers has called a strike in protest at Anne Robinson's 'assisted foot-work' in *Billy Elliot* – the musical that points out the advantages of dancing over mining.

This has plunged the country into chaos. David and Nick Cameron-Clegg have appeared on television this evening appealing for calm and promising that ballet of a high standard will continue to be delivered to audiences up and down the country and that it shouldn't interfere with 'our strong and stable government'.

Bruce Forsyth is quibbling over the bill. He says I only drained twelve bottles when I've billed him for fourteen. I can't be bothered to fight it, but that's the last emergency call-out he gets from me and I strike him from my list.

Filet mignon, cabbage and potatoes parisienne for dinner.

May 15th

The army was called in to replace the National Ballet at last night's performance of *Swan Lake*, and it went ahead with all the roles covered by the Argyll and Sutherland Highlanders in hurriedly adapted camouflage tutus. In the middle of the performance Wayne Sleep threw himself under the Swan Queen in protest, breaking his collarbone, and was dragged from the stage to cheers from the audience.

The Argyll and Sutherland Highlanders managed to pull it together in the second act and delivered what was described by Rupert Christiansen in the *Daily Telegraph* as 'ballet of an extremely high standard, and a treatment of character that was *très sympathique*'. They left to a standing ovation.

May 16th

Mum came back from her WI meeting saying they are planning to do a nude charity calendar and could she do it?

'It was Mrs Riefenstahl's idea. She's so proactive!' she said.

My initial reaction was no. Then I thought I could always tear off her month so I wouldn't have to look at it.

'What month have they got you down for?' I asked.

'April,' she replied.

That's Easter, of course, which is usually pretty quiet for me, so I could probably make do without it.

She explains that since every Tom, Dick and Harry has started doing nude charity calendars they've decided to up the ante and be photographed in graphic sexual positions with the gentlemen of the Bexhill Rotary Club. All to raise money for injured cats.

'It's all simulated,' she assures me. 'Nothing too explicit.'

Cheese balls and breadsticks for lunch, rum baba for pud.

May 17th

Finally got to see the doctor after a six-week wait.

I described my symptoms to him – extreme tiredness after half a wine box.

'Do you ever feel sick in the mornings?' he asked.

'Yes, now you come to mention it, I do occasionally feel physically sick in the mornings,' I replied.

'Well, I *am* physically sick in the mornings,' he said. 'I wonder what it is?'

He sat staring at me for a minute or so, then stood to show me out.

'Well, let me know if you need a sick note, won't you? In the meantime, when the nausea comes on try to think of nice things, like a butterfly, a puppy or a well-toned black man stripped to the waist holding a baby. See how you get on and make an appointment with the receptionist for six weeks' time.'

'Six weeks?'

'Yes, that's when I'm off on holiday,' he said, and slammed the door.

It's a great service, the NHS.

Yellow-fin tuna steaks for dinner, followed by ice cream with wafers.

May 18th

The great dancers' strike continues. The author of *Billy Elliot*, Lee Hall, announced today that he has started writing a new musical expounding the virtues of ballet dancing over being in the army. *Barry Elliot* will, he claims, follow the story of a young lad growing up in Aldershot and whose father, a staff sergeant in the Argyll and Sutherland Highlanders, wants him to join the army like he did. However, the boy discovers an old pair of ballet shoes in a skip and decides he wants to

The Ballet Shoes

dance instead. He starts the training at Sandhurst but is discovered doing a pirouette in the gents' toilets. He is then pursued dancing across the parade ground by his commanding officer to Marc Bolan's 'Get It On'. He is court-marshalled in what is expected to be one of the most moving scenes in the film and is forced to explain why he likes dancing over being in the army: 'There's less chance of being shot.'

Mum had the WI calendar shoot today and came back looking very flushed and with a hickey on her neck. When I asked her how it went she burst into tears and said she wasn't sure about November, then ran to her room.

Fish-paste sandwiches for lunch.

May 19th

The Amalgamated Union of Associated Contemporary and Disco Dancers and Body Poppers, headed by *Pineapple Dance Studios*' artistic director Louie Spence, have decided not to support the strike and agree to stand in for many of the performances that the army can't manage due to other commitments (Afghanistan, Iraq, Notting Hill carnival, etc.). There is pandemonium outside the Sadler's Wells theatre as a picket line of young ballet dancers start setting fire to their ballet shoes and throwing them at the mounted police.

I watch the scenes of young girls with their hair done up in buns and slim athletic men in tights throwing flaming ballet shoes at policemen on the ten o'clock news in disbelief. How long can this go on for?

The treatment the chiropodist gave me for my verruca hasn't worked. Mum says that her hairdresser had used a bit of banana peel, applying it to her son's verruca with some tape at night. She says it cleared his verruca within a couple of weeks. Worth a try, I suppose.

May 20th

Applied the banana skin to the verruca last night and slipped over as I walked from the door to the bed. I'll kill my mum's hairdresser.

Anne Robinson was jostled at the stage door of the Victoria Palace theatre today as she arrived for a matinee performance of *Billy Elliot*, the anti-mining, pro-ballet-dancing musical. At some point someone heard something snap, and her face went back to how it used to be on *Watchdog* before she had all the work done on it and the show was cancelled. She left the theatre with a blanket over her head and went straight round to top plastic surgeon Jan Stanek's surgery, where he worked through the night to put it right, at one point sending out for more string.

Cream of avocado soup for dinner, banana custard for pud.

May 21st

Met the new head of the Bexhill WI today – the mysterious Mrs Riefenstahl. I got home from the ironmonger's just as she was finishing up her meeting with Mum. She froze me with her piercing blue eyes.

'So this is the famous Harry Hill,' she said, a smile playing around the corners of her mouth (where else?). 'Is it true you used to be a doctor?'

'Yes, that's right, *fräulein*,' I said, standing to attention.

'Then tell me, is it true that laughter is the best medicine, ha ha!' She threw back her head in laughter, revealing perfect white teeth surmounting a rim of pink plastic, top and bottom.

'*Auf wiedersehen*, Janet,' she called to Mum, as she brushed past me and strode down the drive, taking care to avoid the widening cracks that have started to appear in the concrete. She left behind her a powerful smell of edelweiss, which we only managed to shift by turning the Glade plug-in up to three.

She's some lady.

Reports tonight that Darcey Bussell today threw herself under the Queen's corgi in an attempt to draw attention to the plight of Britain's ballet dancers, and she appeared on the lunchtime news with Sophie Raworth with paw prints all over her face and tummy. These truly are desperate times.

Wiener schnitzel and cabbage for dinner, nougat for pud.

May 22nd

I phoned up Dave the builder, who put Mum's concrete drive down. It's only been laid for nine months and already huge cracks have begun to appear, which are starting to be colonised by ants. I wasn't even sure why she put down a new drive – the old one was perfectly serviceable. She told me that Dave had explained that she was sitting on a time bomb, that the drive would start to cause problems as the way it had been laid was, in his words, 'unlucky'. By laying a new drive over the top of the old one, for just £12,000 it should reverse the bad luck and put things right.

'That seems like an awful lot of money, Mum,' I said.

'That's what I said, but as Dave pointed out, what price peace of mind and a change in fortune?'

Well, it turns out that according to Dave it's about £12,000.

So I phoned East Sussex Drives, Solar Heating and Replacement Windows, whose headquarters are in Benahavis, Spain.

At first Dave denied all knowledge. Then, when I explained the problem, he offered up this excuse: 'A bit of cracking is normal. In fact, it's supposed to crack to allow the earth underneath to breathe.'

I threatened to get the pint-sized bald trouble-shooter Dominic Littlewood onto him, and he said he'd come and have a look next time he was in England.

'We have had better luck since Dave laid the new drive though, Harry,' said Mum. 'I mean, you've had your teeth fixed, Dog's found love and I've managed to avoid bird flu, so there's obviously something in it.'

'Maybe, Mum,' I said. 'The only small drawback is that we're having to park on the road because it doesn't function as a drive any more. Plus it's overrun with ants. We're going to have to start putting the sugar somewhere high up.'

The most frustrating thing about it is that through the cracks in the new drive I can see the perfectly good old drive grinning at me from underneath.

Over forty regular soldiers from the Argyll and Sutherland Highlanders have deserted and applied to the Royal Ballet School. One young corporal has gone on record as saying it's 'the first time I've ever felt truly alive' and points out that '"battle" is an anagram of "ballet"', which it would be if there were one less 't' and an extra 'l'.

213

An Argyll & Sutherland
Highlander

Asda's own cottage pie for dinner, followed by a sugar-free
gum to take away the taste.

May 23rd

As the sun was out I spent the morning with a magnifying
glass on the front drive burning ants, but have hardly made a
dent in their numbers. As I was lying there, with tiny plumes
of ant smoke all around me, who should wander past but
Mahesh the Jain Buddhist plumber. Tears filled his eyes, he
bit his lip and fled. Actually he's probably got a point this
time. I pop down to Dennis's to buy some ant powder.

'I heard about your mum and the WI calendar,' says
Dennis, winking and poking me with his dirty finger. 'Eh? I
heard about it.'

'What did you hear about Mum and the WI calendar?' I
say rather testily.

'Your mum, with her clothes off, with Alan from the bank,'
he says, gurning and winking in a lewd manner. 'I wouldn't
mind a copy of that calendar! Phwor!'

'SHE'S YOUR AUNTIE, YOU MORON!!!' I shout at him at the top of my voice, shoving 85p in exact money down on the counter, snatching my ant powder from him, marching out of his shop and slamming the door behind me. I catch my reflection in the shop window. My face is red.

When I get home I find that the ant powder is not a powder to kill and repel ants but a carton of powdered ants. I taste a little on my finger. It is tart and rather acidic but very moreish. I suppose this is how Ray Mears gets his kicks.

I suppose I shouldn't have shouted at Dennis. He is my cousin after all. I boil a kettle, walk out onto the drive and pour it down the crack that I have surmised is the ants' headquarters.

'Die! Why won't you die?' I scream, sinking to my knees and snorting a line of ant powder. I think I need a holiday.

Pie for dinner, pie for pud. Ant powder garnish.

May 24th

Went out to inspect the drive this morning and all the ants had arranged themselves in the shape of letters in an attempt to communicate with me. Their message was simple: 'Live and let live.' Then they scattered, scurrying down the huge cracks to the immaculate drive beneath.

The Message that
The Ants had for the
Author

LIVE & LET & LIVE

'Live and let live,' I echoed under my breath. 'Maybe they're right,' and I found myself asking the question 'Just why was I so anti-ants?' Was it a worry about them eating all our supplies of sugar? But these ants hadn't showed any interest in the sugar; besides, it was now safely on a high shelf. Had the ants tried to bite or sting Mum or me? No, no they hadn't. So why do I hate them so? I realise that I have been conditioned from an early age to hate ants and to kill them, but that's only part of it because what the ants represent is a fear of the unknown, and I come to the conclusion that all of us should be more understanding to foreigners.

I realise as I'm thinking it through that this would have made a great election-style anecdote for Nick Clegg of the Liberal Democrats. I've missed the boat with that obviously, but I scribble it down and send it to him anyway. Maybe he can incorporate it into one of his speeches.

I phoned Dave the builder in Spain and told him not to bother repairing the drive. We'll live with it.

May 25th

Still awaiting news about a visa for my fiancée Lay Dee, the Filipina woman whose details were passed on to me by the deadpan comedian Jack Dee. She was previously married to Jack, although according to him the union was never consummated. Knowing I had been somewhat unlucky in love he kindly directed me to the dating website Manila Envelopes. We've never actually met, of course, apart from in the internet chat room of Manila Envelopes, and while these exchanges have always been cordial, it would be nice to meet her in the flesh and see that lovely smile of hers which lights up her entry on her home page. It is clear to me that she is a good sort. Despite Jack's gripes, one only has to read the glowing tributes to her from the men she has dated on the site. Looks like I'm onto a winner!

Thai chicken curry and chips for dinner. No pudding – well, you don't really with Asian food.

May 26th

Overheard Mum plotting to overthrow Mrs Eileen Spencer as head of the WI and replace her with Mrs Riefenstahl.

Dog's new four-poster dog bed has arrived and it seems to have done the trick. Deborah the collie cross stayed over last night, only leaving at 4 a.m. when her Catholicism kicked in and she started to feel dirty.

'Every now and then our relationship will be tested,' said Dog to me on his way out to work at the airport. 'But you got to ride these bumps, take the good times with the bad.'

I must say it is a fabulous thing, the four-poster dog bed. It's made from moulded polyurethane plastic and is flocked so it has a velvety surface. Mum had a go in it as soon as the dog had left and was asleep in no time.

Pork knuckle and broccoli for dinner, Activia yoghurt for pud.

May 27th

Nan called from her Najaf jail cell. She's very homesick. I think her situation has been brought into sharp contrast by news of the upcoming Eurovision Song Contest. I'm sure she remembers the nights we used to spend as a family, all gathered round the TV watching Bucks Fizz and others singing songs in improbable outfits. Although we knew the songs were terrible and no reflection of the modern songwriter's art, in the absence of a proper war we took comfort in beating other countries without a single drop of blood being spilt. In the fallow years we adopted Ireland and cheered to the rafters as Johnny Logan romped to victory. Personally, I think his success in Eurovision played a huge part in rehabilitating the Irish in the eyes of the British and paved the way for the Anglo-Irish agreement.

It follows that to reduce the violence on our streets one could make a strong case for the return of *It's a Knockout!* and its international sister, *Jeux sans frontières*.

May 28th

Finally got round to clearing out Uncle Bob's room. What a mess! Piles of magazines and newspapers, three whole suitcases full of women's undergarments, a number of Chinese and Indian takeaway food cartons, as well as a few fusion and Thai ready meals that had hardly been touched. As I sorted through children's toys, an old radiogram and pieces of used toilet paper I came upon a suitcase marked 'Speshal Fings' in Bob's own hand. I opened it up and inside were scrapbooks in which were pages and pages of carefully pasted cuttings from magazines, newspapers and leaflets detailing the rise of one Harry Hill! The darling man had followed my career and kept a detailed record of it right up until the present day!

I sat flicking through the pages and remembering the old days: 'Balding Comic Wows Them in SE13!' shouts one headline, 'Medium-Size-Collared Loon Rips It Up in N11'; and 'Big-Collared Loon Booed Off in WC2'. There were playbills from my first shows at the Edinburgh Festival and articles showing how I'd won Belgium's answer to the Golden Rose of Montreux, the coveted Golden Sea Swallow of Kernock. I turned over a page and there was a ticket to a recording of my *This Is Your Life* signed by all the guests, including Kevin Keegan and the Marquis of Bath. There was an in-depth interview with Sally Vincent clipped from the *Guardian*, in which she hailed me as 'the new Chaucer', and, most moving of all, a lock of my now vanished hair and all my first teeth on a string.

This has left me rather confused. How did this outwardly potty man get it together to keep this record, and why? I show the cache to Mum, who gets a little flustered. 'I don't know why he would do that,' she says, adding, 'You know him, he's off his rocker!'

I carefully replace the now valuable archive in its mahogany box and continue the job of throwing all his stuff into a skip and fumigating his room, removing all trace of Uncle Bob from our lives for ever.

Ham, pineapple and mash for dinner, pineapple chunks with evaporated milk for pud.

May 29th

I came down this morning to the kitchen and – would you believe it? – the ants have been at the sugar! There was a great big long line of them ferrying the precious granules back to their HQ in the crack in the drive! After all I've done for them! In my fury I grabbed my Lynx antiperspirant spray and, spraying it through a disposable lighter, turned it into a flame thrower, just like Roger Moore did as 007 to that tarantula in the bathroom in *Live and Let Die*. I torched the ants as they stole from me, I followed the line out to the crack and torched that, then mixed up a big bag of cement and poured it into the crack, entombing the evil creatures for ever! 'Live and let live?' I shouted. 'No! Live and let die!' I sang, and dashed round the front garden singing the Paul McCartney and Wings hit at the top of my voice until I was quite exhausted and had to lie down. There's a reason man is at the very top of the evolutionary tree, and it's important that the lower critters understand that.

Caramelised onion soup for lunch, treacle tart for pud.

May 30th

Watched the Eurovision Song Contest last night. In a surprise move Morrissey was representing Great Britain with a song entitled 'Baby on a Treadmill'. The song wasn't up to much – and I say that as a Morrissey fan – but the dance routine that went with it was a real crowd-pleaser. As he got to the chorus:

> Baby on a treadmill
> Algerian man doing chin-ups
> Polish diplomat vaulting in the gym!
> Baby on a treadmill
> So pass me the bottle of Vim!

. . . as he got to this bit he whipped his trousers off (secured at the back with velcro) to reveal running shorts. He then jumped onto a treadmill and started running flat out, as lead guitarist and rockabilly legend Boz Boorer stepped up to the front of the stage and let go with a searing guitar solo. It was actually extremely moving and the Zagreb audience were on their feet by the end.

When the votes came in Mozzer was getting high numbers – eights, nines, even a few tens. The only bum note was sounded by the Algerians and the Poles, who both gave him zero. Otherwise he would have won: he was pipped at the post by John and Edward for Ireland with a self-penned number, 'I Dig Eoghan Quigg'.

Nan phoned during the Irish number in tears. She was watching the contest via satellite on a huge screen in the only Irish pub in Najaf, the Shamrock and Minaret, having been let out for the day. She said she was so upset that she was 'going to take the first plane home'. We managed to talk her out of it. Well, we've got enough going on here.

Trying to steal some of Eurovision's thunder, Channel 4 repeated *Britain's 100 Favourite Trees* back to back with *Britain's 100 Favourite Wood Veneers*, and seeing them so close together I have to say I think the papers were right: *Trees* does seem to be an inferior product.

June

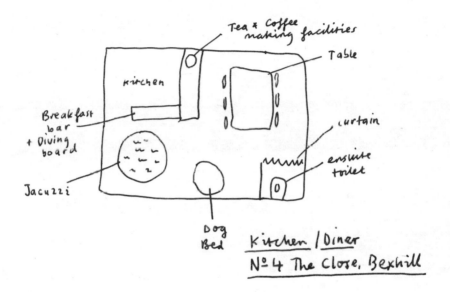

Tea & Coffee making facilities

Table

kitchen

Breakfast bar + Diving board

curtain

ensuite toilet

Jacuzzi

Dog Bed

Kitchen / Diner
Nº 4 The Close, Bexhill

June 1st

I've woken up this morning with a brilliant idea for Ant and Dec, 'Tickle SuBo', where the *Britain's Got Talent* also-ran and Alan Bennett's ex jumps up and down on a trampoline and members of the public have to try and tickle her. OK, it's maybe not a whole show, but it would make a great segment within a show. I jot the outline down and post it off to Gallowgate, Ant and Dec's production company, which they formed with Respect Party leader George Galloway.

silhouette of
Ant & Dec

Cheese tidbits for lunch, half a box of Milk Tray for pud.

June 2nd

Received a parcel today from Nick Clegg containing a pair of underpants. Enclosed with the garment is a handwritten note:

Dear Strong and Stable Government Supporter,
Thank you for your letter. I am happy to enclose the support

undergarment you requested, and fingers crossed they help to raise a lot of money for your chosen charity.

Luv Nick XXX

No Marmite or chipolatas. Coincidentally, at about mid-day here – two in the afternoon Najaf time – we got the good news that Nan has been released from her Iraqi prison unscathed! It's not clear how she has managed to get off without receiving her Sharia-style punishment, but Mum says, 'They probably got fed up with her nagging.' She's heading home to her Najaf bolt-hole.

Marmite on toast for breakfast, sausage sandwich for lunch.

June 3rd

Getting dressed this morning I noticed Nick Clegg's charity underpants on the chair and casually tried them on. They fit like a glove. Result!

Nick Clegg's
Underpants

Mum is spending more and more time down at the WI since this new charismatic leader Mrs Riefenstahl took over from Eileen Spencer. I'm not sure about some of the new rules either. For instance, she has an altogether much more ruthless approach to the summer fête.

'Mrs Riefenstahl says that it's not enough just to compete

in the competitions, our jams and cakes must win!' says Mum with a distant look in her eyes that I haven't seen since she came back from the WI calendar shoot.

Apparently Claire Davies had suggested that 'the taking part' was just as important as winning, and Frau Riefenstahl was very cold with her. The next day Claire's car had been daubed with paint. One word: 'Softy'. She has since left the WI and is helping out with the Girl Guides.

This Mrs Riefenstahl is getting a bit of a name for herself as a ruthless suppressor of dissent.

June 4th

Things seem to be back on between the dog and his girlfriend Deborah the collie cross. A lot of the time he stays over at her place after work for his food, and no doubt other things too. He never stays over all night though – something to do with her not wanting him there when she wakes up because she was brought up a Catholic or something. Often he doesn't get in till 3 or 4 o'clock in the morning. This means Mum gets a good crack at the dog bed, and we've got into a sort of routine where she curls up in the dog bed at half nine and falls asleep and I carry her up to her own bed at about midnight. I then wipe round the bed with Mr Muscle to remove any tell-tale hairs. It does mean extra work for me, but anything for a quiet life. We've both noticed a big improvement in the dog: he is much more chipper, has a real spring in his step. His appetite is up and he's taking a new pride in his appearance, which is 'all good', as Gary Lineker says. It's been 'a long journey', as they say on *X Factor*, but fingers crossed it looks like maybe the dog has found that 'special person with whom to share his life', as they say on *Jeremy Kyle*.

Last night on *Strictly Come Dancing* Bruce came on and said 'Hello to meet you, did well, didn't you, nice' in error and it's caught on. Everyone's using it, from kids in the playground to Nick Clegg in the House of Commons. Amazing, a new catchphrase at that age!

Cheese ploughman's for lunch.

June 5th

As Mum handed me, freshly laundered, Nick Clegg's charity underpants, she asked how they came to be in the laundry.

'I wore them, Mum,' I said, 'and they were a really good fit.'

'Won't that reduce their value?' she asked, and then I had one of those special moments when an idea so good hits you that you feel like jumping up and down on Amanda Holden's trampet.

'That's it!' I cried. 'We get different celebrities to wear the underpants, we photograph them wearing them, we bring out a book of the photos and at the end we auction the pants! All for a charity of our choice!'

'Isn't that potentially rather unhealthy?' said Mum.

'Don't be ridiculous! They've only got to wear the pants for the time it takes to have a photo taken.'

I'm fired up with the idea and start making up a wish list of possible celebs:

Sharon Osbourne	George Galloway
Esther Rantzen	Angie Best

Dappy from N-Dubz	Brian Cox
Seamus Heaney	Shakira Caine
Paddy Ashdown	Noddy Holder
John Redwood	David Quantick
Marguerite Patten	Any of the *Loose Women* team
Peter Purves	Phillip Schofield
Ben Fogle	Tinchy Stryder
Sophie Rhys-Jones	Jimmy Cricket

Looking down the list I start to realise that even if I got these people to wear the pants, I'm not sure it's going to be any good. Plus without a photograph of Nick wearing them at the start of the book the whole project would be pointless.

I carefully fold the piece of paper with the list on and put it in the bin.

Fish nuggets with tartare sauce for dinner, custard sponge for pud.

June 6th

With no further sightings of the Bexhill UFO, whispers have been circulating in the town that Londis manager Dominic has a drink problem. I think this is grossly unfair, although I must admit he does seem to reek of booze. As Mum points out, that's strictly circumstantial evidence and it might be 'a form of diabetes'. Yes, the Londis has taken a bit of a dive in recent months – I mean, all last week there was no milk. But I accepted Dominic's excuse that his supplier had been using a different antiseptic gel to wipe the cows' udders, which had caused a rash, and the swollen teats were less willing to yield their load to the gentle suction cups of the automated milker. Yes, some of the shelves in Dominic's Londis are laden with foods you wouldn't necessarily expect in a convenience store. I don't know anyone around here who likes sheep's cheese, for example, or indeed still uses flashbulbs or slide film, and he claims that his rollmop section is particularly popular with 'visiting Norwegian fishermen who have been blown off course from Dover'. Not sure. Last time I looked the jars were covered in a thick layer of dust. What I will say about Dominic's version of Londis is that there's always plenty of booze, and God knows we all need a drink now and then.

Nan phoned to say that today she received a telegram from the Queen. It read '£20 each way on Asian Temptress in the 2.30 at Haydock Park' and clearly was not intended for her. Nan put the money on the horse anyway and won sixty quid.

Thatched haddock and potatoes parisienne for dinner, Frube for pud.

June 7th

With our holiday to Spain booked for July we need to get a passport for the hamster if he is to come with us. The problem we have is that he won't sit still long enough on the stool in the photo booth in the post office. I wasted six pounds on eight very blurred shots, one of which had the top of my head in as I tried to distract the little critter. I explained to him that if he didn't keep still he wouldn't be coming. This seemed to go in one ear and out the other. I went back in the afternoon with a peanut on a string which I Blu-Tacked to the ceiling of the photo booth so that the nut dangled down above the stool just

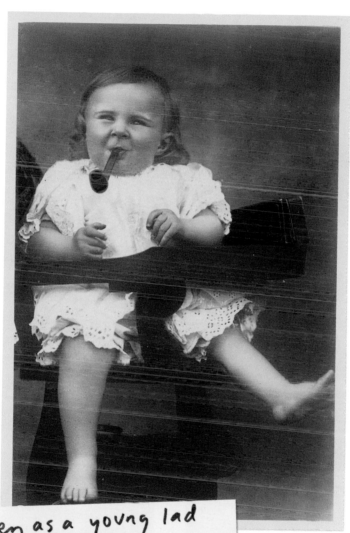

Even as a young lad
I was different

Mum's first boyfriend suffered terribly with excessive hair growth

But she kept in touch with him for years

Dad's scheme to sell cardboard ties to The Mock Tudor Building Industry

never took off

The last photo ever taken of Dad on the day War broke out. Off on his way to Scotland

The Bexhill Players' entry to Britain's Got Talent. Mum 3rd from left

Mum found that if she concentrated hard enough she could hover 18 inches off the ground

15

Mum after her brush with the 50 minute makeover team.

It was probably a mistake to hold the Bexhill Annual Toboggan race in June. Mum 3rd from left

Nan's New Rockery
- Najaf

Kindergarten: The food
and drink was excellent
but ofsted reckoned the
teaching was 'patchy'

Mum claims to have been
one of the first female
Teddy Boys

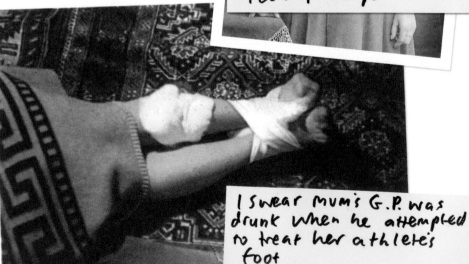

I swear Mum's G.P. was
drunk when he attempted
to treat her athlete's
foot

learning to swim during the drought of 1976

Nan's Tina-Turner-o-grams proved a nice little earner

during the double-dip recession

Otis Ferry and pals help to see off the cockroach infestation at Nº 4.

Brandon Flowers of The Killers shares a bottle of Queen Anne with Princess Beatrice

Faber Summer Party Martin Amis and Lorraine Kelly get intimate

members of West Life applaud manager Louis Walsh at his 70th Birnday Party

Quentin Tarantino Martin Scorsese + friends swap tips on directing at The TV Quick Awards

My 45th Birthday Party
me on the right.
From left:
Rachel Whiteread

Nick Clegg,
Justine Frischmann
Mark steel
Nigel Mansel
Fiona Phillips

From Left to Right:
Charlotte Church
Julie Birchill
Kate Bush greets Lord
Mandelson

Some Guys have all
the luck!
Bob Carolgees being

Mobbed by
Anne Widdicombe,
Sarah Brown and
Carey Mulligan

at the opening of
the De la Warr Pet
Food Pavillion

My wedding day to
Lay Dee showing
the Hill side of the
family

Mum 3rd from left

Dog's Christening

Mum shows off her
entry to 'The largest
piece of Fudge' competition

At the Bexhill
county fair

out of shot. Happily this kept the hamster in position for long enough to get two good shots. I then took the photos along to the vet to get him to sign the back certifying that it was a good likeness of the little fluffer. The vet said he didn't have to sign the back as they're not like human passports, but I say I'd prefer it if he did, just to be on the safe side. The last thing I need is to go to the trouble of filling out the form and getting the photos done, only to have the application rejected for something as silly as not having the photo signed on the back.

'But you don't need me to sign the back,' says the vet.

'Maybe not, but if you could that would be great.'

'No,' he says. 'If I sign yours I'll end up having to sign everybody's. You don't need it signed. I'm not signing it, that's an end to it.'

'It will take you two seconds to sign. Please just sign it. I won't tell anyone.'

'No, it's the principle. It's ridiculous, I'm not doing it.'

'Sign the goddamned photo!' I yell at him.

'No way!' he yells back.

I grab his hand and try to force him to sign, but in the tussle that ensues the photo is flipped over and I end up drawing a moustache on the hamster's face.

'Now look what you made me do!! Sign the photo or I'm going to the *Sunday Mirror* about what you get up to here.'

'What do you mean?'

'Putting your finger places that it shouldn't be.'

'Wha . . .? You're mad! OK, if it gets you out of my surgery I'll sign your photo!'

And so finally he signs the back of the photo. Why can't people just be helpful?

This morning at about half ten the TV presenter and handy-man Nick Knowles surfaced through the parquet flooring in the lounge with a spade.

'Hello!' he said. 'Can I use your loo?'

It seems he's been working on a DIY show where he and a team of builders offer to dig out a member of the public's basement to 'help to realise the potential of your property'. The property in question is in Robertsbridge, some twenty miles away. Nick and the team started digging and obviously took a wrong turn somewhere and have ended up in Mum's front room. Like Nick says, it'll make 'great telly', and we welcome him and his team up through the hole, and after they have all relieved themselves, make them a brew. He explains that the tunnel is oak-lined and has over three miles of wardrobes, a wet room and en-suite bathroom, and will add value to the house in Robertsbridge. He also says that they will make good the damage to the parquet flooring and as a goodwill gesture put up a rosewood corner cupboard in the hallway.

After they've gone it dawns on me that Mum's property is now connected to another property twenty miles away by a tunnel and so is now technically semi-detached, reducing its value substantially. I phone Nick, who promises to cap off the tunnel at the property boundary and thanks me for the tea. I feel a little uncertain about it. I suppose it's just jealousy that these people in Robertsbridge now have all this extra storage and all we got out of it is a lousy corner cupboard. I don't think it's real rosewood either; it's a laminate.

Beef chunks with paprika rice for dinner, lattice almond sponge for pud.

June 9th

The hamster's passport application form was returned today. It has been rejected. The hamster feels bad and is worrying that it is because his family are from Syria. It's true that there is a lot of bad feeling towards the Middle East at the moment, but I can't think that this would count against a hamster. Looking through the form I think that it was rejected because the vet signing the hamster's photo claimed to have known him for at least two years, when in fact the hamster is only eighteen months old. I should have had it checked at the post office, but I didn't want to pay the extra fifteen quid. Oh well, it seems that the hamster won't be able to come on holiday with us.

When I tell the hamster the news he takes it rather badly, saying that he's had a really stressful year and was looking forward to a chance to unwind. I soften the blow by saying that I'll take him for a few day trips when I get back and buy him something nice from the airport, and he seems to accept that.

Asda's own chicken tikka massala for dinner, which was unusually yellow in colour.

June 10th

No news from Ant and Dec regarding 'Tickle SuBo', the game-show-segment idea I had for the popular duo, but I guess it's early days.

Dog is worried that Deborah the collie cross he has been

seeing for over three months is having an affair. When Dog challenged Deborah at work today she admitted that the affair with Chico the Old English sheepdog is back on and announced that she was pregnant with his kids.

I've never seen the dog so low.

June 11th

Mum is pregnant from the WI calendar shoot and has asked me to prescribe the morning-after pill. I calculate that it is in fact more like three weeks. I give her twenty-one morning-after pills to cover it. She ends up having an overdose. The cumulative effect of all the mornings-after send her three months into the future, where she jots down the name of the winner of the 2.30 from Haydock Park on September 5th – Festen Bulbous.

Perhaps next time she'll think a bit harder before allowing herself to be taken advantage of by a local Rotarian.

Bexhill carnival – the disability-vehicle display team were brilliant, until the fire.

Popcorn and candy floss for lunch.

June 12th

Clay-pigeon shooting with Guy Ritchie. After a while he suggested we 'mix things up a bit' and we moved on to clay-Madonna shooting. Life-sized Madonnas in conical bras made from clay were propelled from a cannon and we had to try to shoot them. Fun but kind of dispiriting at the same time.

The dog has been trying to get Deborah jealous by deliberately getting seen walking with Janine the Doberman on Deborah's route home. He just won't accept that it's over and move on.

The thing is, everyone round here knows that Janine is a lesbian.

News from the site of my windmill/station conversion for *Grand Designs*. It seems the decorator has got wallpaper paste mixed up with a bucket of frog spawn. We now have tadpoles hatching underneath the wallpaper and causing air bubbles. Oh, Kevin McCloud loved that!

June 13th

I came down this morning to find that the goldfish has committed suicide. He has been a little low for a while, retreating to his porcelain treasure chest and taking very little interest in food. Then once or twice we found him lying on his side near the water's surface. I said he was attention-seeking. Mum reckoned he was feeling left out after the arrival of the baby and that we should try and make more fuss of him. So we bought him a porcelain castle, complete with a green area in front of it in which a tiny porcelain Elton John is seen playing a tiny porcelain red piano.

It seemed to buck him up for a while, but not for long, and pretty soon he was hanging out in the porcelain treasure chest all the time, only really coming up when I sprinkled his food or, not being that bright, when I pretended to sprinkle his food. Mum called it teasing, but a lot of the time I would do it just to get him out of that chest and stretch his fins. After a while he even stopped coming up for his food.

The vet suggested we crumble half a Prozac tablet into his tank, which we did, but it had no noticeable effect.

Then this morning there he was, by the side of the tank. He'd obviously thrown himself out. He was still alive when I got to him, just. He was mouthing something, but I couldn't understand what. It sounded like 'Pah! Pah!' Was he calling me 'Papa' perhaps? Or was he saying 'Pah!' to life? We'll never know now. I suppose rather than trying to decipher his last words I should have put him back in his bowl, but I wasn't thinking straight – the grief, you see.

The vet put down the cause of death as 'delusions of

The goldfish seemed to be trying to say something to me.....

Amphibia' – the idea that the fish thought he could breathe out of water – but I think he was just sparing our feelings. Suicide, as you know, is illegal and none of us want to see the dead fish behind bars.

It surprises me how badly I've taken it. I mean, I fed him every day, but we weren't that close. Now every time I close my eyes I can see his little face poking out from behind Elton John like an aquatic Kiki Dee. Mum says we should get another one, but I say it's too soon. Besides, the carnival has been and gone – and last time it took seventy-four gos before I got the three hoops over that bowl.

It does solve the problem of who's going to look after him while we're on holiday though.

We put the fish on a bed of cotton wool in a big matchbox and leave it half open on a tray on the bed in the spare room so that anyone who wants to can pay their respects.

I went to pay mine and it had gone. It took ages to get it back off of next door's cat. We shouldn't have left that window open.

Dog, who is very low anyway, determines to stage an all-night vigil.

Scampi and chips for dinner.

June 14th

In the morning we light a small bonfire, place the matchbox containing what's left of the fish upon it and say a few prayers, sing a few hymns – 'Cumbaya', 'Lord of the Dance Settee', finishing with 'I Guess That's Why They Call It the Blues', an Elton John number which just seemed appropriate. Then there was a very strong smell of cooked fish and we all started to feel peckish, so we had an early lunch.

I wake up in the middle of the night worrying whether there was more we could have done to help the fish. Mum brings me a cup of hot milk and plumps my pillow, which seems to calm me, and the sandman is soon there at her side with his fuggy cuddles.

Salmon steaks for dinner.

June 15th

Got a card from Peter Fincham with a scene from *Heartbeat* on the front. Inside, 'Sorry we've had to let you go, good luck in your new job' is crossed out and 'Sorry to hear about your fish' is written over the top in crayon. Sweet.

A lazy day. I'm feeling rather listless and can't settle on anything so I write a list – a shopping list – which helps to shift that listless feeling, and I pop down to Londis for a few bits and bobs. Everyone is very sympathetic about poor Noddy the goldfish. It's at times like this when it's nice to live in a small, tight-knit community like Bexhill.

I drop in to see Dennis at the hardware shop as I have lost the fine red pipe you get with the can of WD40 and so am unable to direct its lubricating fluid with any accuracy. He tells me that you can't buy those red pipes individually and to secure one I would have to buy a whole new tin. Well, we all know how long it takes to work your way through a whole tin of WD40, so it makes no sense at all for me to buy a new one. With this little bit of business over with, Dennis then makes some crack about Mum's recent brush with Alan, the man in charge of repossessions at the Hastings branch of Santander and a prominent Rotarian.

'I hear your mum very nearly got repossessed!' he said. 'I heard he got a very nice Easter present!'

I slapped him round the face and told him to mind his own business, and on my way out I grabbed one of the red pipes off his WD40 display.

I hate that petty, small-minded gossip that you get in a small town, and long once more for the cold anonymity of London.

Boiled egg for dinner, nougat for pud.

June 16th

Rehearsals start for the pilot of the new ITV1 game show *Spot the Difference*, which I'm presenting. The idea is that celebrities attempt to win money for charities that they've only recently heard about – especially children's ones – by spotting the difference between a pair of historical tableaux featuring identical twins. ITV have had a problem (a) getting enough identical twins, and (b) getting enough celebrities.

A lot of the celebs say they'd prefer to keep the prize money rather than have to give it to charity, and remember for a lot of celebs at this level these are the only sort of shows they do, so they end up working for nothing all the time. OK, that means that the public warm to them, but you can't live on charity. Well, you can, but that would make you a beggar, which is not a nice way to refer to these often very talented people. A couple of them have said they'd only do it if they're guaranteed a proper paid job like *I'm a Celebrity . . . Get Me Out of Here!* at the end of it.

The run-through is fraught with difficulties. The producer is having a big problem telling the identical twins apart, and that gets their backs up. There are four historical tableaux: the Battle of Hastings, the Great Fire of London, the Siege of Mafeking and Susan Boyle being beaten by Diversity in the *Britain's Got Talent* finals 2009 (for younger viewers).

The set designer is hopping mad because in an attempt to save money they've decided to do the whole thing in front of a blue screen. So for the Battle of Hastings you've got thirty sets of twins in Norman and Saxon costume – fifteen on each set – against a backdrop of postcards of Hastings beach. There are five subtle differences between the two tableaux and it's up to the celebrities to spot them. The celebrities for the pilot are Vanessa Feltz's personal trainer Dennis and Jan Leeming. Jan's very good at it and spots four of the differences straight away (William the Conqueror has got one sock lower than the other, Harold hasn't got an arrow in his eye, one of the Saxon fighters is wearing a watch and in one of the tableaux there is a donkey). But the fifth one is proving very difficult to spot. There is a very long gap during which Vanessa's personal trainer has a couple of guesses and Jan shares a little historical knowledge about the actual battle, but this is pretty much dead air. The studio audience start to get restless and begin chatting to each other. Then one of the twins in the tableaux shifts his position slightly and Jan, seeing this as a potential difference, points it out. I don't know whether to award the point or not. I'm getting nothing back from the gallery in my earpiece. I look at my watch and two hours have elapsed since the last genuine difference was spotted. The producer now starts shouting in my ear to go to the ad break.

'Will they spot the difference?' I say. 'See you after the break.'

I rip the earpiece out of my ear and storm up to the gallery.

The producer has calmed down and calls it 'a teething problem with the format' and says that I shouldn't worry.

'What is the fifth difference between the two tableaux?' I ask, and it turns out he doesn't know either. The answers are sealed in an envelope held by an Ofcom official in line with the new rules – instigated after the last ITV phone-in scandal.

It takes eight hours to tape the entire show, and neither Jan nor Vanessa Feltz's personal trainer Dennis ever spot more than four differences on any of the four tableaux.

The audience left at midnight to find the multi-storey car park had been locked for the night. They then invaded the set and demanded overnight accommodation.

The finale was supposed to be Susan Boyle herself being lowered in on a wire singing the Sam Cooke hit 'Wonderful World', but she threw a wobbly back-stage so her team of advisers decided against it and she was put on the first bus back to Fyffe.

What a palaver!

The producer was upbeat in the green room after the show, saying that with a bit of music and some dubbed-on laughs it would make 'a serviceable hour of prime time', but I was not convinced.

Sausages on sticks, Mini Kievs, tiny pork pies and salmon vol-au-vents for dinner/breakfast.

June 17th

Brenda our cleaner is not doing a very good job. Mum says the only thing she is cleaning is 'us out of cash'. While I don't think this is a very good joke, I do agree with the point she is making through humour. To be fair, Brenda is an older lady. We don't know how old, but I'm guessing she's in her late seventies. That's part of the problem: she's at an age when a lot of her friends are dying and so she needs time off to attend the funerals in the Philippines. Often she is gone for three or four weeks at a time. In the meantime the dirt piles up – particularly around the cooker. Of course, the other problem is her apparent aversion to elbow grease. Increasingly she is relying on copious amounts of Mr Muscle. At £2.10 a bottle it's expensive stuff, that Mr Muscle, not to mention the effect that the bleach in it has on the environment. I mean, I've seen her with a bottle in each hand, fiercely pumping the handles as she backs into the kitchen and disappears in a fine mist of lemony scourer.

The other week I caught her with two bottles taped together in each hand – that's four bottles on the go at the same time. I said to her, 'It's MISTER Muscle – not MESSRS Muscle!' but I think it went over her head.

I've told her that the bleach in these kinds of cleaners enters the waterways of the world and kills our fish, but she won't listen. She says the best way to kill fish is 'With hand grenade! Bang! Everyone help themselves! Yum yum!'

'No,' I say, 'there will be no fish left for our children's children if you carry on the way you are.'

'Plenty fish for everyone! Bang! Yum yum!' she cries, pumping the twin handles of her Mr Muscle bottles.

She might as well be standing in the middle of the London Aquarium with a baseball bat whacking cod on the head.

She uses it on all the wrong surfaces too. I've seen her cleaning windows with it, wiping the flat-screen TVs . . . Once I caught her spraying a fly with it, and then when the fly crashed to the floor she stood over it with both hands pumping a blizzard of Mr Muscle at it until it stopped moving, shouting, 'Die! Till you dead!'

So I've started marking the level on the bottles and monitoring her usage. I'm feeding the data into my computer and intend to confront her with it in the form of a graph or pie chart at the end of the month.

By rights I should just sack her on the spot, but what can I do? She's very good with visitors.

Kedgeree for dinner, rice pud for pud.

June 18th

Nan phones to say she has extended her Stannah-style chair lift at her Najaf pied-à-terre. Not because she is in any way disabled; it's just that she's lazy and she got one pretty cheap off eBay. The lengths of extra track will take her from her bedroom right to the kitchen, door to door, with 'stations' in-between at the bathroom, the downstairs bog and the living room. It also includes a scenic route out through the French windows, round the bomb crater and back up the side return to the front door. She also has a chicane on order to spice things up a bit in the hallway. You've got to hand it to the old girl. We'll have no problem shifting the place when she finally decides to shuffle off this mortal coil and return home.

Woke up in the middle of the night to an odd grunting noise. Went downstairs to investigate and found that Mum had got her tongue stuck to the ice tray again, and I had to gently free her with a hot flannel.

June 19th

Went to PC World and I'll tell you now, it has absolutely nothing to do with Petula Clark.

Boneless turkey roll for dinner, Yoplait for pud.

June 20th

Amanda H phoned and said she'd been prison visiting. 'It's great 'cos it makes you look, like, compassionate. You should try it.'

I book myself in for a session at Parkhurst.

On his way back from work for the last three nights Dog has seen Deborah lining the route with Chico, the Old English sheepdog. She's been a right cow to him.

June 21st

Got to the till at Londis today and couldn't remember my PIN number. The cashier, bless her, was only trying to help and started suggesting different numbers to me.

'Is it 1?' she said.

'I don't think so,' I replied.

'Is it 2? Is it 3 . . .?'

Which didn't help a bit. While I knew that it must consist of four of the numbers from 1 to 9, her suggesting different numbers only served to confuse me more. In the end I explained that I would have to put the groceries back and find out what the PIN number was. However, as I went to take the card from the machine the cashier grabbed it from my hand and tried to bend it in two and tear it up.

'Oi! Give me back my card!' I cried.

'Can't do that, I'm afraid. The card must be destroyed. You do not know the PIN number. You may have come upon the card in a fraudulent manner!'

I almost managed to grab it, when she stood up. Well, she must have been very near seven feet tall. There was no way I could reach it standing on the floor, so I jumped up onto the side of the till. Thinking quickly she activated the conveyor belt that usually conveys your groceries towards the cashier, but in this case it became a slow treadmill for me to pound as I attempted to wrest the card from her grasp. I got it back, albeit with a thick rumple down the middle where she'd folded it. She reached down and pressed a button which increased the pace of the conveyor belt, and my feet went from under me and I was slung forward, ending up with my head in a carrier bag. Pulling the bag off, I rolled off the treadmill and stormed off. At which point, completely unannounced, my PIN number entered my head. So, returning to the till, I said 'Try it again' and pushed the rumpled card into the card reader.

Oh, the satisfaction of those four little words 'Transaction approved, remove card'! And here's the ultimate revenge: after she'd torn off my receipt I asked for cash back. You should have seen her face!

June 22nd

Yesterday's incident at the Londis has damaged my confidence in remembering my PIN number. In fact, I couldn't remember it again this morning. I phoned the bank to try to find out what it is so I can write it down and keep it safe. The person I talked to wouldn't give me the number because I was unable to remember my password. I can't change the password because I don't know the PIN. If I knew the PIN I wouldn't want to change the password. I hang up in a fit of pique and go and do a sudoku to calm myself down.

Phoned up the bank one more time to see if I could get someone a bit more sympathetic on the other end. The voice on the phone said: 'I just need to ask you one or two security questions for identification purposes. What was your mother's maiden name?'

'Easy,' I said, 'Piedmont.'

'Correct. Where were you born?'

'Surrey.'

'More specifically?'

'Woking.'

'Correct. What was the make of your first car?'

'Austin Maxi.'

'The registration?'

'P reg.'

'The full registration?'

'TNX 420P.'

'I'll give you that – 430P. OK, for a bonus point who starred in the 1978 remake of *The Wizard of Oz*, *The Wiz*?'

'Michael Jackson?'

'Yes. Another . . .?'

'Diana Ross.'

'Correct. And the score was by . . .?'

'Stevie Wonder?'

'No, Quincy Jones. OK, let's add up the scores . . . You scored six points, which takes you on to our bonus round.'

'Hang on,' I say, 'what about my PIN number?'

'Sorry, can't help you at the moment. All our systems are down. I was just trying to keep you entertained until they were fixed. Do you want to play on?'

'Oh, go on then,' I say.

Well, by the time the system came back on I'd got up to level twelve and had won a crystal vase, an imitation leather holdall and a DVD box set of *All Creatures Great and Small*.

Lancashire hot pot for tea, washed down with a glass of hock.

June 23rd

Get a call from the press office at ITV asking me whether I know anything about an offensive message I supposedly left on Andrew Sachs's answer machine.

It's true I did leave a message, congratulating him on his debut on *Coronation Street*. It went something like: 'Congratulations, Andrew, on your grand debut on *Corrie*. It was the daughter of all performances. It is so nice to see an actor playing a proper role rather than having to prostitute himself in an advertisement. All the best, your fan Harry Hill.' It seems that the power supply was faulty and kept dropping out and so only recorded odd words. The message he maintains he received when he arrived home from a late supper and pressed the play button on his answer machine was: 'Your granddaughter is a prostitute, advertise your fanny.'

I immediately phone Andrew at home to explain the situation, but get his answer machine. I leave the message: 'Hello, Andrew, it's me, Harry. I'm phoning you to explain that there's a bug on your answer machine. It keeps turning on and off, so that message was actually: "Congratulations, Andrew, on your grand debut on *Corrie*. It was the daughter of all performances. It is so nice to see an actor playing a proper role rather than having to prostitute himself in an advertisement. All the best, your fan Harry Hill." Apologies for any confusion.'

June 24th

Just when I thought it had all gone quiet on the God Bed front I get a very encouraging letter from the brilliant inventor Clive Sinclair. He's really up for it! Yay! This is fantastic news and just the shot in the arm I need to continue with the project because, if I'm frank, a very small part of me was starting to lose any hope of getting it off the ground. The fact that I've now got the man behind the Sinclair C5 on side means we've got every chance of success.

Sir Clive Sinclair
holding something

'Clive Sinclair?' said Mum. 'What's he been up to? I haven't heard hide nor hair for about twenty years!'

'No doubt he's been working on a top-secret invention, Mum,' I said. People who don't invent things themselves don't really understand how much development time is needed to get a project off the ground. 'No, he'll not have sat idle, mark my words,' I said.

I phoned Nan to tell her the good news, and she reckoned that Clive Sinclair was 'the best prime minister we never had', which was nice, adding, 'Is he still married to Ms Shirley Williams?' 'That's Roy *Jenkins*,' I said, 'and they weren't married.'

'Clive Jenkins, that's right,' she said. There's no point in trying to argue with her when she's in that mood. She said it's still very hot in Najaf, so hot in fact that she has got out the paddling pool.

The *News of the World* phone, asking me to refute claims that I have left two offensive messages on Andrew Sachs's answer machine.

'Two?' I ask.

'It turns out that second one was mangled into "Hello, Andrew, bugger off and your granddaughter is a prostitute, advertise your fanny."'

I will be writing to him to explain.

Nan's in trouble again. Another case of inappropriate nudity, but this time I feel for her because it does seem like a genuine mistake. Apparently she was having fun in her paddling pool and in the absence of a towel decided to sun-dry herself. She slipped out of her wet things and lay on her recliner, which, as she points out, she has a perfect right to do. After about forty minutes she decided to have 'a bit of a work-out' on her trampoline. Forgetting she was still quite naked at this point, she proceeded to bounce up and down. Unfortunately there is only a low hedge separating Nan's garden from that of her neighbours, Mr and Mrs Khan, who were out in the garden with a number of family members celebrating Mr Khan's recent promotion. You can imagine the rest. Nan compounded the insult by waving to the crowd every time she popped up. The local police were called and once again she found herself in custody and facing the sharp end of Sharia law. To be honest I haven't got a lot of sympathy for her. It's almost as if she prefers prison to her own home.

Have finally compiled all the data I've collected over the last few months on Brenda the cleaner's Mr Muscle usage and entered it into my computer. It makes fascinating reading. Phoned Brenda and asked her to get here thirty minutes early tomorrow so I can go through it with her.

June 25th

Brenda arrived early at the house, but during my PowerPoint presentation of the Mr Muscle data she raised her hand and took exception to my methods.

'This is an inadequate sample,' she said. 'Your procedure is flawed. You cannot draw any satisfactory conclusions from this data. All you can do is suggest a trend.'

It seems that prior to coming to England she did a day-release course in statistics.

This is really annoying because, as you know, I spent a lot of time on that presentation, only to have her destroy it in a matter of seconds.

'Class dismissed!' I shouted. 'Everyone out – except you, Brenda. I want you to write out one hundred times "I will not use excess Mr Muscle when cleaning the house."'

She looked mega tee-d off but started on the punishment. Well, I just feel I've got to have some sanctions. As Mum pointed out, it doesn't quite make sense because all the time she's doing her lines she's not cleaning the house, and I'm paying her £9 an hour.

Later on I walked in on Brenda and caught her using eight pens sellotaped together to do her lines. Can no one be trusted in this once proud land?

Roast beef and Yorkshire pud for dinner, pain au chocolat for pud.

June 26th

The phone rang this morning and it was the familiar voice of Clive Sinclair. After a general chat about the practicalities and background to my God Bed idea, he says, 'Why don't you pop over and we can talk things through in more detail?'

'Sure, that would be great,' I say, and we make the necessary arrangements for me to travel to Sinclairville, the experimental community he set up on a disused oil rig in the middle of the English Channel at the height of his success, which houses a laboratory and invention-testing centre. Whoopee!

June 27th

The helicopter arrived to take me to Sinclairville. I say helicopter – it looked suspiciously like a Sinclair C5 with a propeller on top, and although it was cramped it flew OK.

Not long after the white cliffs receded from view there it was, Sinclairville, sticking up out of the sea on giant iron legs. Situated as it is in international waters, Clive declared it independent from Britain and set himself up as head of state. Currently with a population of seventeen, it has its own currency – the Sinclair – its own stamps and its own honours

A Three Sinclair stamp

system. As we hovered overhead I could see the familiar ginger crown and beard of Clive himself, waving us aboard.

Red setters are considered holy here.

'Welcome, Mr Harry!' said Clive, dressed in his robes of office – a marmalade-coloured corduroy suit with rabbit-fur-trimmed collar, a giant belt like the boxers win made from milk-bottle tops, and atop his head a crown made from lamb-chop bones.

'There is no time to waste. Climb aboard!' he said, and with that a flunkey pulled up in a stretch Sinclair C5. Clive and I got in and we were whisked off down a ramp to his subterranean quarters.

We travelled down a dark, dank corridor to what looked like a metal container, where we disembarked. 'That will be all!' barked Sir Clive at the flunkey.

I don't want you to go away thinking that this was like something out of the space age, because it most definitely was not. The whole place smelled of fish, there was a constant drip from the ceiling and the harsh fluorescent strip lights gave everything a ghostly glow, including my host.

'First of all, I love the God Bed idea,' said Sir Clive, getting down to business. 'But I'd like to make a few adjustments.'

'Well, I'm open to any idea that will improve the design,' I said.

'Here, what do you think of this?' He unrolled a large diagram. 'You see what I've done? I've put wheels on it and incorporated an electric motor and battery so that it is now mobile.'

'That looks very much like the Sinclair C5, Sir Clive,' I said, a little confused.

'You got a problem with that?'

'Um, well . . .'

'Why don't you people get it? Plastic electric three-wheeled vehicles are the future! I said it back in 1985 and I say it again now. You've seen yourself how well the infrastructure works here in Sinclairville.'

'Yes, but this was to be a bed, not a vehicle.'

'That's so short-sighted! Why not combine the two?'

'Not sure,' says I.

There is a pause as Sir Clive looks at his drawing, and then the driver (who it turns out is his brother) comes in with a tray of tea and a Kit Kat (which I note is past its sell-by).

We drink the tea in silence.

'It must get lonely here, Sir Clive,' I venture.

'Not at all. We get Sky TV, and I have the full package – movies, sport and lifestyle shows – so there's never a dull moment, and occasionally we get visits from some of the shows on their way to France. Lulu did a warm-up here. We had Jools Holland playing here last month. You don't want my design, do you, Mr Harry?' he said, looking at the rust-encrusted floor.

'Not really, Sir Clive, no,' I answered. 'I feel it is too far removed from my original.'

'But you will stay the night? David has thawed out a chicken.'

'No, I think I'd better get back. I have a call in to Richard Branson. I'm hoping he might come through for me.'

Well, I shouldn't have mentioned Branson! Clive sprung up to his full height and clawed at the air with his fingers, his knuckles white with anger, his face puce with rage. There followed a foul four-letter tirade that I cannot possibly reproduce in a celebrity memoir.

As the Heli-Clair carried me from the deck and Sinclairville gradually receded from view, I was filled with immense pride: pride in the achievements of this man who had bucked the system and come out on top with his own take on society, but sadly a society that was not for me.

Chicken wings and thighs for dinner, out-of-date chocolate instant whip for pud.

June 28th

Had my first prison-visiting session and got Dennis Nilsen. As soon as I sat down he tried to strangle me. So I won't be doing that again.

Peter F left a message on my phone to call him, which I do.

'How about a discussion show with Toby Young, Kirsty Young and Will Young hosted by Jimmy Young and calling it *The Young Ones*?' he says.

'What would they be discussing?' I ask.

'Um, stuff that's happened in the week? Films? Consumer issues? Old stuff that might be valuable? Is that important?'

'I think it could work. They're all really strong broadcasters in their own right and together it could be a very powerful product.'

'Great, thanks, H. Just thought I'd run it past you. Sorry about *Spot the Difference*.'

'Eh?'

'Oh, sorry, didn't you know? It's been pulled.'

Another doomed project bites the dust.

Crisps, Hula Hoops and Frazzles for tea.

June 29th

Sent an anonymous bunch of flowers to *Emmerdale* star Amanda Donohue, as I do every year on this her birthday. I've never met her, but I used to fancy her something rotten when I was in my twenties and just got into the habit of it. Recently I've also taken to phoning her on the set of *Emmerdale*, and when she comes to the phone I sing 'Happy birthday to you' down it. When I do it today she gets very angry and hangs up before I've even personalised the song by putting in her name. She calls me a creep and a weirdo – it's just like something out of *Emmerdale*!

I think this might be the last year I do it.

Something very odd happened this evening. Just as we were sitting down for *Emmerdale* there was a knock at the door, and upon opening it there was Otis Ferry, the notorious fox-hunting son of Roxy Music front man and self-styled lounge lizard Bryan. The young man was breathless and looking anxious.

'Quick, can you hide me?' he panted. 'I'm being pursued by anti-hunt fanatics!'

I let him in and suggested he hide behind the curtains, but before I could say 'Avalon' there was another knock at the door and I was confronted by a motley crew of hunt saboteurs.

'We know he's in here!' they cried, wielding camcorders

and anti-hunt banners. They pushed past me and on into the house.

They went through every room in the house, twice. Yes, every room – which was a bit of a shock because Mum was in the bath. With no sign of Otis, they left grumbling about 'a lack of tea- and coffee-making facilities in the spare room'.

I popped upstairs to check on Mum.

'You OK?' I said. Then out of the foam at the other end of the bath popped the face of Mr Otis Ferry!

After drying his wet things we gave him a plate of cold cuts and sent him on his way.

June 30th

The notoriously controversial comedian Frankie Boyle is in the papers again. He, of course, made his name in the hilarious BBC panel show *Mock the Week*, in which a group of panellists quite literally mock the week. While I must admit I do really enjoy the show – with its jokes about the royals, politicians and flooding in parts of rural Britain – I do come away feeling slightly sorry for the week. I mean, it's not the week's fault that those things happened to it. Maybe they should think about mocking other longer stretches of time, such as a month or trimester – you know, pick on something their own size.

Frankie made a rather cruel joke about Harriet Harman's hands which I couldn't possibly repeat here, and while being very funny is just a little too unkind for me to allow myself to laugh at.

Ham hocks for dinner, strawberry blancmange for pud.

July

The Novotel, Heathrow

July 1st

I arrive at the Faber summer party, which is held in the street outside the Faber building, just along from the British Museum. As all of us authors queue to get into the Pig and Whistle pub, I overhear someone saying, 'I don't honestly believe you can compare Fitzgerald with Nabokov,' and tempted as I am to get involved I realise it's just idle banter between the security guards and decide to keep schtum.

Times are hard in publishing these days. In previous years the summer party had been a lavish affair: free booze and canapés paraded through the throng on the backs of scantily-clad women dressed as some of Faber's most successful authors from the past – T. S. Eliot, William Golding and Ricky Gervais. But as I say, there is a recession on, things are tough, and this year's had more of a street-party feel. There were three large trestle tables in the beer garden, stacked high with sarnies, and at one end were two huge tea urns operated by head of publishing Stephen 'Pagey' Page. There's always a little bit of needle between the novelists and the poets, but this year was the worst ever. A couple of the poets ganged up on Booker Prize-winning Australian novelist Peter Carey. On seeing the situation Kazzy Ishiguro and Hanif Kureishi waded in. Before you could say 'T. S. Eliot' a full-blown fight had broken out. Seamus Heaney grabbed a table and smashed it over Orhan Pamuk's head, giving him a splinter and spilling tea everywhere. Wendy Cope climbed up onto the bar and then jumped onto Tom Stoppard's back, who then proceeded to rotate round at speed until poor Wendy went flying off into an empty barrel, knocking it onto its side. Then off she rolled, out of the beer garden, across the road and into the front courtyard of the British Museum!

I ducked under a trestle table to sit it out and bumped into old Pagey himself.

'If only *Cats* hadn't come off in the West End,' he mourned, producing a hip flask of brandy.

Later on I ducked into Burger King for a BK Flamer and bumped into Peter F. Sitting down opposite him I asked him about his latest project, *The Young Ones*.

'Bad news, I'm afraid, H. Will Young can't do it due to other commitments, so we're approaching Will Self.'

'How does that work? Doesn't his surname have to be Young?'

'That's not an issue now. It's got a bit of momentum behind it – momentum's the key thing in showbiz, you must remember that,' he said, chugging back a chicken nugget.

BK Flamer and six mini-pancakes with maple syrup for pud.

July 2nd

Watched *8 Out of 10 Cats* on Channel 4 for the first time last night, and I must say really enjoyed it. It's great to see the events of the week mocked but not the week itself, like they do on *Mock the Week*. My only problem with the show is that I can't work out where the other 'cat' is. There's the main cat, Jimmy Carr, who is the quiz master, the two team-captain cats, Sean Lock and Jason Manford, and then there are two more cats on each team – usually comedians or celebrities – which makes a total of just seven cats, so where is the remaining cat? Should the show not be called *7 Out of 10 Cats*? Or *7 Out of Nine Cats*? It's a bit of a big mistake to make, isn't it? Someone has obviously not bothered to count up the number of cats on the show. As I say, I enjoyed watching it, but this deficit in the cat department kept playing on my mind and spoilt my enjoyment slightly.

When the show finished I allowed a sensible amount of time for him to get changed and then called Sean Lock, who is one of the main cats on the show, to ask him whether anyone else had picked up on the obvious mismatch between the number of cats advertised in the name of the show and the number of cats on the panel.

'Don't worry, a lot of people have brought that up, Harry,' he said. 'The reason for the mismatch is historical.'

'Oh yes?' I said, sounding interested.

'You don't really want me to go through it, do you? It's just that Jason and Jimmy are here and we were all planning to go down Stringfellahs . . .'

'Could you perhaps just condense it into its basic elements, Sean?' I said, using his Christian name. I could hear Jimmy Carr's voice in the background: 'Get a move on, Sean, all the best booths will be taken . . .!'

'Um, look, I'll send you the detailed printed breakdown that we send to everyone who raises this query, but basically we are not supposed to be the cats mentioned in the title . . .'

'Who are the cats then?'

'It is a reference to an advert for cat food . . .'

'Listen, Sean, I appreciate you've got somewhere to go, but

if you can't be bothered to answer a colleague's genuine query about the show that you're on, then fine, forget it, have a nice life,' I said, and hung up.

It's a shame, because I like Sean, but I will not be made a fool of. Calling the show 8 *Out of 10 Cats* is already signalling to the viewer a cat shortfall of two. To then only feature seven cats is misleading and just the sort of thing that has contributed to the public's loss of trust in our institutions. I will be writing to Ofcom, Nick Clegg and Dominic Littlewood to see if I can't get this wrong righted.

Looking forward to our Spanish holiday in just two days.

Wall's savoury pancakes for dinner, crêpe suzette for pud.

July 3rd

Mr Dalliwal, Dog's department manager at the airport, phoned today saying he wanted to talk to me about Dog's behaviour.

'Not over the phone,' he said. So I told him he'd better come round.

Over a bottle of Pinot Noir he explained that Dog's behaviour at work had become increasingly erratic over the past few months and that he had given him a verbal warning.

'Erratic? What do you mean?' I asked.

'Sexually harassing the other members of the dog staff,' he said. He explained how some of the female dogs had complained that Dog had been making lewd suggestions and touching them in an inappropriate place, such as on the bottom. He'd once even tried to pull down his supervisor's jeans.

'You didn't have any idea this was going on?' he said, looking concerned.

'No, no,' I said. 'I mean, he's always been one of the lads, always liked the girls, but this? No.'

It saddened me further to learn that one of the chief complainants was Deborah the collie cross.

On top of that his drinking has become a problem.

'Miniatures mainly. He gets them from the planes,' said Mr Dalliwal. It turns out that a woman from HM Customs had been tipped off by a 'neighbour' who had noticed a large number of tiny bottles in our recycling bin.

Worse still, it has started affecting his work. Once or twice he's been sniffing while drunk on the job and incriminating people who were later found to be clean.

'That's expected every now and then, but when it's Lord Snowdon – that's when it starts to get embarrassing and questions are asked.'

'What sort of questions?' I say, asking one myself.

'Well, questions like "Are you Lord Snowdon?" and "What was Princess Margaret really like?" – stuff like that.'

'Oh, right,' I say. 'So what's the plan?'

'Well, I've given him a verbal warning. If he doesn't clean up his act he will then get a written warning, then a written warning in a frame, and if he's still not improved he will be fired. Sorry to burden you with this, Mr Hill, but sometimes if there's someone at home to support the offender it can have a better long-term outcome. Burp! Pardon me.'

I'm stunned. I had no idea that things were this bad. OK, his behaviour has been a little erratic, but drinking on the job? Verbal warnings? I decide to chat with Mum about how to proceed.

I thanked Mr Dalliwal and showed him to the door, and

as he drove off I opened and closed it several times to try to dispel the smell of his burp.

Chicken tikka sandwiches for lunch.

July 4th

Talk to Mum about what to do about Dog over a sandwich in the park. As she points out, Dog's been under a lot of pressure lately, what with his relationship with Deborah the collie cross breaking down. As she says, we're off on holiday tomorrow, so maybe a clean break will help him to recharge his batteries and he'll be able to return to work refreshed and with a more positive outlook.

I will certainly be recharging *my* batteries – my camcorder, my phone, my cordless shaver and a number of rechargeable batteries – as the electricity for the week is all in.

Got the printed sheet through from Sean Lock about why *8 Out of 10 Cats* is called this when there are only seven cats on the show, and I now feel a bit of a fool for making such a fuss.

As it's American Independence Day, Mum and me take it in turns to waterboard each other in the bathroom.

The last of the ham for dinner and Magnum Mini for pud.

July 5th

Off to Malaga today for a well-earned break!

Our neighbour Eric Smythe-Wilkes has very kindly agreed to look after the hamster while we're on holiday, on the condition that we repay the favour one day. 'Not a problem,' I say, thinking it's not a problem because I know for a fact they haven't got any pets.

The mini-cab comes to pick up me, Mum and Dog, and Dog insists on sitting in the front because he says otherwise he gets car sick. It's actually quite a nice drive up through East Sussex to Gatwick – a trip that Dog makes every day (but for how much longer?) – until Mum checks the tickets and sees that it's Heathrow we're flying from. By the time we get to Heathrow we've missed the flight. The only thing to do is to book into the Novotel in the shadow of the Heathrow complex – all three of us in the same room to save money.

While Mum and Dog settle down in front of the TV to watch the news on Al Jazeera (to get in the holiday mood), I take a wander back through the covered walkway to take a look around the airport. It started me thinking about that bloke who lived in an airport for eighteen years. It's actually not a bad place to live if you can put up with the sound of the planes. You've got a Burger King, a KFC, a Cafe Nero and a Garfunkel's if you've got something to celebrate. There are various clothes outlets, booze retailers, newsagent's and book shops – all offering reduced prices. Plus it's handy for the airport – for holidays.

I get back, and Mum's unpacked all the suitcases and put all our clothes into the wardrobe and drawers in the room.

'What did you do that for? We're leaving at the crack of dawn!' I say.

'I don't like the idea of living out of a suitcase,' she says. If she's not careful she's going to ruin this holiday.

Later on, after an afternoon nap, we pop out and I treat us all to a slap-up Burger King tea. Then we watch *Gremlins 2* on ITV3. Not a bad start to a holiday, by anyone's reckoning!

Sweet Chilli Chicken Royale for mains, BK Fusion Rocky Road for pud.

July 6th

Up at the crack of dawn and we start repacking the suitcases, only now all the stuff that came out won't go back in again.

'That's often the case when you go on holiday,' says Mum. 'That's why I normally bring a spare bag that's empty.'

'Where is it, then?' I ask.

'There wasn't room in the suitcase for it.'

We decide to dump the tinned food. The dog will just have to take his chances with the local fare.

Going through security we have to remove our shoes, which Mum objects to strongly, claiming that walking barefoot in an area where so many other people are walking barefoot increases her chances of getting a verruca. She's right, of course, but it's a small price to pay for knowing that the person you're travelling with is not wearing exploding shoes.

I've been a bit tight with the flights and we're flying economy class. Mum says we should try to gatecrash the first-class lounge by using my famous face to open the door. It's worth a try, I suppose.

'Hi, I'm Harry Hill!' I say to the lady on the first-class-lounge reception.

'Yes? Can I see your tickets?' she says.

We hand them over and wait for the inevitable rejection.

'Sorry, you need first-class tickets to get in here,' she says.

'I know, it's just that being well known . . . sometimes the rules can be bent.'

'Well known?'

'Yes, Harry Hill, from ITV . . .? The voice of *You've Been Framed . . .*?'

'No, I live in a valley. We don't get very good TV reception there, so I've never seen the show. Hang on and I'll check with my colleague. Valerie?' she calls to another receptionist. By this time there is quite a queue forming behind us. 'Harry Hill? Says he's on ITV?'

'We weren't allowed to watch ITV as kids. My parents would only let us watch BBC1 and 2,' says Valerie. 'They said it was common, and because I've never got into the habit I haven't really watched it since, so I'm afraid it's a no.'

'What about him?' I say, pointing at another airline official at a computer behind them.

'Is there a problem here?' says a rather gruff gent in a Panama hat behind me in the queue.

'No, mate, everything's in hand, ta,' I say.

'I think Dave's busy, Mr Harry Hill. I'm afraid I'm going to have to ask you to leave.'

'Just see what Dave says,' I say. 'If Dave doesn't know me, I'll wipe my mouth and walk away.'

'Dave's busy. Sir, please move away from the desk.'

'You heard her!' says the gruff gent in the Panama.

'Dave!' I call out to the bloke at the computer. 'Cooo-eee! Dave! Over here!'

'Move aside please or I will have to call security.'

We are strong-armed out and adjourn to Garfunkel's. Shame. If I'd just managed to attract Dave's attention I feel sure he would have come through for me.

The flight goes very smoothly. We were served a light

snack: grapes, cheese, cress, a miniature bottle of white wine and a white chocolate truffle, just the sort of thing you eat every day at half past eleven in the morning.

We pick up the rental car at Malaga airport and we're off. Now I'll say from the get-go that I won't drive on the Continent. I'm not the best of drivers in the UK, so the thought of driving from the passenger seat like they do over here fills me with horror. No, Mum drives. She drives on the right-hand side of the road, as their laws dictate, but to make herself feel better if there are no cars coming the other way she scoots over to the left-hand side. In this way she manages to spend as much as 30 per cent of the journey on the British side of the road.

First impressions of the apartment we've rented are not good. The block is situated next to a flyover and overlooks a fun fair; at the back is a golf course and we don't play golf.

our Holiday apartment, costa del sol.

Still, we're very positive people, us Hills, and Mum wastes no time in getting into her swimming cozzy and diving into the swimming pool. Sadly the pool has been drained of all water and Mum takes a nasty knock to the head. It would have been worse but the impact was cushioned by a patch of moss on the bottom of the pool. I couldn't work out why she didn't spot that the pool was empty, but she blames it on her new bifocal swimming goggles, which she says made the surface of the pool seem 'kind of shimmery'. Too bad I didn't get a shot of it on my camcorder. It would have been perfect for *You've Been Framed*, and the £250 dividend would have helped to pay for the Novotel.

I set to filling the pool with a hosepipe, but I have to say the water pressure is very low and I fear that it's evaporating as fast as I'm filling it.

Dog and me then head down to the local Mercadona for some provisions.

Economy burgers in baps, fried plantain for dinner and crème caramel for pudding – well, when in Rome!

July 7th

Didn't sleep well. It was stiflingly hot – my bedroom is directly under the hot-water tank – and the noise from the fairground went on until three in the morning. The 'Test Your Strength' seemed particularly popular. I managed to get used to the rifle range and the 'Hits of 2009' that go with the dodgems, but that 'Test Your Strength' thing – it's so sporadic. I'd just be starting to nod off when a really strong person would step up and 'DING!', the bell would ring and wake me up. Still, we're positive people and with a new day comes a new begin-ning. The fair has stopped, the sun is out, and Mum treats me and the dog to a fry-up on the balcony.

Just as I'm tucking in there's a 'BOP!' and the first golf ball flies over and lands on my fried egg. I wouldn't mind but it was right on the yolk – splat! Yolk all down my Hawaiian shirt and the best bit of the egg rendered inedible. Twenty minutes later the doorbell goes 'RRRRrrrring!' A bloke in golfing fatigues is at the door asking for his ball back. The day continues in this way – golf ball flying into the flat, twenty minutes later the doorbell going. At half past four the funfair starts back up and we get the 'Test Your Strength' bell added to the mix. 'DING!', 'BOP!', 'RRRRRrring!' – it's like having your life remixed by Fat Boy Slim.

Despite the twenty-four hours that have passed there is still only a foot of water in the bottom of the swimming pool. There's nothing for it but for Mum to drive us to the beach.

As she tacks back and forth across the lanes with one eye on the sat nav, I feel a pain in my hands. No, it's not a heart attack, it's my finger nails digging into the palms. I'm so tense!

We get to the outskirts of Marbella and pull up at some traffic lights, and I hear my name being called.

'Hellooo, Harry!'

I look across, and in the open-topped sports car next to us are Dale Winton, Cilla Black and Jason Gardiner from *Dancing on Ice*!

'What are you doing here?' says Dale. 'Why not join us back at the villa for a sundowner?'

Mr. Dale Winton

'Great, Dale, yes!' I call across. Suddenly the afternoon is looking a lot better.

'Follow me!' screeches Cilla, putting her foot down hard on the accelerator. The car growls and speeds off into the distance.

'Quick, Mum!' I yell. 'Follow that car! That's our dinner!'

I've never seen a Fiat Multipla move so fast. In and out of the traffic we wove, Cilla's car never more than a dot on the horizon. At one point we appeared to be gaining on her, but when we came within about fifty yards it was clear that far from being Cilla's flame-red hair sticking out of the top of the car it was someone transporting a poinsettia plant, which was poking through his sun roof; and that wasn't the top of Dale's head, it was an Alsatian; and that wasn't the close-cropped pate of Jason Gardiner, it was a cactus. We'd been following the wrong car. Bang went cocktails by the pool of Cilla and Dale's luxury Marbella villa – and, no doubt, endless nights out clubbing and hobnobbing with the Costa del Sol's elite. What a bummer! Still, there was some great driving from Mum and she deserves a reward. We stop off at Mr Chippy in Puerto Banus, and while she's waiting for the haddock I slip into a newsagent's and buy her a copy of the *Daily Mail*. Well, she's earnt it.

Up all night to the sound of various people testing their strength.

July 8th

The third day of the holiday and the pool's still not full. It comes up to Mum's knees, so we all go for a paddle. Actually the dog's fine, he's able to swim about in it, but because it's so hot and he's moulting the surface of the pool becomes covered in brown dog hairs. When Mum and me get out of the pool the hairs have all stuck to our lower legs. I spend the morning with the pool net dredging it for dog hairs, but it's too big a job. There's nothing for it but to drain the pool and shave the dog. I go down to Mercadona to get some razors and shaving foam.

I bumped into Dave, the builder who laid Mum's new drive, as well as fitting the solar-heating panels and lining her windows with foil. I couldn't be bothered to take him on over the drive, and when I told him about the swimming pool at the apartment he offered to give me a quote. I told him where to get off.

I don't know whether you've ever tried to wet-shave a golden retriever? No? Well, take it from me, it ain't easy. He was wriggling about, not because he wasn't up for it, but because he said it tickled. I had to use eight cans of shaving foam to get a decent froth up and two packs of disposable razors because they kept clogging. He got a couple of nasty cuts on his face and one on his undercarriage, which was far from ideal. In retrospect it was probably a mistake to use aftershave: poor Dog went running round the room in a panic saying his skin was burning up.

Hey ho! I'll know for next time. What a result though! Kind of weird, a naked dog: looks kind of human from certain angles and otherworldly from others. Mum says if he had a longer neck he'd look like E.T.

'Good job I'm on holiday and no one knows me over here,' he says, then 'Ouch!' as a golf ball flies through the open window and lands right on one of his cuts. Well, we had to laugh.

So that's most of that day gone. Just a couple of hours of sunlight left, so we all cram onto the tiny balcony, faces turned to the sun, and guzzle down a nice cup of sangria before the fair starts up.

Spicy sausages and noodles for dinner, pineapple fritters for pud.

July 9th

Dog has woken up with really bad sunburn. Of course, we hadn't thought about it, but his hair was acting as a natural sunscreen, so now we have to spend the first twenty minutes of the day applying factor 20. I must admit I feel sorry for the poor fellah, standing there with no hair, covered in white, greasy cream – no chance of a holiday romance for him.

We're all really tired – it's been three nights now with virtually no sleep.

'Maybe we should all go back to the Novotel,' says Mum. 'That's when we were happiest.'

She's right, and I'd be lying if I hadn't thought about it myself.

'We don't quit!' says Dog defiantly. 'We're not quitters and we don't quit! Mum? Get the car ready, we're gonna have some fun!'

Dog was right. Suddenly we were excited again, united, a team.

'Where we going, Dog?' I said, sitting back in the car with him in the driving seat.

'To the fair!' he said, revving the engine.

'What do we need the car for?' said Mum.

'You'll see!'

And off we went, down the drive, round the corner and through the entrance to the fair, sending the fairground barkers running for cover. Past the dodgems Dog drove, round the helter skelter and the roller coaster and slap bang into the 'Test Your Strength' machine with a 'Ding!'.

'OK, guys, job done,' says Dog, parking up. We high five and stroll out of the fair like three Wild West gunslingers.

Of course, none of the above actually happened; that was a daydream I had.

'Yeah, let's go back to the Novotel,' said Dog.

'OK,' I said, and I got on the phone and booked some flights for the next day.

July 10th

Dog's hair has started growing back and he now has all-over designer stubble. He's getting a lot of attention, and at one point a policeman approaches him and tells him to 'cover up. No nudity please, there are children. Cover yourself please, Sir.' So we take him to one of the airport stores and buy him a pair of Speedos and a T-shirt.

While we're waiting to check in at the airport, Dog gets mistaken for George Michael. There is a resemblance, particularly with the sunglasses, and Dog plays along, offering to sign autographs.

'What happened to your hands, George?' says one roly-poly girl from Essex with a puzzled look on her face.

'Oh yeah, the fingers got a bit worn down with all that

strumming,' says Dog, which she seemed to accept.

Then there's a problem at passport control. They won't let Dog through, saying he doesn't look anything like his passport photo.

Mum shows them some photos that she had taken while I was shaving him. Soon the security guys are laughing and calling to other airport officials to come and have a look at the pics. I have to admit they are comical. I suppose by the end we were surrounded by about fifteen passport and customs officials, and they were happy to wave us through, slapping us on the back as they did so.

I must say it was good to get back to the Novotel. We even managed to get our old room back. Mum put the TV onto VH1 and we jumped about on the bed in celebration.

'The holiday starts here!' shouted Dog, and I took their orders and headed off to Burger King.

Smoked Bacon and Cheddar Double Angus for dinner, BK Fusion Mint Choc Swirl for pud.

July 11th

Had a great night's sleep, breakfast in the room and then spent the day mooching round the shops in the Heathrow Village. Thought I'd better get Eric Smythe-Wilkes a little present for looking after the hamster, so I settle on a giant Toblerone – you can't argue with that. OK, you can get Toblerone in the UK, but the big ones are quite difficult to find and so are a bit special, a bit of an occasion. Oh yes, he'll be pleased with that. Who wouldn't be?

In the afternoon I took a trip on an open-top bus to Staines.

A Giant Toblerone

There wasn't a hell of a lot to see, to be honest. Had a picnic lunch in the Elmsleigh shopping centre, and got moved on for not eating food bought on the premises. It's true that we had made the picnic from bread rolls and cheese that we had snaffled from the buffet breakfast bar at the Novotel on the way out, so hands up, guilty as charged.

Had a bit of a pow-wow and decided to head home tomorrow. Well, the Novotel experience, while being fun, is very expensive. We're already down on the deal having forked out for the apartment.

One last Burger King dinner and then watched *Ferris Bueller's Day Off* on ITV4 while charging my phone, camcorder and car battery.

July 12th

Our neighbour Eric Smythe-Wilkes called round with the hamster, and I gave him the Toblerone.

'Just a little token of our appreciation,' I say.

'I thought you went to Spain?' he says.

'That's right.'

'Well, Toblerone is Swiss.'

'Er, your point being . . .?'

276

'Just seems a funny souvenir of Spain, that's all.'

Some people!

Peter F calls to tell me that Jimmy Young's pulled out of his pet *Young Ones* project and that he's now going for Jimmy Savile.

Fish fingers, oven chips and peas for dinner, vanilla soft scoop for pud.

July 13th

Up to town to meet London mayor Boris Johnson, who wants to talk about the opening ceremony for the 2012 Olympics.

He explains over coffee and ring doughnuts that he wants something cheap but spectacular and quintessentially British, but also to show Britain's cultural diversity and 'maybe to have women in it too'. After much discussion we settle for a Dalek racing round the track waving a Union Jack, hotly pursued by Shirley Bassey, while Brian May plays the theme from *Chariots of Fire* on his electric guitar.

Watching Ant and Dec's show tonight I was incensed to see an item called 'Scratch Anthea': there's Anthea Turner jumping up and down on a trampoline while members of the public try and scratch her, with a different number of points for different parts of Anthea's body. This is basically my 'Tickle SuBo' item dressed up. I scribble a note threatening legal action and post it to George Galloway himself.

July 14th

Popped into town on Mum's disability scooter to get one or two items from Londis and a top-up present for Eric. As I came past the pub I could have sworn that I saw Dog in the beer garden nursing a pint, but I was travelling at speed so might well have been mistaken.

Returned with a bottle of Spanish wine and dropped it round at Eric's.

'What's this?' he said.

'Um, it was the other part of your present I got from Spain as a thank you for looking after the hamster,' I said.

'Why's it got a Londis price sticker on it then?' he said rather contemptuously.

Well, I made my excuses and left. There's no pleasing some people.

Creamed pork for tea, ice cream for pud.

July 15th

I have joined the local residents' group opposing the conversion of Bexhill's art-deco landmark, the De La Warr Pavilion, into a pet-food factory. The council say that as a venue for live music, entertainment and seaside shows it has been losing money hand over fist for years and something needs to be done. They let the situation be known, and local pet-food company Choppingham Meats approached the council with plans already drawn up to convert this concert hall, which has played host to the London Philharmonic Orchestra, Vera Lynn and Rod Hull and Emu, into a pet-food factory.

In response to complaints about possible smell pollution, Choppingham have said that it wouldn't be dog food the entire time – which along with cat food creates the most smell – and have drawn up a timetable: Monday, small rodent food (hamsters, gerbils, etc.); Tuesday, small mammal food (rabbits, guinea pigs); Wednesday, dog food; Thursday, cat food; Friday, budgie food a.m., dog food p.m.

This has gone some way to alleviate my fears, and on the plus side it does mean that we won't have to put up with all those dreary concerts.

At the meeting I get talking to Major Peter Andrews from the Devolution for Bexhill Party, who explains that if given the go-ahead the pet-food factory will bring employment to the area. 'And I will see to it personally that no jobs go to any of the chavs and drongos from Hastings,' he says, although it isn't clear how he plans to achieve this. On balance, I now think that the De La Warr Dog Food Pavilion is a good idea.

Peter Fincham phones to tell me that Toby Young and Kirsty Young have pulled out of his pet project *The Young Ones*, so the line-up is now Jimmy Savile in the chair, Will Self, Jackie Stewart and Sylvia Kristel (the French actress who played Emmanuelle in the seventies).

July 16th

Caught Mum trying to force a two-pence piece into the SIM-card slot of her Pay As You Go mobile phone. I explained that the payment had to be made over the phone using a credit card, but the slot is bent now and the SIM card won't fit back in.

July 17th

Noticed this morning that Mum has got a blue tongue, and suspecting some sort of lack of oxygen in the blood immediately called an ambulance. When it arrived she was reluctant to get in, protesting that she was feeling 'as right as rain'.

Admittedly she didn't seem unwell, but at her age you can't be too careful.

The doctors seemed a little puzzled by her case and admitted her for observation.

Me and the dog took the opportunity of an empty house to have a bit of a boys' night in. We opened a few tins of Skol lager and put on an old VHS of *Emmanuelle 2*. Well, that's what I thought it was, but I must have put the wrong video back in the case. But after the initial disappointment me and the dog really enjoyed *Digby – The Biggest Dog in the World*. Jim Dale underplayed it beautifully.

Ham sandwiches with the crusts cut off for tea, strawberry Frube for pudding.

July 18th

I am woken in the middle of the night by the dog howling. Went down to investigate. He'd had a nightmare, probably brought on by *Digby*. It took me a while to calm him down. His eyes were wild and he was panting 'Please tell me it could never happen.'

Unfortunately I was unable to give him this assurance as I believe that with advances in molecular biology it will one day be possible to increase the size of a dog to giant proportions. I think I worsened his anxiety by adding: 'By then Jim Dale won't be alive to sort it out for mankind, like he did in the film.'

Of course, thinking about it in the cold light of day, what

really upset him was watching a film glorifying an Old English sheepdog when his girlfriend has been carrying on with one behind his back. It was thoughtless of me. I shouldn't have put him through that.

The hospital phoned at about noon asking me to come and pick Mum up. All their tests, from blood tests to full body scan, were normal. It seems that the blue tongue was due to her sucking the end of a felt-tipped pen. She mentioned it to the ward sister when they threatened to take blood from her tongue. The sister was very curt with me when I went in to get her and accused the two of us of wasting valuable hospital resources. It's almost as if they would have been happier had she been seriously ill.

I am a bit annoyed with Mum though, to be honest. Still, it's nice to know she's got a clean bill of health – all thanks to a felt-tipped pen.

Bubble and squeak for tea.

July 19th

Mum's disability vehicle is missing. She got up this morning and was feeling particularly lethargic, and so thought she'd use it to go and get a bun to cheer herself up. But when she went to get on it, it wasn't there, so she fell over, very nearly injuring herself

'If you're not careful, Mum, you're going to end up having to use one of them for real,' I joked, enjoying the irony.

She was most upset, and jumping up and down claimed it was a symptom of broken Britain.

'They've got no jobs, they live off the state, many of them

are on drugs . . . I hate pensioners!' she shouted. 'If I find out who's nicked it, I'll pull their tongue out by the roots!'

Well, I calmed her down and accompanied her to the police station to report it.

The policeman, one PC Firminger, was not very helpful. 'Probably resprayed and in Rio by now,' he said with a smirk.

'There's no need to be facetious,' I said.

He said he would 'keep an eye out for it' on his travels, and suggested we put the word out and have a look round ourselves.

Mum suggested setting up roadblocks and challenging anyone on a similar make and model, but PC Firminger wasn't keen.

Then, on the way home from the police station, I saw an elderly lady on a similar scooter. I ran up to her, and when I challenged her she did a quick twist of the wrist and sped off. They only have a top speed of twelve miles per hour and a maximum range of twenty miles when the batteries are fully charged, so I ran after her, jogging behind, biding my time for about five miles, I suppose, till the battery ran down. Then she tried to make a break for it over the fields, but being elderly and clearly having some indeterminate disability she didn't get far. I grabbed her and pulled her down onto the soft grass. Then, before I knew it, she'd plonked a kiss on me and her fingers were fumbling with the toggles on my duffel coat.

'Oi!' I exclaimed.

'Don't be shy, laddie!' she honked back at me.

I pushed her over and pinned her to the ground.

'I'm engaged to be married,' I growled. All I needed was

for it to get back to Lay Dee that I'd been groped by another woman and my nuptials would be off!

I challenged her about the scooter, but she produced her papers proving ownership: a receipt from Gran's Hatch, Bexhill's premier disability-vehicle outlet, and a photo of her riding it while reading a newspaper with a headline about the successful 2012 British Olympic bid, pinpointing her ownership to before Mum's had been stolen.

Actually I had known she wasn't riding Mum's scooter from about two miles back. As I'd got close I could see the trim was slightly different – blue vinyl instead of Mum's charcoal grey – and there was no sign of the scuff marks that Mum had sustained in that prang with the bottle bank outside Tesco Express. Mum's is a Kymco Maxi L Mobility Scooter, and this lady was riding a Rascal 329LE.

I let her go. Well, in fact I had to push her two miles down the road to the nearest shop, where the proprietor very kindly let her plug in and rejuice. A bit of a waste of a morning, to be honest, and always in the back of my mind was the thought that it had allowed the real thief to make good his or her escape.

July 20th

Dog didn't come home last night.

Then this morning I get a phone call from PC Firminger saying he'd found Mum's disability scooter being driven by a dog that claimed our address as his residence.

We both went down to the police station, where PC Firminger was sitting at his desk looking apparently very pleased with himself.

It seemed that the dog, being late for work, had borrowed Mum's mobility scooter. On the way back in the evening he had jumped the traffic lights on the corner of Sackville Road and was pulled over by the police on the dual carriageway (A259) and found to be behaving rather erratically. PC Firminger breathalysed him personally and found him to be three times over the alcohol limit for a dog. His driving isn't good at the best of times, but drunk? It's a wonder he didn't get himself killed.

'What now?' I said to PC Firminger.

'We can't really let it go, Harry. He will appear before the beak in the morning.'

We took him home, the three of us balanced precariously on the scooter, with Mum driving.

Sausages and two-minute rice for dinner, sherbert fountain for pud.

July 21st

A very contrite Dog appeared in court number three, Bexhill magistrates court, this morning. I would feel sorry for him, but he's brought the whole thing on himself.

I looked across at one point to see Deborah the collie cross

Bexhill Magistrate's Court

in the public gallery dabbing her eyes with a handkerchief. Perhaps I had her wrong after all?

Dog will now have to get the train to work. Serves him right.

July 22nd

The dog confessed to me this evening that he was made redundant from his job at the airport. In fact, he hasn't been working at the airport now for a week due to being the subject of a claim of sexual harassment in the workplace.

Unable to cope with the shame of being unemployed he has been getting up every morning as usual and pretending to go to work. Instead he's been going to the park until the pub opens, where the dog that lives there has been serving him drinks.

I am completely nonplussed, firstly because I don't believe there is any shame in being unemployed, and secondly because I'm disappointed that the dog didn't feel able to tell me of his problems. I'm also annoyed that he's been served alcoholic drinks in the pub when he's clearly under eighteen.

'I'm thirty-seven in dog years,' he says, but it's quite clear, I think, that the legal drinking age is supposed to be in human years. 'Most dogs don't live to eighteen, and by that reckoning we'd never be able to have a drink,' he adds.

Maybe I'm old-fashioned but I don't see a problem in that. I happen to think that dogs should only drink water (or Lucozade if they're ill).

The dog says it's nice to have a glass of wine with a meal, but I saw the way he acted when I let him suck the wine-soaked tea towel at Christmas: he charged around barking and trying to have sex with the leg of anyone that would have him. I didn't like it and I didn't like seeing him being unfaithful to my leg in this blatant way, particularly in front of Amanda Holden, and was embarrassed for him.

I am having to come to terms with the fact that my dog is an unemployed sex-pest alcoholic.

Sole à la bonne femme for dinner, tangerine segments for pud.

July 23rd

Great news: the De La Warr Dog Food Pavilion has been given the go-ahead! Work to convert the concert-hall interior into a state-of-the-art offal and condemned-meat salvage factory starts forthwith. They reckon it will be ready by the autumn. This is great news for the prosperity of the area.

The dog's confidence is on the floor and he spends much of the day in his bed. He has even stopped running to the door to see who it is when somebody calls because he says it's never for him. It is interesting the way the dynamics between him and Mum have changed. Previously he was the main bread-winner out of the two, but now he kowtows to her, letting her use his bed whenever she likes.

He's spending more and more time in his bed – not the new one with the four posts on it but the old one. He says the new one just reminds him of failure and what might have been.

Peter F's pet project *The Young Ones* went on air tonight with the following line-up: Jimmy Savile in the chair and

Will Self, Jackie Charlton and Koo Stark on the panel. And you know what? It worked a treat. There was great chemistry from the start, and I predict it's going to run and run.

Prawns for tea.

July 24th

Poor overnight ratings for Peter F's pet project *The Young Ones*, so ITV1 have pulled it.

Dog was out all day, and when he came back around midnight he was completely plastered. He was rude to Mum and defecated on the rug in the lounge. I gave him a strong coffee and walked him round the garden to try to sober him up.

I could hear him sobbing for most of the night.

Tuna-in-brine salad for dinner, cherry chocolate log for pud.

July 25th

Peter F phones to try out an idea on me, again.

'You know how successful *The One Show* on BBC1 is?' he asks.

'Of course. Adrian Chiles and Christine Bleakley have a brilliant sexual chemistry, plus a lovely touch on serious issues, so you never really get frightened.'

'Exactly!' he says. 'How about doing our own version and getting Gok Wan to host it and calling it *The Wan Show*?'

'Hang on. Let me get this right: you'd trick people into viewing your show by making them mistake it for the real thing?'

'Exactly! And once they're tuned in we keep 'em there with even stronger sexual chemistry and an even more superficial content! This is new territory for ITV and it's very exciting,' he says, and hangs up.

You've got to admire him. He's not let the cancellation of his *Young Ones* project get to him; no, he's straight in there with a new idea.

Of course, after that all I could do was sit down and try to think of some other shows with names that sound like those of the presenters. These are the ones I've come up with so far:

Anne D's Roadshow – antiques show presented by Anne Diamond.

Pam or Armour – current-affairs programme fronted by Pam Ayres.

Cash in the Attic – Craig Cash (from *The Royle Family*) looks through people's heirlooms.

Anton Du Beke's Saturday Night Takeaway – magazine-style show with the public trying to win prizes and getting humiliated in the process.

Hobley's City – hospital drama featuring Tina Hobley (even though Tina's currently in *Holby City*, things change and every girl has her price).

Reginald's News – the news from your area hosted by Radio 1's Reggie Yates.

Kym Dine with Me – show where Kym Marsh gets cooked for in other people's houses.

I think you'll agree, not bad for half a day's work!

July 26th

The good news (and boy do we need some good news round here!) is I've won the Cuppa Cino cafe Network South-East franchise from National Rail, which is fantastic. I tell Mum, and straight away she pre-orders a croissant and a frothy coffee. I thank her for her support but I'm not prepared to let her have goods at today's price tomorrow. She then storms off, saying that I can stuff it and that she'll 'take a packed lunch'. Family, eh?

Phoned Kevin McCloud of Channel 4's *Grand Designs* to crow, but couldn't get through.

Went to see *Webtangle*, a new play at the Royal Court about lying.

Taramasalata for mains, tiramisu for pud.

July 27th

I have had to banish Dog from the house. His behaviour has become completely unacceptable. Most of the time his breath smells of booze. I found a quarter bottle of vodka hidden in his bed. He has been sick twice late at night on the rug, and by the time I've got to it in the morning and alerted Mum she has found it extremely difficult to shift. The front room now has a background smell of sick, which I can't see going before Xmas. He has become increasingly amorous towards Mum – and, for that matter, anyone who comes through the door. I won't go into details (it's not necessary here), but suffice to say that Mum doesn't have the strongest of pins at the best of times and on two occasions she was worried that she might dislocate her hip.

So I explained all this to Dog and gave him a clear option: either he moderate his behaviour or sling his hook. He chose the latter. He got his stuff – his Lynx spray, a quarter bottle of vodka, some photos, his iPhone and a duvet – and packed it all into his bed and started dragging it towards the front door.

'No, the bed stays,' I said. He looked at me with real venom in his little toffee-coloured eyes and asked for a carrier bag. Then he was off. I don't know where he'll go but I think he needs to reach rock bottom before he realises what it was he had, and maybe that will make him want to heal himself.

That's what it said on the internet, anyway.

July 28th

At last a quiet night, with none of Dog's bad behaviour, and there is definitely less of a smell in the lounge too.

There's much excitement in the town at the news of the new condemned-meat processing plant that will soon be opening. Already a number of top jobs are being advertised in the *Bexhill Gazette*:

Condemned-Meat Masseur – an important part of the process is tenderising the meat, as the toughest cuts are often used. The Meat Masseur would be required to pummel the meat with a series of sticks as it passes along a conveyor belt. Strong upper body essential.

Terms: £8.50 an hour and six weeks holiday a year, plus complimentary twelve-pack of dog food.

Offal Shaper – responsible for forming the lumps of offal into shapes attractive to dogs, such as rabbit, bone and cat shapes. The successful candidate will have an art background, preferably with a sculpture/ pottery or woodwork GCSE.

Terms: £10.50 an hour and four weeks holiday a year, plus complimentary fourteen-pack of dog food.

Slurry Chunker – responsible for forming the slurry of reclaimed meat into chunks using spatulas of varying sizes. The successful candidate must have a good eye for chunks and like working with slurry.

Terms: £6.50 an hour and three weeks holiday a year, plus complimentary eight-pack of dog food.

Pipe Stuffer – responsible for stuffing the main food pipe with dog-food ingredients, which then feeds the various tins. Good aim required, so a background in darts or badminton a plus. There are two jobs – left-handed pipe stuffer and right-handed pipe stuffer Ambidextrous applicants will be considered for both.

Terms: £7.85 an hour and one week holiday a year, plus complimentary forty-four-pack of dog food.

Artist in Residence – fully-trained artist trained in figurative oil and/or watercolours required to paint scenes of the dog-food manufacturing process for the Choppingham Meats archive and visitors centre. Must have proper art qualifications, preferably in painting food and/or tins.

Terms: £7.50 an hour and two weeks holiday a year, plus complimentary four-pack of dog food.

Mum fancies the job of Condemned-Meat Masseur, but I don't think she's got the upper body for it.

Meat stew for tea.

July 29th

Caught Dog begging outside the station this morning. It's partly my fault I suppose. I taught him how . . . for biscuits . . . when he was very young – but it was for fun. I didn't expect ever to see him depending on it for his survival. He was sat there with a piece of cardboard that had 'Homeless' written on it and with the upturned lid of his Lynx spray in front of him. He had about twenty pence in it, in coppers. I bent down and suggested to him that he go down to the De La Warr Dog Food Pavilion and see if there are any jobs going, but he said the smell would drive him mad and that he was 'fine where I am'.

July 30th

Found Mum at the table trying to paint a tin of dog food this morning. She says she's now after the artist-in-residence job at the dog-food factory. It wasn't a bad picture, in the Fauvist style, but she's got a long way to go to get her folio in shape as I know that this job is to be keenly contested.

Stephen Page from Faber texts me, saying, 'Could there be more stews and casseroles in your diet pls?'

Casseroled sausages for dinner, mango slices for pud.

July 31st

Caught Dog busking outside the station. At least this is an improvement on begging. He had a child's guitar and a mouth organ and was doing a lot of Dylan. Takings were clearly up, but I couldn't help thinking he should be doing some more modern numbers. I went round the corner to the internet cafe and wrote out a suggested set list and downloaded the chords. I don't know if he'll be interested but I still feel some responsibility for him, and maybe this busking is the first sign that he wants to get back into society.

Beef stew for dinner.

August

The Pear growing in the garden
of Nº 4 The Close, Bexhill

August 1st

As I came past the station today there was a small crowd gathered around Dog. He was in the middle of a kazoo solo in what turned out to be 'Poker Face' by Lady Gaga. The

A kazoo

crowd broke out into spontaneous applause as he finished and most of them threw coins into his Lynx lid. As the people wandered off, I walked up and asked him how it was going.

'OK, yeah,' he said, towelling the sweat and saliva from his jowls. 'Thanks for the chords and the set list.'

'That's OK,' I said. 'Have you thought about maybe changing the order slightly?'

'Go on,' he said, interested.

'Well, "Poker Face" is a great number, but I think to finish go for "Bridge Over Troubled Water" – you see, it really builds, and by the time you get to that high note at the end you're going to have them eating out of the palm of your hand.'

'You think?'

'Yes, and don't start with "Blowin' in the Wind".'

'But it's classic Dylan!'

'Exactly,' I countered. 'It's what people expect. It keeps you in their minds as just another busker. Shake things up a bit, go for something modern, something up-tempo that will pull them in. I could get you the chords to "Single Ladies (Put a Ring on It)", the Beyoncé number?'

'Would you do that?'

'Sure.'

'Hang on, that's got a rap, hasn't it? I can't rap.'

'Simple, just bark.'

'Bark?'

'Yeah, bark – that's what you guys do, you're a dog. Mark my words, they'll love it.'

'OK, yeah, "Single Ladies", great,' he said, then there was a pause. This rapid exchange had conjured memories of the closeness that we once shared.

'How's Mum?'

'She's fine.'

'And Nan?'

'No recent stonings, but she's still in prison.'

'Give them my best.'

'OK then, I'll get those chords for you.'

'Yup.'

I wandered off. I don't know if he's still drinking. I hope not, and I hope he's reached rock bottom and is on the upturn.

Steak-and-ale pie for dinner without the pie bit so it's like a sort of stew, sherry trifle for pud.

August 2nd

Mum took her portfolio with her for the artist-in-residence job at the dog-food factory. She was very nervous.

The interview panel included Anish Kapoor, Brian Sewell and Rolf Harris, as well as a smattering of Choppingham Meats top brass. They were very dismissive of her work, Rolf in particular, who said that the work lacked depth and that her use of paint was sloppy. He said that he should be able to smell the gravy but wasn't getting anything back off her 'primitive daubings'.

She didn't get the job but has been asked to consider the post of left-handed pipe stuffer. Yes, it's a bit of a come down from artist in residence and no, it wasn't what she'd had in mind for her retirement, but as she said, 'It's nice to be asked, and the money and dog-food allowance will come in handy.'

Got a text from Dog in the evening: 'Goosebumps towel senior yoghurt toddy, muscular au pair.'

Which I took to mean: 'Good to see you today, much appreciated.'

August 3rd

Huge crowd round Dog this afternoon. I could hear the applause as I came round the corner from Dennis the ironmonger's. There were people hanging out of windows, others standing on the roofs of their cars, all craning to hear the singing dog. I tried to push through to the front but was held back until the last strains of 'Bridge Over Troubled Water' died down.

'That was dynamite!' I said, patting his warm back.

'Did you see them?' he gushed, his eyes alive as he counted out the change. 'You were right about the Beyoncé number, it just pulls people in, and "Bridge" is a brilliant closer.'

'Have you thought about maybe getting some gigs?' I said. 'You know, in pubs or clubs? You've got a real talent there.'

'I wouldn't know where to start,' he said.

'I could look into it for you if you like.'

He agreed that I would work on an ad hoc basis as his manager. We shook hands and I set off back home to see what work I could get for him.

Everyone I phoned was interested until I said the words 'singing dog'.

Corned-beef sandwiches with side order of corn for dinner, cream horns for pud.

August 4th

An odd thing happened today. I went up the graveyard with the strimmer to get rid of the long grass over Dad's grave. Dad isn't in the grave, no. Mum had it installed to throw the military police off the scent. It also acts as a focal point for our grief – grief that he left with such huge debts and never got in touch again. So I did Dad's grave with the strimmer, and then looking over at the one next to it I noticed that it was a bit unkempt, so I started strimming that too. I was halfway through when a woman turned up and harangued me for doing it. She said she liked the grass long as it attracted butterflies, which reminded her of her sister who was buried there. I dunno, you try and help someone . . .

Phoned up all the local clubs again and disguised my voice

by holding my nose and speaking with a pencil clenched in-between my teeth. A couple of people mistook me for Michael Winner. I told them I represent a new singing sensation who's doing an 'open-air concert' down at the station and that if they wanted to be part of 'the biggest singing sensation to come out of Bexhill since Pat Farnborough', they'd better get down there, and that if transport was a problem I would be passing by in a minibus with the intent of transporting local promoters. A lot of them sounded interested. You'll note I've made no mention of a dog. My plan is to hook them in on his talent alone.

Sausage rolls, cucumber and crisps for lunch.

August 5th

Mum has won the weekly competition on Radio 4's *In Our Time*, the discussion programme hosted by Melvyn Bragg. She had to count the number of times he said the phrase 'the examination of the psychology of religion as a means to explore not the doctrine of belief but the nature of the indi-vidual's experience itself'. The answer was twenty-three. The prize is to spend a week with Lord Bragg himself at Center Parcs on the Purley Way, Croydon.

'What if we don't get on?' Mum whined to me. 'What if I don't like him? I mean, I like him in half-hour spurts broken up by other guests, but a whole week just me and him, what will we talk about?'

'You'll be fine,' I said, trying to reassure her. 'If he starts getting on your nerves, pretend to be asleep.'

Center Parcs is a fabulous destination, and she'd be a fool to miss out.

August 6th

The pear tree has produced just one pear this year. This is very disappointing as last year it produced two, which did at least mean one each for Mum and I. Still, I suppose half a pear is better than no pears. This does mean that with only one pear on the tree I'm going to have to keep a close eye on it. A number of dangers face the pear as it matures over the next few months: fire blight, the insect psylla and its associated black mould, and of course predators such as birds, who love

A Psylla, the natural enemy of the pear

the young pear buds. It's going to be tough, plus with just the one pear it's crucial that I get it right. The stakes couldn't be higher. It may sound strange but in many ways I wish the tree had borne no fruit at all rather than just one. Then the pressure would be off. One pear is a worst-case scenario for the pear cultivator.

Angel-hair noodles, tufu and bacon off-cuts for dinner, apple fool for pud.

August 7th

Mum is dragging her feet over setting a date for the Center Parcs trip with Lord Bragg. Every time he phones her she tells me to say she's out, and I don't really like lying to Lord Bragg.

He often tries to keep me talking on the phone in the hope that she'll come back while he's on the line, little knowing that she's actually sitting on the sofa listening in.

Freed up the bolt on the bathroom door with a little WD40. I've been meaning to do that for weeks.

I inspected the pear tree's precious cargo this morning and it's looking good. No trace of any disease, the fruit is swelling nicely and the stalk is sound.

Ham, egg and chips for dinner, Jaffa Cakes and condensed milk for pud.

August 8th

Feel a bit let down. I hired a minibus and drove all round the back lanes of Bexhill, picking up various local promoters and fixers: Clive and Greg Bell at the Two Tuns; Joyce Bleckley at the Priory Court Hotel, St Leonard's; Graham Ham of the Red Lion, St Norman's Bay, which has a function room that is renowned locally; and Patrick Abrahams of the Duke of Cumberland, Guestling, which last year held a barn dance that locals are still talking about. So quite key people in the local music biz.

It took me about two hours to pick them all up. When we got to the station I was pleased to see a reasonable crowd of people and parked the van. Would you believe it, Joyce Bleckley turned to me and said, 'Thanks for the lift! Be seein' ya,' and got straight on a train to Victoria without so much as a peek at my star-in-waiting. I bent down to grab a handful of dirt to throw at her but thought twice about it and let the grit fall from my hand. I ushered the others to the front of the throng and nodded to Dog, who was now on a break and chatting with a couple of teenage poodles. Five minutes went by, then ten. I leant in and whispered to Dog to 'get going', but he brushed me off, saying he'd start his next session when he was good and ready. My local promoters were getting restless. There was only so much I could do to hold their attention. I told them Dog's back story, his 'journey, emotionally'. I did a brief potted history of the station buildings, which I had to make up due to lack of local knowledge. When I found myself demonstrating how to make a mouse out of a hanky I knew the game was up. After twenty minutes they all filed back into the minibus, and I took them back to their gaffs.

I was furious.

'You've blown it!' I shouted at Dog as the sun set slowly over the seafront. 'You only get one chance in this business, and you've blown it! I put my neck on the line for you today and you embarrassed me. That's why you'll only ever be a rank amateur. You'll never turn pro!'

He just shrugged and sucked on a chewy shoe.

I shouldn't have said those things, but I was angry. It was another two hours taking the promoters home, and not one offered any petrol money.

At about half eleven at night I got a call from Joyce Bleckley asking me whether I'd pick her up from the station. I won't repeat what I said to her, but it was not pretty and contained an Anglo-Saxon word that was not 'Beowulf'.

Frikadeller, smoked-salmon pinwheels and chips for tea.

August 9th

Lord Bragg phoned fourteen times today asking to speak to Mum. In the end I turned on the answer machine and ignored the calls. Mum really does need to address this. Does she want to go on the trip or not? If not, she needs to let Lord Bragg know, as it's really not fair on him. She asked me to phone up Radio 4 to ask whether she could go with Andrew Marr instead, as she reckons he seems more of a laugh, but I refused.

August 10th

Lord Bragg phoned again and pretended to be from the gas board. He asked to speak to Mum about changing her gas supplier, and I put her on the line. He then revealed his true identity and asked her why she was avoiding his calls, which put her on the spot rather. She denied she was avoiding him and said that I hadn't been giving her the messages. He said that he really needed a break and was dead keen to book the Center Parcs thing so that he had something to look forward to during the next series of *In Our Time*, because he said that some of the experts – 'especially the historians' – get on his nerves 'with all their facts and figures'.

Melvyn kept her talking for about forty minutes I suppose, finally pinning her down to a date in September.

Mum came off the phone looking all flushed and said she was still not sure about it. But at least she's talked to him and got a working date.

Cheese-crusted beef roll for dinner, choco liqueur for pud.

August 11th

Mum says that she's been having extremely vivid dreams about Melvyn Bragg at Center Parcs. Essentially what happens is, they are both queuing for the water flume, and when he gets to the top he lets his mat go on its own and then turns round and nicks hers, leaving Mum to go down the flume without a mat, which leaves her with severely chafed thighs which Melvyn then offers to apply E45 cream to. Usually as he delves about in his satchel for the cream she wakes up, so he never actually lays a hand upon her.

I say to Mum that it's extremely unlikely that Lord Bragg will (a) let go of his mat, and (b) try to steal hers, but part of me thinks that maybe he is the sort of bloke that would fool around at the top of a water flume.

Of course, a psychologist would have a field day with Mum's dream, and it hasn't helped Mum's feelings of concern about the planned trip.

The pear continues to do well. With the recent dry spell I've been careful to keep it well watered as they do not tolerate dry conditions at all well, and the last thing I want is a gritty or woody texture to my pear.

August 12th

Lord Bragg phoned again today three times, asking Mum what she was taking with her, whether he should take woollens or a mac, whether there would be a washing machine or an ironing board, and what the dress code was at dinner. He also suggested they pre-book some of the restaurants and also some of the activities, like the jazz brunch buffet and sports cafe disco, which are bound to be popular. Mum found the whole thing quite awkward. It's a shame when one half is so keen and the other reticent. Having made the decision to go, I just wish she'd throw herself into it more.

The papers came through today with a date for Dog's trial on the drunk in charge of a mobility scooter rap. I suggested we hire that top lawyer who got the comedian Jimmy Carr off his speeding fine, but Dog said, 'Save your money, I'll defend myself.'

I point out that he has no training in the law. He says he'll go down the library and get a book out on it. I think he's being very silly but, still, if that's what he wants to do, who am I to stop him?

August 13th

Phone call from Peter Fincham at ITV asking would I make up the numbers for *I'm a Celebrity . . . Get Me Out of My Tree If I Don't Like It?*

They've already got Sir Trevor McDonald hosting and commitments from Cilla, Cannon and Ball, Sharleen Spiteri, Baz Bamigboye and Sylvester Stallone's mum to live in their favourite species of tree for three weeks, surviving only on food that is brought to them partly digested in the beaks of specially trained birds. I say that in principle I've nothing against being fed partly digested food by a bird; in fact, that aspect of it intrigues me. No, my problem with it is after the furore over my list of Britain's 100 top trees I really can't be seen now to favour any particular tree.

'What about if the type of tree was chosen for you?' he says.

'By whom?'

'Well, I'm thinking on my feet here, could it be chosen by a cancer charity?'

'I'll think about it.'

I'm torn because I know these reality shows can really improve your popularity with the public – provided you are able to keep a lid on your nasty side – but at the same time I don't want to be known simply as 'that tree bloke'. I phone him straight back and agree to go 'into the forest'.

Pruned the pear tree today, taking care not to over-prune as this encourages the parasitic insect psylla, which feeds on pears.

Sweet-sour gammon for dinner, peach halves for pud.

August 14th

Peter Fincham phoned first thing.

'We've got a bit of a problem,' he said. 'The tree the cancer charity have chosen for you is the horse chestnut.'

'You mean . . .?'

'Yes, the conker . . .'

'Absolutely not!' I bellow down the phone. 'Get them to choose again or get another cancer charity involved!' I hang up on him as he splutters about 'damage limitation' and 'Ofcom guidelines'.

I sit up at Mum's breakfast bar eating a piece of toast and thinking I can't have all that conker stuff come out again. I can just see Dizzee Rascal teeing up for another stab at the charts with 'Conkers Two'. In my mind's eye I can see him in his Hampshire flat with the rhyming dictionary turned to

'–onkers'. No, never again. The other thing that perturbs me rather was losing my cool with Peter F like that – do that in the jungle and I'm very much like the scorched bread I now scoff (that's right, toast).

Marmite toast for tea, Tunnock's tea cakes for pud.

August 15th

The cancer charity are refusing to budge on their choice of tree for me to live in for the new ITV show *I'm a Celebrity . . . Get Me Out of My Tree If I Don't Like It*.

I phone the chairman of the charity myself. He explains that they're concentrating on 'men's cancer' this year and so the conker is a good association for them. I suggest the acorn would make a similar connection. He says, 'Speak for yourself.' In the end we reach what I think is a reasonable compromise and agree that I will live in a walnut tree.

This could work out quite nicely for me in that the walnuts should provide a pleasant change from the pre-digested food that the birds will be feeding me.

August 16th

Mum's birthday. She was up with the lark and knocking on my bedroom door asking for her present. I got her the usual – a scented candle and a box of Celebrations to open now – but her main present was a trip on the Eurostar. Just to Ashford, but she likes the shops there and there's a very good Mexican restaurant where you get a free hat if you spend over thirty quid.

We travelled second class, but for a £5 supplement you

The Eurostar

could use the sauna carriage. It involved getting changed in the toilets, which wasn't very pleasant as the toilet had become blocked and so I had to stand on my shoes. Mum and I then had to walk through the buffet car in just our towels to get to the sauna carriage. All went well for the first ten minutes or so – lots of lovely hot steam, soothing music (you know, whale noises and waves breaking on the shore, plus the odd pan pipe) – I was really starting to chill, then Mum went and opened a window. All the steam cleared in about ten seconds flat. The other passengers, including some notables – Yusuf Islam, Mike Morris, Anne Diamond, Wincey Willis and Rusty Lee on a TV-am reunion jolly, all half-cut – were furious, and the two of us beat a hasty retreat back through the buffet car. Unfortunately the toilet was now out of order, so we had to tramp through five further carriages in our towels before we got to one with a working loo.

When I got back to my seat someone had nicked my free hat.

When we got home there was a lovely posy of flowers on the doorstep from guess who? That's right – Melvyn.

Cheesy nachos, chicken fajitas and trifle for lunch.

August 17th

The story about me appearing in *I'm a Celebrity . . . Get Me Out of My Tree If I Don't Like It* and living in a walnut tree has been leaked to the press, and Jan Moir in the *Daily Mail* accuses me of 'rank hypocrisy', pointing out that I only placed the walnut tree twenty-third in my list of Britain's 100 favourite trees 'and now he's come out and said it's his favourite'.

The *Daily Star* print a picture of a walnut on the front page 'wearing' a big collar and my glasses.

A 'spokesperson for Harry Hill' is quoted as saying that the original Channel 4 list was not a list of Harry's favourite trees but was chosen by a committee, and that the choice of tree for *I'm a Celebrity . . . Get Me Out of My Tree If I Don't Like It* was made by a cancer charity keen to highlight men's cancer. The *Mail*'s editor says, 'It's still a bit bad.' I get a message of support from Alex Salmond, and the International Walnut Dashboard Appreciation Society send me a key ring.

Applied a little fertiliser to the pear tree today, which should see it through my absence. Hopefully not too much as this encourages the parasitic insect psylla, which can wreak untold damage on my diminutive pear harvest.

August 18th

The *Sun* announce that their guest columnist for the duration of *I'm a Celebrity . . . Get Me Out of My Tree If I Don't Like It* will be none other than my nemesis – Dizzee Rascal. Great. I'm already wondering whether it's too late to pull out.

Photo shoot at ITV centre with some walnuts.

Bump into Cilla Black, who says she's regretting plumping

for the poplar as she hadn't realised how bendy they are.

Mum cooks me a big roasted joint with all the trimmings as a send-off but won't tell me the nature of the meat.

August 19th

First day of the *I'm a Celebrity . . . Get Me Out of My Tree If I Don't Like It* shoot. I wave goodbye to Mum, who, as she holds me to her, whispers, 'Don't fall out,' which was sweet.

I'll miss her. I'm also a little anxious at leaving the pear tree unattended for such a long period of time, but give Mum strict instructions on how to look after it.

I am taken to a hotel on the outskirts of Crawley, where I am introduced to the other contestants: Cilla (the poplar), Cannon and Ball (the laburnum), Sharleen Spiteri (the oak – lucky swine!), Baz Bamigboye (the flowering cherry) and Sylvester Stallone's mum (the Canadian redwood).

They all seem very nice. We are briefed about what will happen tomorrow. We will be taken by helicopter to the forest area and dropped on bungee ropes into our trees, where we will stay for the duration of the show – two weeks. The producer explains to us that it's not actually a forest but a man-made copse formed in the car park of the TV studios in Teddington. There is a layer of astroturf with the trees planted at intervals of about ten yards. It's at this point that the producer explains that there is a problem with one of the trees. We all sit forward, hoping that it won't be ours. He explains that while most of the trees were imported from China, one of them – the Canadian redwood (Sylvester Stallone's mum) – was due to come in from Canada. However, due to its size it had to be floated over behind a tug boat. He goes on to say that after a heavy storm three days ago they lost contact with the tug boat and haven't heard from it since. He says that another redwood is being chopped down and floated over 'as we speak', but it won't be here till the second week of the show at best. Poor Sylvester Stallone's mum. Her face crumpled and she bawled her eyes out. We all gathered round her like we've seen them do on those American programmes and put our arms round her, but it didn't seem to do any good.

I sidled up to the producer and demanded to know what was going to happen, as there were only five trees and six top celebrities who needed a tree. He said that the rest of us would draw lots live on TV to see who got lumbered with Sylvester Stallone's mum. Of course, it's just the sort of drama they like on these reality shows. I was worried that this lack of a tree would create a swell of public sympathy towards Sylvester Stallone's mum and that it therefore was not a level playing field, and I put this to the producer, who told me to 'grow up'.

The fact is, I want to win this thing.

After a light buffet lunch, we all go back to our rooms and chill. I phone Mum and tell her about Sylvester Stallone's mum, and she says that a large red tree has been washed up on Bexhill beach and that it could be the one that Sylvester Stallone's mum was planning to stay in. I tell her to get down the beach and stop anyone from trying to steal it. I then call the producer, who says he'll look into it.

We start the day with the draw for who's going to get 'lumbered' (by the way, coming up with these tree-related gags is absolutely effortless for me!) with Sylvester Stallone's mum. It takes place on the balcony of the producer's hotel room, overlooking the busy A23.

Guess what? That's right, she's staying with me in my walnut. Fan-flaming-tastic or what? I could not freaking believe it. She hardly said a word to me. She's taken the lack of a designated tree really badly and gone from being the lively Italian matriarch to a slack-jawed zombie overnight. Don't get me wrong, it's not that I don't like Sylvester Stallone's mum, it's just that I had plans for that tree. I sidle up to the producer and ask him whether sharing the tree will also mean that I'm going to have to share the walnuts too.

'Get a life,' he snaps. I think he's got a problem with me. I think he sees me as trouble.

At the first opportunity I get on the phone to Mum to see if there's any word on the tree that was washed up on the beach.

By the time she got there, she said, the tree, which she positively identified as a Canadian redwood ('It was so big you could drive a car through it!'), had been loaded up onto the back of four flat-bed trucks and was heading up Bexhill High Street. Fortunately she got the registration numbers of the lorries, which I duly forward on to the producer.

We are taken by helicopter from the hotel car park and follow the curve of the A23 as it snakes past Carshalton to Teddington and the so-called forest, where we are attached to our bungee ropes as we hover.

I must say I was nervous sitting there with my legs over the edge of the helicopter and nothing between me and certain death but a length of elastic, and I was just about to tell them that I wasn't going to go through with it when the producer pushed me out. It was an odd feeling falling towards that walnut tree with Sylvester Stallone's mum on my back, and unlike anything I've ever done before. As we got within touching distance of the tree canopy I grabbed hold of a branch and released the bungee rope from around my waist, dropping easily into the sturdy branches. Unfortunately Sylvester Stallone's mum was not quite so deft. Forgetting to loosen her bungee belt she went flying back skywards towards the helicopter and its rotating blades. I could see the look of panic on the producer's face. 'Grab her!' he cried. Sylvester Stallone's mum did not pass through the rotating blades of the Westland helicopter. No, she hit the underside of it with a crack and started back down towards me.

'What do I do?' I shouted at the producer.

'Cut the rope!' he shouted back. Well, that's easier said than done. As she came towards me I reached up behind her and tried to cut the thick rubber cord, but to no avail. With no foothold in the tree I was propelled up on Sylvester Stallone's mum's back towards the helicopter. Fortunately, as any physicist will tell you, the force in the bungee rope had diminished enough for us to avoid the helicopter, and we headed back down towards the tree, but not far enough to get near it. We bounced up and down like that for forty-five minutes until eventually we came to a halt and the helicopter lowered us both to the astroturf floor of the car park, where a man with a short ladder helped us climb into the tree. I tell you, I've never been more pleased to see a tree in my whole life.

So there we were, me and Sylvester Stallone's mum alone in a walnut tree.

I wasted little time in tying up my hammock and getting some rest.

Walnuts for dinner.

August 21st

Would have slept well if Sylvester Stallone's mum hadn't kept falling out of the tree. She's black and blue. Every time I helped her back up I'd look over to see Sharleen Spiteri beaming back at me from her oak. She's loving every minute of it.

From my tree I can see all the other contestants. Baz Bamigboye is in his flowering cherry, while Cilla, from what I could see of her, spent the entire night standing up clinging to the branches of her poplar. She really hadn't thought that one through. You see, the way the poplar carries itself with its branches almost vertical there really is no place to build a little camp like me and Sylvester Stallone's mum have started to do. Cannon and Ball appeared to be doing some sort of tribal dance through the night.

She's not all bad, Sylvester Stallone's mum. She brightened up a lot once she'd had her tablets and unpacked her little case.

At breakfast the first of the birds turned up with our food in their beaks. Mine was some sort of parakeet, and I did as I had been told to do – just sat as still as I could, tilted my head and opened my mouth. The parakeet stood on my chin and regurgitated some Rice Krispies into my mouth, then flew off

me being fed by a bird

for some more. Actually being bird fed sounds worse than it is. The Rice Krispies were sweeter than usual, probably due to the enzymes in the bird's saliva breaking down the starches into sugar. No, they tasted more like Ricicles.

Fate finally smiled on Sylvester Stallone's mum. Her bird was a pelican – all she had to do was reach in, and there was a round of toast and a soft-boiled egg. I think this was the producer trying to make amends for the abortive bungee jump and lack of designated tree.

We spent the rest of the morning reading our books.

August 22nd

I was kept awake late into the night by Cannon and Ball's singing. It was nice at first but soon started to grate. At intervals they would shake their tree too, making a rattling noise.

I finally got to sleep, only to be woken by Sylvester Stallone's mum asking me whether she could bunk up with me in my hammock. Bit of a liberty, but I agreed. I've no idea what this looks like on TV.

At tea, as the parrot finished regurgitating some fried mince, onions and mashed potato, it spoke to me.

'You're doing great,' it said. That was all. A short message, but what a lift to the spirits!

August 23rd

This morning I awoke to find that Baz Bamigboye's tree is no longer where it should be. I slept through it, but according to Sylvester Stallone's mum in the middle of the night Baz had tried to light a fire for warmth, the whole tree had caught fire and he had to jump to safety. Later today there will be another draw to determine whose tree Baz will be sharing until a replacement flowering cherry is found. Presumably that won't include me and Sylvester Stallone's mum.

August 24th

In the draw today Baz was allocated to stay in Cilla's poplar. That should be fun for them both! Honestly, what a silly tree to choose to live in!

August 25th

This morning we were told that Cilla Black has had enough, has left her poplar, is back at the hotel in Crawley and will not be returning. That's a shame for Cilla, but I'm afraid her failure was due to poor arborial research. But there's no room for sentimentality. As far as I'm concerned it's one down, four to go.

Baz now occupies her vacant poplar, and using his powerful arms has woven three of the lower branches into a sort of nest, thus stabilising his position.

August 26th

In the night Tommy Cannon had a panic attack and had to be taken out on a stretcher. They're falling like flies and we haven't even had the first public vote! When the news is announced I look over at Sharleen Spiteri, who just smiles back, but it's the smile of someone who is confident of victory.

Bobby Ball strips to the waist, daubs his upper body with bird droppings and wails like a banshee all night. An odd tactic.

August 27th

Oh sweet baby Jesus! It was the first public vote today and Spiteri was sent packing. Can't believe my luck.

I try to gauge how I'm coming across by asking the parrot that feeds me, but he's staying tight-beaked.

'Just keep going,' he says, in-between coughing up blobs of cauliflower cheese.

August 28th

At rather a low ebb tonight. The parrot that feeds me spoke to me again in a rather dispiriting way. As he regurgitated some hot potato waffles and bacon he leant into my ear and said, 'You're all washed up, you're going to fail.' His voice sounded different, one I vaguely recognised but couldn't quite place. It's a waiting game now.

August 29th

A difficult night, with Sylvester Stallone's mum snuggling in for warmth and that parrot's creepy voice echoing around in my head. Feel like packing it all in. Keep thinking of Mum in that nice warm dog's bed.

At breakfast this morning the parrot again leant in and whispered in my ear. What he said was quite horrid and was couched, I'm afraid, in the sort of language I couldn't possibly repeat in a celebrity memoir. Suffice to say, I slapped the parrot round the face and pushed him away without bothering with pudding. As I watched him fly off I found myself close to tears. That voice – familiar, yet I cannot put my finger on it.

In the afternoon we were allowed some messages from home, delivered to us via a TV screen while they film us in the hope that we will cry. Odd to see Mum and Dog, but there they were sitting up at the breakfast bar. Sadly, rather than an uplifting message detailing how proud they are of me and how well I'm coming across, Mum listed all the little chores that are outstanding and that will need my attention when I get back. I must say I was surprised to hear that the bolt on the bathroom door is still sticking as I had freed it up with a little WD40 before I left.

Oh well, it was nice to see them, and I'm sure that the buzzing noise made by the dimmer switch in the lounge is long-standing and only occurs when turned to low.

Sylvester Stallone's mum had a very funny message from Sylvester. There he was, dressed as Rambo, spouting off. I spotted that it wasn't a specially recorded message from him – rather a short clip from *Rambo 4* – but it seemed to cheer her up so I didn't tell her.

I put my fingers in my ears as the parrot fed me mushed-up pellets of sausage and potatoes parisienne.

August 30th

Rather a slow morning. Took a massage from Sylvester Stallone's mum, but she was a little rough. I combed her hair in return and formed rough bunches out of it, secured with strips of walnut bark.

At lunch today I looked across at Baz as the parrot hovered over him splattering food out of its beak onto his tongue. Baz seemed to be talking to the parrot, and then it dawned on me. The parrot's voice – it was that of Baz Bamigboye! He's been teaching the parrot words and phrases that he knows will lower my morale! The dirty double-crossing douche bag!

'Right, if he wants to play dirty that's fine by me,' I thought. When the parrot came to feed me, I taught it to say, 'You're coming across really badly, Baz.'

At tea time, after the parrot had fed us, I heard sobs coming from Baz's tree. It seems he can dish it out but doesn't like to take it!

August 31st

The walnut supply is getting low and I'm rationing Sylvester Stallone's mum and me to only eight a day.

Second public vote and Bobby Ball went out. Nice guy.

Mind you, I won't miss his night-time caterwauling.

September

some Wind Turbines

September 1st

At about midday today there was a huge commotion as Sylvester Stallone's mum's Canadian redwood tree finally turned up on the back of four flat-bed trucks. It's a real monster! You could drive a car through it! Boy, am I pleased to see it, as it's been getting pretty cramped in the tree, and although strictly they belong to me, I've felt obliged to share the walnuts.

It takes them several hours to get the redwood into the ground, by which time it's dark and Sylvester Stallone's mum asks whether she can stay one last night with me. I let her. Well, she's not really any trouble.

I wake up in the night to see her going from bough to bough picking my walnuts and stuffing them into her under-garments. I manage to wrestle four off her but let the rest go.

September 2nd

I wave Sylvester Stallone's mum off to her new tree. She inches along one of the great boughs, turns and waves at me, and I wave back. As she waves, a walnut drops from her sleeve. She's a canny operator, and if I was a betting man I'd put my money on her winning this.

I'm missing Sylvester Stallone's mum terribly and try to train the parakeet who feeds me to take a message to her, but with no success. It just keeps repeating Baz's foul-mouthed diatribe.

In the afternoon I drew a face on a walnut shell until I was satisfied that it looked like Sylvester Stallone's mum. I talk to the walnut and it makes me feel better.

September 3rd

I have been voted off *I'm a Celebrity . . . Get Me Out of My Tree If I Don't Like It*. I can't say I am surprised. I was aware that I wasn't doing much to entertain the viewers. I mean, all yesterday I just sat in one of the boughs of my tree and talked to my walnut. Compared to Bobby Ball's shenanigans – hopping about, singing, shouting the names of people he's worked with over the years at the top of his voice – I'm only surprised that I didn't go sooner.

I descend from the tree and walk up the astroturf to the waiting press. There are only two papers represented, the *Teddington and Hampton Wick Gazette* – a local paper – and the *Sunday Express*. It seems the ratings for the show have been disappointing, and after three episodes it was transferred from mainstream ITV1 to midnight on ITV2, after the bingo.

I have a brief chat with the *Express* and then spend nearly forty minutes with the *Teddington and Hampton Wick Gazette*, mainly talking about my favourite haunts in the borough. I am then taken to be interviewed live by the show's hosts Kate Thornton and Des O'Connor. They play back my 'best bits' to me, which I'm aware is very short, much shorter than you normally get on these sorts of shows. Most of it is me arguing with Sylvester Stallone's mum about walnuts. Then they say they want to know all about my little walnut friend, and play a long clip of me talking to the walnut I painted to look like

Sylvester Stallone's mum. As I see it come up on the screen I start to weep uncontrollably. Des tries to make light of it, but Kate is uncomfortable, and through my tears I can see that she is crying too. Des announces an advert break, but this catches the production team out. They're not quite ready and there's an embarrassed silence, me and Kate crying and Des sitting with a fixed grin on his face which is gradually dying away. The first advert to come up is for Saniflo, the macerator-blade effluent disposal system for toilets that are not on main drainage.

I left during the advert break and got a car home. When I watch it back on the ITV Player on my computer later it continues after the ad break with just Des on the sofa, talking to a walnut painted to look like Kate Thornton.

I got home about midnight and Mum greeted me with 'Where have you been?'

'I've been on *I'm a Celebrity . . . Get Me Out of My Tree If I Don't Like It*,' I said.

'Have you? I thought that had finished.'

It seems that my stint on the show has not had the profile-raising effects I had hoped for.

I tune into the live feed of the show, just to catch a glimpse of Sylvester Stallone's mum really. She looks so vulnerable crouched in her giant redwood, taking sustenance from a chiffchaff.

My sleep is interrupted at intervals by vivid dreams of being strangled by bindweed.

September 4th

On my return to Bexhill I wandered out into the garden and, horror of horrors, noticed a tiny red insect on the pear tree which I believe to be psylla. That is, of course, every pear grower's nightmare as it sucks the juice from the fruit. What alerted me to it was the honey-like substance that they secrete, which had then attracted a black, sooty mould that looks similar to fire blight but washes off.

I destroyed the insect and gently washed the mould from the fruit. I suspect I applied too much fertiliser earlier in the year or perhaps over-pruned the tree in the early stages. Thinking about it, I should probably have used branch spreaders to increase air circulation.

I think I've caught the pear early enough to have averted any permanent damage, but it was a close-run thing. I have decided to check on the pear twice a day from now on until the harvest.

Told Mum about the brush with psylla, and she said, 'I haven't seen hide nor hair of her since *Blind Date*.' We both laughed heartily at that. It's not true actually. Cilla stood in for Paul O'Grady on his Channel 4 talk show for a week, and Mum and me both watched it, and of course she was also in *I'm a Celebrity . . . Get Me Out of My Tree If I Don't Like It*, so she's not being entirely fair, but it was a good joke of Mum's nonetheless.

September 5th

It's my birthday in a couple of weeks so I spent the morning doing the thank-you letters. Just generic 'Dear (Blank),

Thank you for my present. It is proving very useful. Another year under my belt, eh? Who'd have thought it? 46 years old! 4 years older than Elvis when he bit the bullet and 14 more than Jesus. Thanks again, Harry.'

It just gets me ahead.

Waved a very nervous Mum off on her holiday to Center Parcs today. Melvyn picked her up about half past eight. I must say he's quite the gent, holding the door open for her on his Seat Ibiza.

'Don't worry, H, I'll try to bring her back in one piece,' he said with that trademark grin. 'Kenny are playing in the ballroom tonight,' he added excitedly.

'Kenny?'

'Yes, had that hit in the seventies – "Do the Bump". It's not the original line-up, but it's still lead singer Rick Driscoll on lead vocals.'

I smiled at him and nodded.

I told Mum last night that if he tries anything she's not happy about, she should give me a ring and I'll get down there straight away to pick her up.

Mum was right. The winner of the 2.30 from Haydock Park was Festen Bulbous, but the silly mare forgot to place a bet.

Checked on the pear tree, and the pear looks good and healthy today with no recurrence of the dreaded psylla. The fruit is swelling nicely and I have every hope that in about a month's time it will be a sweet and juicy pear.

September 6th

Sylvester Stallone's mum has won *I'm a Celebrity . . . Get Me Out of My Tree If I Don't Like It*, a fact that has been ignored by all the daily papers except the *Express*, which put it on the front page and supplied a special pull-out section all about her fourteen days in a tree. I bought a copy, but reading it it's as if I was never in that specially adapted car park in Teddington. There are a couple of shots of me in the group photos and one where I can be seen in the background of a shot of Baz. I browse through the editorial and find it surprisingly moving. It's basically the story of one woman's journey, a battle with the elements and a return to a more simple way of life. It finishes with a quote from Bobby Ball: 'Darwin was right, we can live in trees.' I feel a bit better about myself now. As Bobby points out, yes, it was a TV show, but it was an important anthropological experiment too.

Mum arrived home last night by minicab. She looked pale and shaken but refuses to go into the details of what happened.

If I ever set eyes on Bragg again, he'd better watch out.

Kidneys in red wine for dinner. No pudding.

September 7th

While I was away Mum was sold a wind turbine by a door-to-door salesman. When I ask where it is, she points out into the English Channel and says, 'There, that one, second from the left.'

'That's your turbine?'

'Yes, the electricity from it is mine and I can sell it back to the National Grid and offset my electricity bill with it once I've paid off the cost of the installation.'

'How much did it cost?'

'£750,000 in 16,000 monthly payments, but if I should die before I've paid it off it automatically transfers to my next of kin – you.'

'Great. What about the fourteen-day cooling-off period?'

'I don't want to cool off, I want the turbine. It's the way forward for the world, providing energy for my grandchildren and their children after that.'

'You're thinking of Ribena.'

'That's right, Ribena.'

'Besides, you haven't got any grandchildren,' I point out as I'm dialling the bank's number to cancel the cheque.

The pear continues to swell nicely. Not long now. In a funny way I've enjoyed looking after this one pear more than overseeing a whole tree full. It's been like guiding a lone fishing boat into harbour, and this will sound ridiculous but I almost feel as if I know the pear.

Checked through the CCTV footage from the time when Mum was sold the turbine and spot the door-to-door salesman. It is quite clearly Dave who laid the drive and sold her the foil and the solar-heating panels, wearing a beard and sunglasses.

Fish fingers and mash for dinner, chocolate coins for pud.

September 8th

Princess Anne came down to Bexhill today to open the De La Warr Dog Food Pavilion.

She was a little testy before the opening, refusing to shake hands with local schoolchildren because she'd forgotten her gloves. Eventually one of the catering staff found an oven glove, which did the job. I understand Anne's point – royal protocol is there for a reason – but it didn't look good, she standing there shaking hands with an eight-year-old wearing a novelty oven glove in the shape of a cockatoo. She didn't stay long either. A couple of quick photos and a whirlwind tour of the offal and condemned-meat processing area and she was away. She passed on the tour of the Choppingham Meats Through the Ages Experience, in which you are taken on a fairground ride through the story of Choppingham Meats, narrated by Boy George. Since Choppingham Meats was only established in 1986 it's not particularly enthralling, but George does the best he can, finishing on 'Karma Chameleon' and changing the words to 'Karma, karma, karma, come to Choppingham Meats – red, gold and brown, red, gold and brow-her-her-hown . . .'

So anyway, Anne didn't sample its delights and was off back down the A21 before you could say 'Pedigree Chum', with, it must be said, eight complimentary trays of Choppingham Meat dog food (two rabbit and lamb, two chicken and pea, two pork and beef, and two pheasant and ptarmigan) sitting on the back seat of her Land Rover Discovery.

Not a bad day's work!

Liver and bacon for dinner, rice pudding for afters.

September 9th

Woke up to a strong smell of rabbit and lamb. Couldn't work it out at first, then remembered the pet-food factory. You

330

get used to it pretty quickly but it's absolute torture for poor Dog. He's been constantly salivating and asking what time dinner is. We have let him move back into the house while he works on his defence for his upcoming drink-driving court case. Touch wood, he seems to have stopped drinking. Maybe he's starting to turn his life around.

He has been working all day and most of the night on the case law. So far he says he can find no successful prosecution of a mammal, apart from a monkey that was hung for treason in Hull during the Second World War. He's turned up one failed prosecution – of a squirrel in Burnley for arson in a naval dockyard, but the squirrel died before the case came to trial. He's pretty confident that he can get himself off.

With daily headlines of binge drinkers and broken Britain, I fear that the judge might make an example of him.

Very cold today, so I went out and put one of my old socks around the pear to insulate it against any potential early frost.

A couple more days and the time will come to harvest it.

September 10th

Mum's first day at the De La Warr Dog Food Pavilion as a left-handed pipe stuffer. She was talked through the job by the outgoing left-handed pipe stuffer, Bill, whose left hand was terribly swollen and red ('Almost like a lobster,' said Mum). He explained that the trick was to have the pipe stuffed and ready for discharge before the distal end meets the proximal tin.

The council have introduced a new household-waste regimen. Not content with reducing collections to alternate weeks for recyclable and non-recyclable waste, they are now asking us to sort out the waste in more detail. We will now need to sort it out into separate bins thus:

1. Paper
2. Card – including soup cartons, but not greetings cards. They go into . . .
3. Cardboard (inc. greetings cards)
4. Plastic bottles
5. Cartons but not soup cartons (see cardboard)
6. Meat waste (not pork)
7. Tins and cans (not soup)
8. Italian food waste
9. Indian food waste
10. Food waste of indeterminate ethnic origin (including British)

That means we'll need nine new bins!

Chicken tart for dinner, apple tart for pud.

September 11th

I head up to London for a meeting with Eric Fellner, the head of Working Title pictures, about my idea to make a film about Flipper the dolphin turning his back on the sea.

'It's a kind of fish-out-of-water flick,' I say.

'Dolphins are mammals,' he replies.

'Yes,' say I.

'You said "fish",' he says.

'Figure of speech. It would be a CGI dolphin with a bad attitude who wears Gucci, smokes a cigar and dates *Playboy* models.'

A Dolphin

'Who would do the voice?'

'Bernard Cribbins,' I ventured. He liked that.

We agreed that the film would be better if we could get across some sort of eco-message about dolphins being caught in tuna fishing nets, but at the same time avoiding a strong anti-Japanese message as Japan is a big market for this sort of film.

'Got anything else?' he said.

'How about the life story of the Olympic swimmer Mark Spitz?'

'What's the story there?'

'Well, it would be a fish-out-of-water story again . . .'

'But he's a human who makes his living from being in the water.'

'Exactly.'

'Keep me in the loop,' he said.

It must be hard work trying to get money for films all the time.

September 12th

Eric Smythe-Wilkes called round today and asked me about returning the favour of looking after our hamster. I'll be honest, I was more than a little puzzled because, as previously outlined, one of the reasons I chose Eric for the job was that he didn't have any pets.

'It's Betty's mother,' he says. 'She's got dementia, so we can't take her on holiday because she would ruin it for us. Could you take her, just for a long weekend, while we're on holiday in Eastbourne?'

'Oh!' I was taken aback rather. 'Is she . . .'

'Fully house-trained yes, but a danger to herself so she can't be left alone. It's just that you did say . . . about the favour . . . so I'm calling it in.'

'I don't remember you saying that the favour had to be returned,' I said, back-pedalling like mad.

He produced a small hand-held tape recorder and proceeded to play back the conversation to me. I heard myself saying, 'Of course, not a problem, I will be happy to pay back the favour.'

I suppose I could have argued the toss with him, about the difference between looking after an elderly lady and looking after a hamster, but technically he had me. Besides, as Eric points out, it's only Eastbourne, just ten miles up the road.

'Yeah, just drop her off on your way,' I say. Well, it might be fun to have a new face round the house.

September 13th

Mrs Doreen Smythe-Wilkes arrived today for her week's stay

with us while Eric and Betty go off to Eastbourne.

Received a cheque for £45 from those two thieving magpies Anton Dec and Declon McAnt for the 'Scratch Anthea' segment on their show, with a letter apologising for any copyright infringement, so I'm satisfied. Result! Forty-five quid, nice one! Just shows you, sometimes you really have to stand up for yourself and what you believe in.

Chinese takeaway for dinner, no pud.

September 14th

Sad to say that Mrs Doreen Smythe-Wilkes has not been out of her room. Mum took her a bottle of water and some food, but there was no response, so she left them outside the door.

September 15th

It seems Mrs Doreen Smythe-Wilkes is dead. Seeing her food and water untouched this morning I broke the door down, and there she was, stiff as a board in her nightie and with GMTV on the portable TV. This is extremely embarrassing as Eric and Betty are due back in two days and I know that Betty in particular was very fond of her.

Mum suggested I go round to the Nemesis rest home and

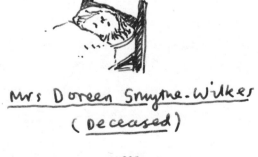

Mrs Doreen Smythe-Wilkes
(Deceased)

335

see if I can spot another old lady who looks similar and do a substitution.

It does seem the only possible solution. As she points out, if I could get an old lady who was confused and maybe didn't have that long to go, that would be the best option. I think I'll sleep on it.

Spring rolls, prawn toast, sweet-and-sour pork balls, spare ribs, chicken with cashew nuts, crispy chilli beef and egg fried rice for dinner. Drank two litres of water before bed.

September 16th

Went round to the Nemesis rest home first thing, and on an initial viewing spotted a couple of old girls that would fit the bill. It's really just a question of working out how to sneak one of them past the matron.

Mum comes up with a plan which at first glance seems pretty much foolproof. I go to the home with Mum on the pretext of looking for a home for her. I swap Mum for one of their old ladies. I take the new old lady home, leaving Mum at the home. I get the old lady home and swap her for Mrs Doreen Smythe-Wilkes. I then return Doreen to the nursing home, explaining that I picked up the wrong one and exchange her for Mum. Then I take Mum home.

The obvious pitfall is that I am swapping a live old lady for a dead one. Mum had the idea of painting eyes onto the closed lids of Doreen's eyes. I don't think there'll be any need for that if I choose a busy time like lunch. I could be in and out before anyone's realised that she hasn't touched her jelly.

There is no time to lose as Doreen is beginning to get a

bit gamey. Make an appointment to 'look round' the nursing home tomorrow morning.

Smoked-salmon pinwheels and cheese pinwheels for dinner, strawberry mousse for pud.

September 17th

Took Mum to look round the home. I've got to hand it to her, she did a great job at pretending to be old. I know she's seventy-three, but you'd never know it normally. However, this morning she looked about ninety, mumbling, dribbling – an absolute *tour de force*. Once we were through the door the staff pretty much left us to it. We got straight round to the target old lady's room and got her on the disability vehicle, leaving Mum in her bed with the covers over her head. Then we made a beeline for the exit. I say we – I had to lean over the old girl and put my hands over hers to operate the throttle and brake.

The whole swap couldn't have taken more than forty minutes and went smooth as clockwork. It didn't take long to cover the two miles back to Mum's house.

As we pulled into the drive who should I see waiting by the front porch but Eric and Betty Smythe-Wilkes. It seems they'd had to cut short their holiday due to 'dental pain' and had come to 'pick up Mum'.

'Here she is!' I said brightly.

'Don't be silly, that's not Mum,' said Betty.

'Isn't it?' I said, doing a double take and feigning surprise.

'Stop messing about, Harry,' said Eric, peering through the lounge window. 'Where's Mum?'

Well, I had to do a lot of quick thinking at this point.

I don't think I've crammed that much thinking into such a short space of time since Amanda Donohue caught me going through her handbag.

All I could come up with was the truth.

'You'd better come in, guys,' I said. Once I'd got them sat down with a cup of tea I let them have it.

'I'm afraid she's gone.'

'Gone where?' was the rapid response from Eric.

I then found myself saying, 'Kidnapped!'

'What?!'

'Yes, they wanted £10,000 or they'd kill her!'

'Why didn't you contact us?'

'We didn't want it to spoil your holiday!'

'Who's she?' said Eric, pointing at the old lady from the nursing home, who was now waving at him.

'A friend of Mum's we were going to use as a honeytrap to lure the kidnappers out.'

As I was saying all this I was thinking to myself, 'If I get out of this mess without a criminal record I'm going to drink that bottle of Piat d'Or I've been saving for a special occasion in one.'

'Where's the ransom note?'

'I lost it!'

I managed to get them to agree not to contact the police and to see my plan through, and encouraged them to go home and unpack and await further instructions.

As soon as they were out of the house I whipped the old lady back to the home, where they hadn't even noticed she was gone, and recovered Mum, who was fast asleep in the old girl's bed and was a little resentful of me waking her up.

Once back at the house we got the body of Mrs Doreen Smythe-Wilkes and under cover of darkness carried her to next door's front step and, I'm ashamed to say, left her there – the implication being that the kidnappers had acted upon their threat.

It was Mum's idea to ring the front doorbell, which meant we had to hot-foot it over the hedge.

A very sad Eric and Betty called round some ten minutes later with the tragic news that Doreen had been killed by her kidnappers, and we all joined in a few prayers. Once they'd gone I drank two-thirds of the bottle of Piat d'Or before collapsing onto the couch.

September 18th

The police came round this morning asking all sorts of tricky questions about the kidnapping, but I think I managed to fob them off. Finished off the other third of the Piat d'Or for lunch.

The good news is that Mum actually quite liked the rest home and says she would be happy to go and live there should the need ever arise, even though there is no 'clubhouse'.

Poor Joe Pasquale turned up last night to play the De La Warr Pavilion with his *Cheeky Cheekiness Show*, only to find that it is now a dog-food factory. No one had bothered to inform him of the change in use. Mindful that if he cancelled the show he wouldn't get paid, he insisted on performing the entire thing, including interval and encore, in front of the twenty-one staff on the night shift as they went about their business of processing condemned meat and offal. He received a standing ovation. Good for you, Joe.

The first day of Dog's trial for being drunk in charge of a mobility scooter. I don't fancy his chances much: there are three cats on the jury!

The prosecution put what seemed to me a pretty cast-iron case against him. He'd been caught driving the vehicle and had given a positive breath test and urine sample.

'How's he going to wriggle out of this one?' I whispered to Mum.

Dog opened his defence by stating that he would be claiming mistaken identity, and then called his first witness, one PC Firminger.

'Are you sure it was me that you pulled over and breathalysed that night, Police Constable?'

'Quite sure,' said Firminger.

'Quite, quite sure?' said Dog.

'Quite, quite, quite sure,' said Firminger, playing along.

'Then what if I were to tell you that I am not who you think I am?' said Dog, and with that the door of the court burst open and in walked an identical dog.

'Because I am not the dog who lives at number 4, The Close, Bexhill-on-Sea, but his brother!' said the dog in the dock.

'And I am the dog in question,' said the identical dog.

There were gasps from the public gallery, and the journalists from the *Bexhill Gazette* scribbled furiously in their notebooks.

'B-but the name on your collar!' spluttered Firminger.

'A tuppenny trinket purchased from a pet shop!' said the brother.

'Case dismissed!' cried the judge, and the court descended into complete uproar, with Dog and his brother being lifted shoulder-high by the jurors, including the cats.

The two dogs held a makeshift press conference on the steps of the court, during which it became apparent that Dog's brother was indeed his twin, separated at birth and sent to a different home. While Dog had gone into the sniffer business, his brother had trained in law and was one of Kent's foremost canine lawyers. Dog had tracked him down using techniques he'd gleaned from watching *Who Do You Think You Are?* on TV.

PC Firminger approached us, stony-faced.

'Congratulations, Dog,' he said ruefully, 'but I'll get you one of these days.' And turning to me he added, 'Unfortunately there is no sanction today for this dog being caught drunk in charge of a disability scooter, but if I were you I would punish him severely. Withdraw any treats, get him to do some chore or other thing that he doesn't like doing, so he gets the message that what he did was wrong.'

As the crowd dispersed an elderly lady monkey approached Dog. I'd noticed her sitting in the public gallery earlier in the trial.

An Elderly lady chimp

'Too bad you weren't in Hull in 1941. You could have saved my husband,' she said. Then, producing a banana and a bag of nuts, she wandered off towards the station with her carer.

There's a three-star review in *The Stage* for Joe Pasquale's show at the meat factory last night.

Boiled beef and carrots for dinner.

September 20th

In view of PC Firminger's advice, Mum and I have decided that the best punishment for the dog would be to make him do the washing-up for a week and stop him watching *Coronation Street*.

Get a call from Dickie Woolfe, the head of Channel 5, asking me whether I would be interested in fronting a programme called *The World's Most Dangerous Roads*. It would involve me, a camera crew and a quantity surveyor travelling to famous accident blackspots and demonstrating why they are dangerous, with the quantity surveyor providing details of the surrounding geography, slope of the road, moisture levels and soil analysis.

My initial reaction is 'No, this sounds like a terrible idea,' but the fact is I do have a bit of a gap in my autumn schedule and this is paid work; plus, as the controller points out, I would get to see some of the roads that 'I've only heard about on the news'. So I say yes. He says he'll get back to me at the end of the week when the producer has come up with a detailed schedule, and in the meantime he will send me a map. He gives me the number of Bob the quantity surveyor and suggests we meet up and get to know each other because

'You will be seeing a lot of each other over the next few weeks and will be sharing a room.'

Before I could challenge him on the room-sharing bit he'd rung off.

September 21st

Bit bored so I phone Bob the quantity surveyor. We start chatting about the project, and he's a bit dull to be honest, but it's one of those situations where he thinks he's being interesting and I don't really have the social skills to get him off the line. He starts telling me about how he saw his brother at the weekend and how his brother has bought a new digital camera – a Panasonic one with a Leica lens – and how he fancied one himself. Then, when he'd looked into it on an internet chat room, he'd discovered that Leica actually make the body for the Panasonic camera too. All this kind of stuff, down the phone, bearing in mind I phoned him out of boredom in the first place and now I'm getting bored – plus I'm paying for it.

I try to bring the subject round to the TV show by saying that he'll be able to get some good photos on the shoot, but he keeps on and on about whether he should buy the Panasonic camera or the Leica.

In the end I say that I've got to go because my tea's ready. He points out it's a bit early for tea, and he's right – it's only half past four – so then I have to lie and say that I'm going to see a show. He says, 'What show?' Thinking on the hoof I say '*Chitty Chitty Bang Bang*'. He says, 'That came off in September 2005.'

So I say, 'No, it's an amateur production.'

He says, 'How do they get the car to fly?'

I say, 'Magnets.'

He says, 'How does that work?'

I say, 'Um . . . north-facing magnets on stage repel the north magnets in the car, so it kind of hovers.' It's sort of plausible, but I can't resist embellishing the story by saying, 'That's why you are encouraged not to wear a watch if you're sitting in the first two rows.'

He doesn't buy it, though. He asks me where the production is being staged, and I say I can't remember because Mum got the tickets and booked it. In the meantime he's Googled it and declares that the only current production of *Chitty Chitty Bang Bang* is in Mozambique. Just my luck.

'That's right,' I say, 'Mozambique. That's why I'd better get a move on.'

He suggests we meet up when I get back from Africa, and that's when it all went wrong.

I innocently asked him whether he would be bringing his 'telescope on legs', and he completely hit the roof. He was shouting down the phone at me, saying, 'It's not a telescope, it's a theodolite, but everyone calls it a telescope!' and 'What's wrong with this ****ing country?!!!' and 'Why don't they teach quantity-surveying in schools?' He gave me a real earbashing, said 'Enjoy the show,' then slammed the phone down.

The thought of having to share a room with him for three weeks has rather taken the shine off the money I will make presenting *The World's Most Dangerous Roads*.

September 22nd

Disgusted to find that the dog has been using the jacuzzi to do the washing-up. Mum and I were sat in it for elevenses when she found a broad bean in a personal place. I put my goggles on and had a look round (she'd got out by this stage) and found some bits of broccoli, a partially degraded corn-flake and a chop bone. This just won't do. I dried myself off and phoned PC Firminger for his advice.

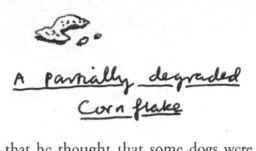

A partially degraded
Corn flake

He said that he thought that some dogs were good and some bad, and that we'd 'got ourselves a bad 'un'. Which wasn't very helpful.

I drained the jacuzzi while Mum did the washing-up.

Screening calls for ten days just in case Bob the quantity surveyor phones up.

Mulligatawny soup for lunch, Viennese fancies for pud.

September 23rd

Sadly we are having difficulty getting all my fiancée Lay Dee's paperwork together for the immigration office. This is due in part, I suspect, to her previous convictions. But I'll say this now: I for one do not believe for a second that she was ever involved in an organ-smuggling ring, and most of the evidence I've seen – except that of a human liver being discovered packed in ice in the glove compartment of her Nissan Sunny – seems to me to be circumstantial. Besides, it was a long time ago and she has served her time for it.

No, rather than believe the information that my so-called friends have discovered about Lay Dee on Google I'd rather believe the fine character references that stand next to her photo on Manila Envelopes: that she is indeed a 'Very nice lady, very good massage, likes Shakespeare and *On the Buses*.'

There's a girl after my own heart. I yearn for the time when we might sit together, her massaging my feet and reading *Troilus and Cressidus*, as we both enjoy Reg Varney and co. and the crazy goings-on down at the depot.

I resubmit her visa application form, enclosing a cheque for £75 as a donation and to cover costs.

Must get that verruca sorted out though or she will become a carrier.

Rissoles for dinner.

September 24th

At breakfast today Dog appeared with a rucksack on his back saying that he has decided to have a gap year, that he plans to travel the world in an attempt to 'find himself'.

'What will you do for money?' I asked.

'I will always have my music' he said, holding up his guitar.

'Keep in touch,' I said. 'I'll give you a lift to the station, if you like.'

'No!' he said. 'No, I need to do this for myself.'

Off he went. I have to say I admire Dog for that. Maybe he'll come back in a year's time happier and more at peace with himself, having come to terms with his demons. He nearly got run over crossing the road though – no road sense whatsoever.

Hadn't briefed Mum properly about not picking the phone up to Bob the quantity surveyor, and she answered the phone this morning and it was him.

'Hang on, I'll just get him,' she said.

Thinking quickly, I said that we were having our calls redirected to Mozambique, and that *Chitty Chitty Bang Bang* had been OK but the special effects were a bit disappointing. While all this was going on, I got Mum to put on Paul Simon's *Graceland* album – you know, the one with the African beats?

'What's the weather like over there?' asked Bob, sceptically.

'Um, let me see,' I said, buying a little time as my fingers frantically Googled the weather in Mozambique. 'Sunny!' I said. That seemed to satisfy him.

Sausage-meat-and-sweetcorn pie for dinner, fruit flan for pud.

September 25th

Received another letter through the post from me.

The postman keeps returning mail that I've just posted. He's reading the sender's address instead of the recipient's. He says it's because he's left handed, so that if he's looking at a parcel the right way up the back is the front.

'What do you want me to do?' he says. 'Stand on me head?'

Is it too much to ask that a letter is delivered to the address on the front of the envelope?

He's also been delivering me letters intended for another

H. Hill in Bexhill, whose address is nothing like mine. He sees the name H. Hill and sticks them through my letterbox. OK, the book tokens have been very welcome . . . I'm kidding, but it does mean another trip to the postbox for me, and no doubt this stupid postman probably then looks at the back and delivers them back to the sender. I think he probably needs to go on a course.

'Yes, a course of lethal injections,' says Mum, and I laugh heartily. Then she says, 'First a sedative to send him to sleep, then an injection of sodium thiopental to paralyse the respiratory muscles, then an injection of potassium to stop the heart.'

She spoilt it with that really. A lot of being good at comedy is knowing when to leave a joke and move on.

September 26th

Today I received the very exciting news that Madam Tussauds wish to form an effigy of me from wax!

'What, for the chamber-of-horrors section?' says Mum.

This is a response I will learn to get used to over the coming weeks as I announce this most prestigious news to the world. It seems I am to travel to their Baker Street headquarters (and other body-quarters no doubt!) to be measured.

September 27th

Went up to the Baker Street headquarters of Madam Tussauds today to be measured up for the forthcoming wax effigy of myself.

I was curious to know whether I was to be part of a tableau

and who else my doppelganger would be rubbing shoulders with.

'Peter Sutcliffe!' came the reply. 'We're putting you in the chamber of horrors!'

I laugh politely.

'I bet you've been getting that a lot, haven't you?' said Shirley the sub-manager. 'Now strip off, and let's get you measured up.'

'Strip off?' I said, a little nervously.

'Yes. Go into the toilets there and get all your clothes off, as we need to measure and photograph you in minute detail so we can make the wax effigy exactly the same as you.'

I duly obeyed her orders, and emerging from the toilets was ushered into a sort of wet room, where two burly blokes turned high-pressure hoses on me.

'Just so you're all nice and clean. It's a health-and-safety thing,' she said, 'to protect us. You don't mind if Joel helps us with the measuring?' she added, beckoning in a lanky fourteen-year-old boy. 'He's on work experience, and obviously it's important he sees every step of the wax-effigy process.'

'Yeah, I suppose so,' I said, looking at my verrucas.

'Then let the measurements commence!' said Shirley, and with that the door burst open and I was set upon by a group of experts.

At the end of the procedure, which lasted about twenty minutes, my clothes were slung at me and I was left to sort myself out.

Well, the whole thing was totally humiliating, and as I left I felt quite dirty, degraded and smelling of wax. I composed a letter of complaint on the train home, but probably won't send it. They've got you over a barrel really. They know just how desperate light entertainers like me are to get into this grand old house of wax, and are therefore pretty much able to make you jump through any hoops they choose.

Crunchie on the train home.

Stuffed vine leaves for dinner, Greek yoghurt for pudding.

September 28th

I log on to the Manila Envelopes website and activate the webcam that is supposed to be trained on my fiancée Lay Dee twenty-four hours a day. It was a terribly grainy picture. We exchanged pleasantries for a few minutes, but then she started to get impatient, and it ended with her right up close to the camera shouting, 'Get me passport!'

It may just be the quality of the picture, but I hope those are not her real teeth.

Mum keeps asking me when I'm going to pick my little friend, the pear, from its tree.

'Surely it's ready by now,' she says. 'If you leave it too long it will fall from the tree and its flesh will be bruised.'

She's right, the pear is probably at a point now where it should be picked, but I am conscious that I am holding back and putting off the harvest, as I know that I am going to miss the routine of checking it. And if I'm honest, I must confess I have, over the last few weeks, been confiding in the pear, talking to it about my hopes and fears for the future, my ups and downs with Lay Dee, my concerns over Dog's drinking. The great thing about the pear is that it is a great listener. It will just sit there on its stalk and take it all in. It won't pass judge-ment like a friend or relative might. Nonetheless, I resolved to pick it in the afternoon, but when the moment came my hand faltered and I allowed it another couple of days to soak up the sun and earth's goodness.

September 29th

Sad news today as I learn that the producer of *The World's Most Dangerous Roads* has been killed in a car crash while on a reconnaissance mission for the programme. Bob the quantity surveyor was also in the car as it hurtled off the Kingston bypass and is in intensive care. In his semi-conscious state he has been calling for, of all people, me. It seems he has no living relatives and after our recent phone calls has put me down as his next of kin. The ward sister says that it would be 'really good if you could come and see him. It might just help to bring him through this, a voice he knows.'

I explain to her that I've never actually met the guy, and also detail his expletive-ridden outburst when I bad-mouthed his theodolite.

'That's a quite understandable response,' she said. 'I went out with a quantity surveyor once and he absolutely hated me referring to his theodolite as his silly little telescope thing on legs.'

I said to her that I didn't call it a silly telescope, just a telescope on legs, but she wasn't really listening.

'I once referred to his as a didgeridoo on a tripod,' she said. 'He didn't like that either, but the one that really got his back up was when I called his theodolite a dog's penis riding on a

A Theodolite

spider. He walked out and I never saw him again. Can I tell Bob you'll come?'

'I suppose so,' I say.

Great. A boring visit to see a semi-conscious boring person I don't know.

Where are you tonight, St Rabbit's Foot, god of luck?

September 30th

Ah! My birthday at last! Mum pretended that she hadn't remembered. By the time it got to 8.30 a.m. and no present was forthcoming I started to believe her. Then she admitted that she wasn't quite ready to give me my present, and implied that she was awaiting a delivery of some description. At about 11 a.m. she said she was just popping out. When she came back she had a loaded Londis bag with a roll of wrapping paper sticking out of it and she disappeared into her bedroom. I could hear the familiar sound of sellotape being torn off its roll and then she appeared in the breakfast bar, where I was opening cards, and gave me my present.

This year my mum bought me for my birthday a tube of

toothpaste, a variety pack of cereal, a jar of rollmops, a corn-cob pipe and a tin of Yardley Black Label talc. All really useful stuff on their own, but oddly together they have rather a low impact.

Got a card with a 2,000-dinar note from Nan, which when I checked the exchange rate turns out to be worth about two quid.

My sister in Canada sent me another bottle of maple syrup. Auntie Jill and Uncle Stanley sent me *The Best of Kirsty's Home Videos* DVD, with a note saying, 'Maybe there's some stuff you could use on one of your shows.' Uncle Peter gave me one of his unique scrimshaw carvings – a figure of Holly Willoughby whittled from a chicken thigh bone – and that was pretty much it.

It seems I have overestimated the number of thank-you letters I would need by one – there was nothing from my godmother, Auntie Shirley. When I pointed this out to Mum, she said, 'Oh, didn't I tell you she died in March? Sorry, I thought you knew.'

OK, I haven't actually seen Auntie Shirley since my chris-tening in 1965, so yes, she hasn't really provided the support and moral compass that she'd agreed to at that ceremony, and yes, she wasn't really my auntie, and no, I didn't hear from her at any other time apart from my birthday, ever, but I was banking on that ten quid.

Mum hastily cooked me a birthday cake. She explained that it was supposed to be in the shape of a heart, but where the cake mixture had sunk in the middle leaving a hole it looked eerily like a noose.

We both stayed up and watched *Jools Holland's Hootenanny*

2004 on video. A particularly strong line-up – Brotherhood of Man (original line-up), Jennie Bond singing 'Downtown' with Salman Rushdie on trumpet, Charlie Drake, Roy Wood and Wizard, and Marilyn Manson.

At about 10.30 I got a text from Dog: 'Hazardous bifurcation.'

I knew what he meant.

Not the best birthday I've ever had, I'll admit. In fact, never have I so looked forward to Morpheus's sweet embrace.

October

A Typical Tesco Express

October 1st

Popped into Londis this morning and tried to get Mum's money back on the jar of rollmops to make up for Auntie Shirley's shortfall, but Dominic wasn't having any of it, pointing out that the jar was past its sell-by date. Of course, it was old when she bought it, but he had me and he knew it. When I managed to drag him down to the rollmop counter, all the jars were gone.

'Norwegian trawler docked last night. Cleaned me out, mate,' he said.

He's a slippery fellow, but what can I do? His Londis has a stranglehold on supplies to Bexhill.

Woke up to the strong smell of cat food. I suppose I'll get used to it. Mum has been sick twice. It's at times like this that I think maybe Vera Lynn and Rod Hull and Emu weren't all that bad.

Stir fry for dinner, blancmange for pud, but it all tasted of cat food.

October 2nd

Head down the A308 towards Kingston hospital, and as I get onto the bypass I hit the bend too fast, slide through the line of oncoming traffic, flip the car and skid for 200 yards on the roof. It's true what they say about accidents: it does all seem to happen in slow motion. The actual skidding seemed to take about an hour and a half, and aware as I was of time slowing down, I thought I should take the opportunity to catch up on my reading. I read a whole chapter of *On Cheshunt Street* by Ian McEwan (the follow-up to *Chesil Beach*, only based around an MOT certification centre in Walthamstow) and then had a snack. I was just thinking about flossing my teeth when the vehicle came to a halt, some thirty yards from the hospital.

'That was a lucky escape!' I said to the paramedic.

'The A308 is the world's third most dangerous road,' he said. 'That's why they built the hospital here.'

I'm in the lift, bracing myself for the meeting with Bob. If he starts up about that flaming camera again, I tell you, I'm going to walk straight out.

I walk into the intensive-care unit, and a nurse takes me to Bob's bed.

I've never met him before, of course. He's younger than I had envisaged.

'What are those wires for?' I ask the nurse.

'Oh, they take electricity from the plug socket there to the CD machine that you can hear playing,' he says.

'Not those, the ones attached to his chest.'

'A simple heart trace.'

'Oh yes, of course,' I say. God, I'm rusty!

'Hello, Bob,' I say. Bob looks up at me, confused. 'It's Harry,' I say.

Bob tries to speak, but there's a tube coming out of his mouth.

'Is that tube completely necessary?' I ask the nurse.

'Yes,' he says, 'it carries oxygen into his lungs. You see, the heart is divided into four chambers: the atria and the ventricles . . .' He produces a diagram of the circulation of the mammal, one half coloured in red, the other in blue.

Every time I try to interrupt he ploughs on.

'. . . This differs from the heart of the bird in a couple of important ways . . .' he continues, and produces a diagram of a two-chambered avian heart.

Fortunately the man in the next bed, who had been extremely restless since I'd arrived on the ward, constantly jerking his arms and neck, fell out of bed with a terrible crash, and so the nurse had to go and help with that.

I looked at Bob and felt so sorry for him – semi-paralysed, yet able to hear everything that was going on. Stuck for what to say, I started to test him on the parts of the mammalian heart, holding the nurse's diagrams up and getting him to indicate what was what with his eyes. With the best will in the world, it was very difficult to tell exactly where he was looking.

When I scored him two out of ten, he started crying.

I thought that the only decent thing to do was to ask him about his camera. 'Did you buy the camera?' I found myself saying. 'You know, the Panasonic one, but the workings are actually made by Leica?'

He looked blankly at me – not the reaction I'd expected at all. I racked my brains for more details – technical specifications, all the stuff he'd told me on the phone.

After I suppose about forty minutes of talk about memory cards, high-definition format and number of megapixels, the nurse that I'd talked to on the phone came over to me.

'Dr Hill?'

'Yes, that's right.'

'Nurse Ellis, we talked on the phone?'

'Oh yes, that's right, with the boyfriend with the didgeri-doo . . .?'

'Ahem, yes. You're talking to the wrong Bob there, I'm afraid. Your man's in that bed there.'

I looked over at the man who had fallen out of the next bed. He waved at me and made a noise. 'Hammar.'

'Eh?'

'Hamma!'

'Sorry?'

'Chamma!'

'No, not getting it.'

'Camra.'

'Not sure what you're . . .'

It was going to be a long visit.

Sandwich from carousel for lunch, Twix for pud.

October 3rd

I had to be quite firm with him in the end. I said, 'Look, we don't really know each other. I don't have any interest in cameras, we have never met before today and it looks like the TV show is off, and so there's not really any reason to continue this liaison.'

'Shanks shoror feeing sho nonesh giv gee,' he said.

'Shash OK!' I said back, and as I left I turned to wish him luck. 'Nood shuck!' I called to him from the door.

'Eh?' he said.

'Nood shuck!'

He stared blankly at me.

'Oh, forget it.'

With that I was away, free of Bob the quantity surveyor for ever.

October 4th

Weather-wise we're having a bit of a heatwave here in Bexhill and the stink off the dog-food factory – particularly on Wednesday, Thursday and Friday afternoons – is like being mugged by a French kennel maid. The council are mega tee-d off because the day trippers have been staying away in their droves and going up the coast to Hastings.

In the meantime the solar panels that Mum had installed on the roof of the house are working overtime, pumping out heat like nobody's business. The house is like a sauna – even the water out of the cold tap is hot. The plugs are hot and the light bulbs are so bright I've got a permanent dot at the front of my field of vision. I've been wearing the sunglasses Nan was given after her cataract operation, even at night, and we've had to buy a couple of cheap air conditioners to help cool us down, which goes against the whole energy-saving idea of solar power. At this rate the panels will never pay for themselves.

I agree with Mum to pick the pear tomorrow morning and perhaps poach it in a little Armagnac for dessert.

Salad for lunch, ice cream for afters.

October 5th

Went into the garden this morning and someone or something's only had the flaming pear off the tree! Excuse my language, but really! Months I've spent nurturing that pear, and some bastard's gone and whipped it from right under my nose! What a diabolical liberty! I am absolutely furious about it. Initially I assumed it was Mum, and while I was a bit miffed that she might have picked it without asking me, I could see her point. But she says she never touched the pear and seems as up in arms about it as me. Although I tend to believe her, I must confess I checked the bin and the compost heap for a discarded pear core. While I suppose she could have disposed of it down the shops or flushed it down the loo (the Saniflo would probably cope with a pear core), I suspect she's had nothing to do with the pear's sudden disappearance.

Spent the evening trawling through the footage from the CCTV camera at the rear of the house to see if that offers some clue about the pear's disappearance (or 'disa-PEAR-ance,' as Mum said), but there's a lot of it.

October 6th

Eureka! At four this morning, looking through the CCTV footage I spot a figure approaching the pear tree. As it moves away from the tree it looks up at the camera, and it is quite clearly Otis Ferry, the notorious hunter. I immediately write

Mr Otis Ferry

stiff letters to (1) Otis Ferry, (2) Bryan Ferry, (3) Francis Stafford, director of the neighbourhood-watch scheme, Bexhill, Fairview Ward, and (4) Major Peter Andrews, leader of the Devolution for Bexhill Party, enclosing details of the offence and stills from the CCTV footage.

October 7th

Shirley from Madam Tussauds phoned to explain that they've made an error with some of my measurements.

'If these measurements are correct it would mean that you have severely deformed legs and should seek medical help,' she said.

I pulled my trousers down and looked at my legs in the mirror.

'No, they look fine to me.'

'Oh, OK, that's what I thought. It's just that you do sit behind a desk on TV, and someone said that maybe you did that to hide the deformity.'

'Are these by any chance the measurements that Joel took?' I ask.

'Well, let's not get bogged down with trying to attribute blame,' she says.

'What do you want me to do?'

'I need you to come back in to be measured again.'

'Can't I just tell you my leg measurements over the phone?'

'No, I'm sorry, we're a highly professional outfit here, and if we make an inaccurate wax effigy the press will be all over us and it will damage the good name of Madam Tussauds.'

'What are you talking about?' I say, getting a little

angry now. 'Your Colonel Gadaffi looks more like Fatima Whitbread, your Duke of Edinburgh looks like Max Wall, and your Gordon Brown looks more like Fred Flintstone! The shape of my legs are the least of your worries!'

'There's no need to get nasty,' she says, not rising to the bait. 'Besides, we do reuse some of the older effigies and redress them to look like today's stars. For instance, we are currently using our Fred Flintstone as Gordon Brown, and before you say it, we are also recycling Boris Yeltsin as Boris Johnson, Ben Elton is now Yasser Arafat, and our David Gest has been sprayed brown and is now doing some nice business as Jay-Z. If you'd prefer, we could always look at our back catalogue and do the same for you. I think we still have a Kojak knocking about somewhere . . .'

'No! No, that's fine, I'll come in,' I say. Well, what choice do I have?

Lamb parcels with fruit sauce and duchesse potatoes for dinner, chocolate eclairs for pud.

October 8th

News from the Home Office regarding Lay Dee's visa application: it has been turned down again. The form itself and the cheque for £75 have been returned with a rather gruff letter accusing me of bribery. What kind of society are we living in where all sorts of riff-raff are allowed to come over here, seeking refuge from so-called tyranny, and yet a gentle soul like Lay Dee – misunderstood, yes; forced to commit organ-smuggling crimes to make ends meet, probably; a talented masseuse, certainly – is banned from entry?

I write a strongly worded letter to Miss Joanna Lumley to see if she can help.

4 The Close
Bexhill-on-Sea
East Sussex

Dear Miss Lumley,

Knowing you as a passionate fighter for relaxing the country's immigration laws, and applauding the success you have had importing Gurkhas into our towns and cities – a proud race who, let's face it, only take up half the space of a native Brit! I agree with you that every town should have one, especially with knife crime on the up. Good on you!

Knowing this – and, of course, being a big fan of *The Avengers* – I write to you to consider the plight of another would-be pint-sized immigrant. I speak of none other than my fiancée and talented foot masseuse Miss Lay Dee. A gentle soul, you only have to take a brief glance at the website Manila Envelopes to realise that she is popular with menfolk the world over, a girl who through no fault of her own other than the ownership of a Nissan Sunny and clean driving licence was sadly recruited into a team of organ smugglers, but she swears to me she thought it was legal as she'd read on Wikipedia that you only need one kidney anyway and that the liver 'grows back' by itself. A girl, Joanna, determined to break out of the small rural village into which she was born and, in the words of Eddie and the Hot Rods, determined to 'Do anything you wanna do'.

Cupid knew nothing of this when he decided to let fly his little arrows of love – one to me and one, presumably from the same quiver, to her – and we fell in love, a love that sadly cannot be consummated due to our draconian immigration laws. This is where you come in,

Joanna. If you would see fit to lean on whoever it was that opened the door to your little Nepalese friends, that would be wonderful, and you can be sure there is a seat at the top table for you and a friend come the day of our nuptials.

This poor girl lies in some foreign field while Mr Abu Hamza and his behooked legions of terror kings roam the streets of Finsbury Park emploring our young to go on team-building white-water-rafting holidays in Wales.

I hope and pray you can help.

Up the Gurkhas!

Yours sincerely,

Harry H
P.S. I enclose a cheque for £75 to cover costs.

Finishing this letter I notice the page is wet. I realise I have been weeping. This cannot fail to stir the great lady into action.

Tongue sandwich for lunch.

October 9th

The big story today is the huge pubic-hair blockade at the mouth of the River Thames. It seems that with the increase in the number of bikini waxes and widespread depilation in general there has been a gradual build-up in the number of pubic hairs entering the country's waterways. They started to collect around the Thames Barrier, with the result that basically a huge underwater pubic bush has formed and is preventing the normal passage of shipping up this crucial transport artery into London.

London's waterways are at a standstill. The press is referring to it variously as:

'The Bikini Triangle – Nothing Goes In or Comes Out' – the *Independent*
'British Hair-Ways' – the *Sun*
'Never Mind the Tube, Here's the Pube' – the *Mirror*

The London mayor Boris Yeltsin – sorry, Johnson, I always get those two mixed up. Which is the fat blond one who drinks too much and seems to speak a foreign language? That's right Boris Johnson! Ha ha! Just my little joke. Actually, thinking about it, that's just the sort of joke they could do with on *Mock the Week*.

Anyway, the London mayor has appealed for calm and engaged a team of divers to go down into the water with clippers and in some cases shears to free up the structure. He is urging beauticians to dispose of all pubes responsibly and calls for a return to 'the ancient practice of singeing', demonstrating how it is done by pulling down the waistband of his trousers and applying a lit disposable lighter to the tongue of hair that radiates from his belly button. There is a flash of light, and when the smoke clears the hapless mayor has a large red blister on his tummy that looks like it needs a dollop of Savlon on it. Say what you like about him, but he's certainly managing to keep London in the papers.

You can see he's in pain as he finishes his address by saying that 'We definitely need to get rid of this pube-ball before the 2012 Olympics or we're going to look a right bunch of Charlies.'

I fax my Boris joke through to the producer of *Mock the Week*. He faxes me straight back, pointing out that it would be perfect for them were it not for the fact that Boris Yeltsin died in April 2007. Fair enough, I suppose.

October 10th

Back up to Baker Street to be re-measured for Madam Tussauds. Thoroughly degrading again. The kid on work experience, Joel, was still there, sniggering, but I wouldn't let him anywhere near my legs.

Popped in at the Showbusiness Disease Centre on the way home just to clear out the last few bits of paperwork and furniture, and was greeted by a French woman in a basque holding a whip. I won't go into the whole sordid details of the thing, but it seems that in my absence one of the lookalikes has been running it as a brothel.

If the press (and Madam Tussauds) gets hold of this I'm dead.

Waiting for me upon my return is a rather rude letter from Jo Lumley saying that the case for the Gurkha was very different to the one I set out for my Lay Dee and that she doesn't want to be involved. She also made a rather lewd accusation regarding my motives. What's more, I see from my files that she's cashed the cheque! I am shocked and extremely discouraged by her attitude. The very suggestion fills my mouth with the taste of last night's supper.

I dash off a terse reply.

Dear Lumley,
Thank you for your letter. I am naturally disappointed that you do not want to get involved in the case of Lay Dee, a foreign national in a fix, a girl of honour and by all accounts some manual dexterity who has fallen victim to the organ-smuggling trade and who now plans to

put all that behind her and start a new life by the side of the man she loves – namely, me. I must say I take exception to your suggestion that my sole intent is to 'get my leg over'. The very idea that I would spend all this time to secure safe passage of my belle simply to satisfy some base animal instinct is quite anathema to me. If I needed to release any sexual frustration I have the mobile number of Amanda Holden, with whom I have an understanding. It makes me think that perhaps you are projecting your own nefarious desires onto my innocent project. Perhaps, Miss Lumley, it is you who wishes to have a leg thrown over yours, and an imported Gurkha leg at that. Stick that in your khukuri and smoke it!

Please do not contact me again.

Yours sincerely,

Harry H
P.S. I hope you're enjoying the seventy-five quid.

As I finish printing the letter off I note that the bottom of the page is wet again. This time the tears are those of anger.

Squid for dinner.

October 11th

The letter to Otis Ferry has been sent back to me marked 'Return to Sender'.

Mum caught stuffing her pipe with her right hand and given a verbal warning. It seems she had been grassed up by the right-handed pipe stuffer, so there was a bit of an atmosphere in the canteen at lunch.

She says that because of the strong smell permeating the factory whatever she has to eat tastes like dog food. I point out that in that case it would be cheaper just to eat dog food. She says that this would be the start of a slippery slope.

October 12th

The front page of the *Bexhill Gazette* has the headline 'Disa-PEAR-ance: Pear Stolen from Entertainer's Garden'. I'm not sure how they heard about it but I've got a pretty good idea (i.e. Mum).

Coincidentally I receive a standard letter from Bryan Ferry apologising for Otis's bad behaviour and a voucher, seemingly designed and printed on a home computer, for two free tickets to the next Roxy Music concert. When I went online to investigate concert dates I found that there aren't any. Still, the thought's there. When they've had their break I'll be up at the front in the mosh pit, singing along to 'Avalon' and 'Let's Stick Together'.

London W8

Dear HARRY

Thank you for your letter. I'm so sorry that Otis has offended you in this way. He's a high-spirited lad and feels very strongly about certain issues, issues that I do not necessarily agree with, but what can I do? What would any father do? Blood is, after all, thicker than water.

I hope that the enclosed voucher will go some way to easing the inconvenience that the young rascal has caused you.

As we always said in Roxy Music, 'Let's stick together!'

Thank you for your interest, and see you at the concert!

Yours,

Bryan F

The talk in the town is of plans to build a Tesco Express opposite the station. When I dropped into Londis Dominic produced a clipboard and pen.

'Sign the petition to stop the Tesco Express?' he said. 'It'll kill off a lot of the local shops, kill the character of the place and turn the high street into just another bland string of corporate outlets that you could find in any town in Britain.'

'I've got one word for you,' I said. 'Rollmops!' And with that I paid for my goods and left.

Yeah, I'm a great one for a grudge.

Liver balls en casserole and potatoes parisienne for dinner, egg custard for pud.

October 13th

Received a single pear packed in bubble wrap with a compliments slip from Bryan Ferry begging me not to take it further. Also received a basket of pears from Mr Saddler, treasurer of the neighbourhood-watch scheme, Bexhill, Fairview Ward, and a nice 'In Sympathy' card from Major Peter Andrews. So then, a sudden surfeit of pears!

This doesn't stop me, however, from dreaming at night of my lost pear, of cupping its bell-bottomed end in my hand and sinking my teeth into its soft ripe flesh, as sweet pear juice drips from the corners of my mouth, running in twin rivulets down my chin and joining in a common tributary down my neck and between my 'moobs'. A tiny trickle pools in my belly button, and I look up to see Princess Anne with a cotton bud in her cockatoo-mittened hand, mopping it up. She then sucks the sodden bud with a smile and a flutter of the eyelids.

To be honest, I often wake up in a sweat and have to have a drink of water.*

October 14th

Sad news: Bob the quantity surveyor died this morning. He's left his funny telescope thing to me in his will.

Phone call from Shirley at Madam Tussauds (I shudder when I hear her voice these days). She says there's a problem with my effigy.

The good news is it doesn't require me to go in, strip off and be measured again. It seems that with the rise in bikini waxing there is now not only a huge sub-aquatic pubic bush blocking the Thames but also a national wax shortage. She says that what they'd like to do is to make the face and torso in wax and finish the rest off in 'rendered pork fat'.

'It does mean that the effigy must be kept in a sub-room-temperature environment, and that we do have to label it as offensive to Jews and Muslims, but we don't really have an option if we are to keep to our schedule,' she says.

Well, what choice do I have? I give her the go-ahead, but I'm not happy about it. She assures me that when the Thames pubic bush is removed and they can get a new delivery of wax, they will make the necessary adjustments to the model, but for me it's just another bad experience at the hands of M. Tussaud.

Beef stew, dumplings and baked beans for dinner, fruit compote for pud.

* Sorry, Princess, if you're reading this, but it's my subconscious mind and I have no control over it. Respect to you, particularly the way you handled that kidnapper.

October 15th

Attended the Faber authors' winter party and have a lovely long chat with the prominent Chinese journalist and author Xinran. We were talking about the money that can be made from books, and I make a rather good joke about 'the Xinran Revenue'. As we chuckle together who should walk up and slap me round the face but Joanna Lumley! Before I could catch my breath she'd started laying into Xinny.

'I suppose this is your fancy piece, is it? You managed to get her in after all. Well, hold onto your livers, everybody,' she shouted, causing everyone to stop what they were doing and stare over at us. 'This little lady will have 'em off you!' She then hurled a glass of wine at the poor woman. It was not without some satisfaction then that I watched the figure of Joanna Lumley being dragged screaming from the Pig and Whistle pub, Charlotte Street.

I apologised to the notable author, made my excuses and headed back to Charing Cross.

Quavers, cheese straws, crabsticks and one chicken vol-au-vent for dinner.

October 16th

An unexpected visitor calls – would you believe, one Otis Ferry! I opened the front door to find him in full fox-hunting regalia and armed with a big basket of pears. He was pretty contrite. He explained that on the night in question he had been on the run from hunt saboteurs and had darted through our garden as a shortcut. His body contorted with hunger he sought valuable energy in my pear. I invited him in for a cup of tea. He's very charming.

As he was leaving I turned to him and said, 'How was it?'

'What?'

'The pear, how was the taste?'

'To be honest, a bit gritty,' he replied, climbing onto the back of his horse and riding off into the distance.

I don't believe it for a minute.

October 17th

Planning meeting for the proposed wind farm today, and tensions were running high.

The situation has been made a whole lot worse because it seems that the nearby wind farm out in Bexhill harbour, which was opened by Keith Harris in 2008, was installed incorrectly, and far from generating electricity has been using it up to power the fans, to make them go round. We were all looking at them as they spun – even in situations where there was no reported wind – thinking what a great idea they were, when in fact what breeze we could feel on the shore was being *generated* by the fans. The only person who seems satisfied by this is Andre the mobile kite salesman, who has never shifted so many units and can't believe his luck. The problem they now have is that they can't get close enough to the fans to switch them off because when they get their boats within fifty yards they get blown back to shore. Some bright spark on the council is suggesting that they build a further set of wind turbines facing the existing ones, which could then harvest the wind they are creating so that at least they would be breaking even, and this seems the most likely course of action that they will take.

The fact is, people don't really like farmed wind. They prefer wind that is naturally occurring.

Had a couple of the pears tonight. Mum suggested pear boats, where the poached pear is split in half lengthways, a cocktail stick inserted with a rice-paper sail and the 'boat' then floated on a sea of blue jelly – chopped jelly if you are looking for a more dramatic seascape. Pretty yummy, but of course my mind couldn't help but think about what might have been – you know, if it had been my own little pear.

October 18th

The day of Bob the quantity surveyor's funeral, at which I am to give the eulogy. Bit of a tough one because I don't know much about him, apart from his indecision regarding the purchase of a new digital camera.

The congregation is made up of a large group of representatives from the National Society of Quantity Surveyors.

I start the address by pointing out the few things I know about Bob.

'Bob was a male Caucasian of medium build who worked as a quantity surveyor for much of his life,' I say, reading from notes. 'A job that would have taken him to various building sites, to places where a road or dwelling was to be built, to areas where the land was perhaps uneven or sloping, or indeed to land with no particular features of interest to a quantity surveyor . . .'

I could sense the audience getting restless and so I skipped a couple of pages.

'When I last spoke to Bob he said that he was planning to buy a new digital camera . . .'

As I ploughed on with the pros and cons of the Leica and Panasonic cameras I felt the whole mood of the crowd shift. Suddenly they were interested! They sat forward, craning their necks, anxious not to miss a single detail. Some of them took notes; others nodded in agreement.

'. . . but which camera should Bob have bought?' I say, finishing up. 'The one camera, built by Leica but labelled Panasonic, or the other, labelled Leica? To all intents and purposes the same two cameras, but one with a slightly better build quality and bearing the prestigious camera-maker's mark. Sadly, we'll never know. He takes that secret to the grave, but you know what?'

At this point all the quantity surveyors sat forward.

'I like to think it would be the Leica.'

The whole lot of them erupted into spontaneous applause. As I walked back through them, stopping only to kiss Bob's coffin, I was lifted shoulder high by the quantity surveyors and cheered to the rafters.

Later, as the coffin is lowered into the grave, one of the quantity surveyors is heard to comment on the level of the surrounding terrain.

Chicken done in the slow cooker for dinner.

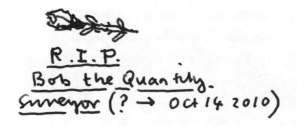

R.I.P.
Bob the Quantity
Surveyor (? → Oct 14 2010)

October 19th

Get a cheque through from *You've Been Framed* for £250 made payable to L. C. Twix – the false name I submitted the hilarious Rebekah Wade pork-ball footage under. They are terribly slow payers. That's something they don't tell you on the show – 'You could win £250 for every clip, but you'll have to wait six months, by which time you'll have forgotten all about it and the clip itself will have been repeated about eight times, and each time you see it go out you'll turn red with rage because you haven't been paid yet.'

Of course, I hadn't thought about my alias. I'll either have to try and open an account under that name or track someone down with the same name and get them to pay the cheque in, with some sort of kickback for their trouble.

I look up the surname Twix in the phone book, and there is one L. C. Twix. Even if their name is not Lee Con Twix this would still do.

I phoned the number. A lady answered, but I immediately hung up, not really having a plan. She then dialled 1471, leaving me in the awkward position of not really being able to explain why I'd phoned her. In the end I said I was cold-calling regarding installation of solar panels.

L. C. Twix said that this was an odd coincidence as she had been thinking about putting solar panels on the roof, and would I care to call round at some point to do a quote? I agreed to pop round in two days' time to 'assess' her roof.

Barbecue pork ribs for dinner, lemon meringue pie for pud.

Called round to L. C. Twix to assess her premises for installation of solar panels, wearing a wig and slightly different glasses. I took a notebook and a leatherette folder that I got free with some holiday tickets last year and the theodolite that I so recently inherited from Bob the quantity surveyor.

Mrs Twix is a very nice lady, with a genuine concern for the environment and the future of the world. She says that I look familiar, but we agree we have never met. I nip to the loo and take the opportunity to tug the wig a little further down my forehead.

Leslie makes us each a cup of milky coffee and we spend about twenty minutes discussing global warming and polar bears. Then the conversation broadens to cover *Springwatch*, and we both agree that Bill Oddie rather hogged the camera and should have let Kate Humble have more of a go, but now that he's gone we miss him and wish he were back and kind of understand what he was doing with Kate now.

'Well, I'd better do the assessment,' I say, draining the last drops of the coffee – including the skin. I wander outside with my notepad and the theodolite and make much play of jotting down various numbers, occasionally holding my pen up as if assessing the angle of the roof. My mind goes back to Bob the quantity surveyor – he'd be proud if he could see me now! He'd be so . . . well, he'd actually be incredibly angry at my misuse of his equipment, but never mind.

After about fifteen minutes I go back into the house to find Leslie Catherine Twix, pretend to do a few last-minute calculations, then let her have the bad news.

'I'm afraid, Leslie, that because of the pitch of your roof and the nature of your central-heating system your house is not suitable for solar-panel installation.'

There is a stunned silence from Mrs Twix, then . . .

'How do you work that out?' she says.

'Well, as you can see, I have my theodolite here, which . . .'

'What can you tell with that silly jumbo sausage on three long chips?' she says.

Even though I'm not a fully qualified quantity surveyor, that hurt. I could see why Bob got so angry about slang terms for his theodolite – it's different when you're actually working with one.

'Besides, I thought you needed two people to work one of those, you and another person at the other end with a pole.'

'No, not when assessing roofs for solar panels,' I countered. 'I know this isn't what you wanted to hear, Leslie, but I'm afraid there's nothing I can do. Your roof is, I am afraid, not suitable for solar panels, and there's nothing I can do to change that fact.'

'Well, how come next door has got them?' she said, pointing through the window at a house virtually identical to hers and sporting a full set of solar panels on each side of its roof.

'Um . . .' I faltered.

'We're semi-detached. How come he's got them and I can't?'

'I can't be responsible for other cowboy solar-panel companies installing them in inappropriate roofing situations,' I say.

'Why has your folder got "Gemini Travel" embossed on it?' she says, her suspicion growing. I explain that we also do holidays.

Here we go again, I thought.

'Hang on a minute while I just check my readings again,' I say, flicking through some pages of a travel brochure from last year's holiday in Majorca.

'Um . . . actually, just looking through that I've realised that yes, you can have solar panels on your roof.'

'Are you sure?' says Leslie Catherine Twix.

'Yes.'

'It's just that a moment ago you said that I couldn't.'

'The sun's moved,' I say.

'Get out,' says Mrs Twix.

'Would you cash a cheque for me?' I ask as I am half pushed through the front door.

Surprisingly she agreed to cash the cheque, but insisted on a 25 per cent commission. What choice did I have?

Sun-dried tomato salad and sausages for dinner, banana custard for pud.

October 21st

Up to Madam Tussauds for the unveiling of the new wax/rendered-pork-fat effigy of me.

Shirley kicks off by asking me whether I've put on some weight since the measuring session, then says she's not that pleased with the likeness.

I can see what she means. It looks a lot like ex-*Sun* editor David Yelland. She says it's one of the few that they've had to put a label on to reduce the number of enquiries about who it's supposed to be, plus of course it's in the non-Muslim/non-Jewish section of the exhibition next to George Bush, Mel Gibson and Salman Rushdie.

The wax/pork fat Effigy of me in Madame Tussauds

I pose with it for the cameras, and as I get close I notice that there is a very strong smell of pork.

October 22nd

The great Thames Pubic Barrier has finally been cut free, and not a moment too soon. London mayor Boris Johnson has announced that it will be first combed through, before being put on permanent display outside the Tower of London. Judging from the photos in the paper, it's going to be quite a crowd-puller. It's massive and dwarfs the mayor as he poses in front of it with a hairbrush.

I receive an invitation to be the main speaker at the National Society of Quantity Surveyors' annual dinner in December. There's no fee, but there's a free meal and disco, plus complimentary quantity-surveying for one year from that date. I agree to it straight away.

Took a trip out to Damien Hirst's rival dog-food factory near Littlehampton. It's impressive, featuring state-of-the-art stainless-steel meat-recovery systems, such as the Kartridge Pak Yieldmaster and Weiler Beehive S44C separator/de-sinewer.

'Very impressive kit, Damien,' I say to the *enfant terrible* of the reclaimed-meat and dog-food processing world.

'Yeah, it's bespoke, the best in the world,' he says, removing his glasses and wiping off a piece of liver. 'I took back control of the art world and I'm going to do the same with meat reclamation. Choppingham Meats had better watch out.'

'What next after that, Maestro?'

'The autopsy and funerary business,' he says, unrolling a huge diagram of a world-beating mortuary. 'With violent crime on the increase there's never been a better time to be in the death business.'

We shook hands, he called me a minicab and I left, up the A259.

He's an inspiration to artists everywhere.

Beef jerky snack on the train and maxi-pack of crisps.

October 23rd

Such excitement! The doorbell rang this morning and there was a big lorry outside. The driver told me he had a special delivery, and when he opened the back up and lifted a tarpaulin there were fifteen Filipino people and, at the centre of it all, my own Lay Dee! To be honest, at first I didn't recognise her. The long journey overland from the tiny village of Bulb Dim in the Philippines had clearly taken its toll, plus she has put on a considerable amount of weight since her photo was posted on the Manila Envelopes website. I think her teeth must have been capped too at that stage because I spotted at least two gaps on the one occasion that she smiled. Certainly a bridge or veneers would improve that aspect of her appearance – that and a liberal amount of hair dye and make-up. Looking past the heavy jowls, the poor dentition and the grey roots surmounted by coarse purple-black hair I could see it was my own Lay Dee. I went to kiss her, but she brushed me aside and led her troops indoors and to the fridge, where she gorged herself on two loaves of bread and a whole tub of Cookeen. Her terse demeanour is entirely understandable considering her long journey, but there's really no need to snatch the TV remote control, is there?

Her English is not as good as I had been led to believe either, but she's fresh off the lorry. Let's not prejudge; let's take stock and in a week's time perhaps draw up a list of priorities.

As Mum said, 'She's here now, that's the main thing.'

Pizza and ice cream for tea.

October 24th

Disappointment for me last night. After the long wait I'd assumed . . . well . . .

'Let's take it slow,' snapped Lay Dee, quoting from the Toni Braxton song and slapping my hand from the buttons of her cardigan.

'Fair enough. I've waited this long,' I thought. She preferred to share my bed with one of her cousins, and I slept in Mum's bed. Mum slept in Dog's four-poster.

Good job Uncle Bob isn't here. I don't know what he'd make of it!

Still, it's wonderful at last to have her home.

I must say I hadn't expected her other fourteen friends to be staying as well, but Lay Dee explained that some of them are cousins, nephews and nieces, and thus soon to be my relatives too.

October 25th

As Mum points out, Lay Dee has rather hogged the TV remote control since arriving. In fact, we haven't seen hide nor hair of it for three days. The TV is permanently tuned to the Filipino-language channel Astro Wah Lai Toi, which needless to say doesn't run *EastEnders*.

I sent Mum down to Londis to get her a toothbrush, some floss, a bottle of Listerine and a Lynx body spray.

This morning Lay Dee disgraced herself rather with the postman when, wearing only a flimsy kimono-style dressing gown and black satin pants, she asked him if he would like to marry her niece, whom she pushed forward and tried to man-handle onto the saddle of his bike. Mike was most embarrassed (he's in his sixties and, as a matter of fact, bats for the other side). He made some excuse that he had an urgent delivery for next door, managed to gently push the niece off his bike and peddled as fast as his old legs would carry him down the drive.

He has delivered me one of my own letters again.

She certainly is an odd cove is Lay Dee, a rough diamond if you will, and one which I intend to polish, even if, at the moment, the polishing is rather one way.

Still no sign of the TV remote control.

Must get her signed up with a good NHS dentist.

Really getting into some of the shows on Astro Wah Lai Toi.

October 26th

Lay Dee and her cousins were caught shoplifting today in Londis.

I had to go down personally and vouch for them, paying for a wine box of Zinfandel white, four jars of Sherwood cook-in sauce, a six-pack of pot noodles and a Twix that would otherwise have ended up in the big pocket that she has sewn into the inside of her coat. The good news is, while searching said coat I found the remote control for the television.

A Twix broken in half

I explained to Dominic that she is a guest in this country and not familiar with our customs. He pointed out that he wasn't aware of any country that provided free Twixes. I promised him that Lay would be down later in the day to give him a foot massage, gratis, and he seemed to accept that.

I think I've managed to avoid a very embarrassing incident. I was determined to keep the police out of it, or she'll be sent home and I'll end up in the papers again.

After lunch I sent Lay Dee down to Londis with her essential oils to look after Dominic's needs.

Stir-fried pot noodle for dinner with small amount of Twix to follow.

October 27th

Dominic the manager of Londis phoned to ask about his foot massage on the house, and Lay Dee looked rather sheepish when I asked her about it. She claims to have got lost on the way, but I have my suspicions.

The landlord of the Jolly Sailor called and asked when I would be going down to settle the bill. I wasn't sure what he meant, but then the story came out. Apparently Lay Dee was down there all afternoon drinking cider. She got so drunk that she ended up standing on the table singing Abba songs phonetically, and when the landlord wouldn't serve her she started knocking back her essential massage oils.

I thought her breath smelt a little of calendula last night as I tucked her up, but I'd assumed it was a satsuma repeating on her.

October 28th

Tried to get Lay Dee in to see a local NHS dentist, but none of them will touch her, saying they aren't able to put aside that sort of time. There's a dental hygienist, Pete in Pevensey, who claims he is keen to get a foot on the ladder with other dental work, and while not properly trained he's keen and has access to the necessary equipment, if only at night. His rates are very reasonable too, so I book her in for a late-night session. I admire someone like Pete, who's keen to make a go of it in life, despite not having the necessary qualifications. He reminds me a little of myself at that age when, with only a City and Guilds qualification in taxidermy, I was able to blag my way onto the hospital wards and work as a doctor. I dare say if there hadn't been that mix-up with the transfusion I'd still be there now. To me all the bags of blood looked the same. Of course, that's where the training would have come in handy.

October 29th

The shortlist for the Rear of the Year has been published, and I've been passed over again.

1. Suzanne Dando
2. Joan Bakewell
3. Lorraine Kelly
4. Eamonn Holmes
5. PC Firminger of the Bexhill constabulary

They now have three weeks in which to parade their rears and try to garner votes.

I find myself growing quite fond of Lay Dee. Admittedly when I first saw her I was rather taken aback, and indeed fired off an email of complaint to Manila Envelopes. But now, now she's had the first stage of her dental work and, as I say, I'm beginning to warm to her and her quaint ways.

She's still making me wait, though.

Thick oxtail soup for lunch, individual caramel custards for pud.

October 30th

Caught Lay Dee kissing her so called cousin in a rather intimate way. She made out it was a normal thing in the Philippines, but I'm not stupid. I asked her to leave, and the fifteen of them have barricaded themselves into the spare room and are refusing to come out.

I have a crisis meeting with Mum, and we agree to try and starve 'em out.

'Remember Mafeking!' shouted Mum through the keyhole

to the spare room. Well, I don't remember Mafeking – and neither, I think, does Mum – but I think they got the message.

In the middle of it all Dominic the manager of Londis phoned and asked whether there was the possibility of a massage today and that he didn't mind paying for it this time. I explain that now is not a good time, but he threatens to go to Nicky Campbell and Fiona Bruce with the CCTV footage of the great Zinfandel/pot noodle/Twix heist.

I dispatch Mum to Londis in Lay's stead.

Nan phones and I explain the situation to her regarding Lay Dee and co., and it turns out she does remember the siege of Mafeking. In fact, she did the catering for it. She explained how as supplies dwindled she had to be ever more inventive with the food they had left. The last menu she can remember scrawling on the blackboard outside Lord Baden-Powell's billet was 'Mouse thighs in ditch-water sauce served on a bed of moss, with green grass on the side, followed by whipped damp.' Fortunately they were rescued before the last mouse was felled. She said that Baden-Powell was a nice bloke but completely obsessed with knots.

Mum had not returned from the trip to massage the manager of Londis's feet by half past eleven, so I wait till after lunch and call her on her mobile.

When I finally do get through she says that she is in love.

She says she'll be back later to get some clean clothes. She can sense that I'm a bit annoyed and attempts to cheer me up by saying she has accrued a 'huge number of Londis reward points'.

I bet she has.

October 31st

Mum came round with Dominic trick-or-treating. She was dressed as a white witch and he as the devil – very apt, I must say.

I'm not a big one for Halloween, resenting the American commercialisation of what was essentially a beautiful pagan celebration of Satan and his dark works. However, Mum loves it. Last year she spent a good couple of hours perfecting her make-up, planning to trick-or-treat as one of the undead. In fact, so realistic was the transformation that many of the children ran off in tears. They then reported what they had seen to the town elders, who then proceeded to march up the Bex Hill with flaming torches, chanting, 'Death to the monster!' I went out on the front doorstep and appealed for calm, but ended up having to give out four bags of Haribo jelly sweets.

Mum was quite shaken by it and just sat there with a mug of Cup-a-Soup, saying 'Four bags gone!' over and over again. Well, she couldn't go trick-or-treating after that and so ended the night with a sweet deficit. Not a great start to the pagan new year.

Frankfurters for mains, pineapple rings for pud.

November

A Fixed Caravan

November 1st

Mum is spending most of her time down at Londis, just to be close to the manager, Dominic. I have said I don't want him up at the house as it is an insult to the memory of my poor dad.

Dad was an early victim of the Second World War. As soon as he heard that Britain had declared war on Germany he headed up to Scotland and was never seen nor heard of again. For a while me and Mum carried on as if nothing had happened. We laid a place for him at our table every night and Mum cooked him a dinner, which she then proceeded to eat. Over the course of the war she put on eight stone. It got to the stage where, if she was honest, she didn't really want him to return because she'd miss the extra portions. He never did.

I often wonder what became of him, and even now when I hear a key turn in the lock I think for a moment maybe it's Dad returning from his Scottish sojourn, but then realise it can't be because we had the locks changed pretty much as soon as he'd gone.

Now I know a lot of people reading this will think, 'Hang on! Harry Hill isn't old enough to have lived through the Second World War.' Well, you're right, it wasn't the Second World War, it's another war, and I have changed the name of the war to protect the people involved.

Corned-beef hash and ship's biscuits for dinner, all washed down with a cup of NAAFI tea as a tribute to our brave forces.

November 2nd

Mum came into my bedroom first thing in tears, saying that Dominic, the manager of Londis, doesn't want to see her any more.

'Where are we going to get our weekly groceries from?' I ask.

'No,' she says, 'it's not that he doesn't want to see me in the shop. He doesn't want to continue our relationship.'

Naturally I'm upset for Mum, but also because we've been getting some nice perks from her dalliance with Dominic: she's been getting first dibs on any stuff he's throwing out, as well as ham at cost price.

'What reason did he give you for the split, Mum?' I ask.

'He said that the relationship was past its sell-by date.'

'Right, Mum, from now on we're strictly Ocado!' And with that I flipped open my laptop and tried to log in.

Three hours later and my job was done. I'd ordered the week's food and booked a delivery for the nearest convenient time – three weeks on Wednesday. Quite how we will survive until then is not clear. We have enough tinned food and various pastes to see us through to the weekend, which leaves twenty-one days on diddly squat. As Mum points out, man is one of the most resourceful creatures on earth and we will find a way. There's also that box of Celebrations left over from her birthday in case of an emergency.

Heinz spaghetti hoops for dinner, tinned peaches for pud.

November 3rd

Went down to the kitchen in the night to get a glass of water, only to find Mum with her hand down her box of

Celebrations. She'd pretty much scoffed the lot, except the tangy orange creams.

'I panicked!' she said.

So this is the first proper day on zero rations and all I can think about is food – roast legs of lamb, stews, cold cuts, charcuterie of every description and lashings of gravy. Every magazine I open has pictures of food, every programme I turn to on the TV shows food being prepared, and even Radio 4 today broadcast three whole minutes of sizzling during *You and Yours*.

Mum points out that leather is 'made from animals' and so technically just the same as crackling, so we cut the tops off her shoes, make cuts in them, rub them with salt and pepper and put them in the oven on a high heat for thirty minutes and then down to gas mark 4 for a couple of hours to make them tender.

They were delicious! I had the right one, Mum the left. Still hungry we turned our attention to an old sheepskin coat of mine that I haven't worn since *Minder* was on TV.

'That'll be lovely roasted with a little mint sauce,' said Mum. I filled the pockets with fistfuls of rosemary, rubbed a little olive oil into it, added salt and pepper, parcelled it up with some string and popped it into the oven.

It was a bit dry, to be honest, and could have done with some gravy, and it wasn't as nice as the shoes and left something of an aftertaste that I couldn't quite put my finger on (I think it was the biro in the inside pocket), but it took the edge off the hunger pangs.

But by tea time those pangs were back with a vengeance, so there was nothing for it but to head down to Martin's the newsagent's and buy us all a Peperami and a Picnic bar each.

November 4th

Mum says she's so depressed over the break-up with Dominic the manager of Londis that she wants to kill herself. I suggest a trip to that Swiss euthanasia clinic, and she jumps at the chance. I get on the phone and book the tickets for tomorrow. I figure as it's a one-off we'll fly first class, maybe get there a couple of days early and see a bit of the country before the big finish. This will also solve our food-shortage problem.

Sandals and leather waistcoat for dinner, frozen water for pud.

November 5th

Arrive in Lucerne and check into the hotel, thinking we'll drop our luggage and go and look at a few of the sights. As I help Mum into her room, a man in Swiss national dress jumps out of the wardrobe with a pillow and tries to smother her. After quite a struggle I manage to fight him off.

It seems there's been a misunderstanding. Mum has opted for the lethal-injection method* and not, as the management of the hotel had thought, surprise smothering. I check she's OK and say I'll meet her in the lobby in about twenty minutes – just enough time for her to freshen up and make use of the complimentary tea- and coffee-making facilities. Then, as I walk into my room, the same thing happens: different man, similar cupboard, a spirited attempt to smother me. I was pretty knackered from the first time and at one point very

* Slightly more expensive, but you get what you pay for.

nearly let death take me, but something in me kicked in – call it self-preservation, call it an unwillingness to let the complimentary tea- and coffee-making facilities go to waste (not to mention the Corby trouser press and toiletries). I found a reserve of energy from somewhere (it may have been the Highland shortcake biscuit I had in Mum's room) and fought back. I forced myself back off the bed and slammed him into the cupboard door, knocking him unconscious. When he came to, he begged me not to tell the hotel management, as his last two attempted smotherings had ended in failure and he was worried about losing his job. I let him sit on the bed for a while so he could get his breath back.

'I've got a busy day ahead,' he said in a thick Swiss accent. 'Four more smotherings, and we only get half an hour off for lunch.'

I felt sorry for him. 'Listen, I'm sure things will pick up. You've got the makings of a first-class executioner,' I said.

'You think so?' he said, stowing his pillow into a duty-free bag.

'Yes, maybe try an energy drink mid-morning – you'll find that sees you through to lunch. Now, go do your thing,' I said, and waved him on his way. I then phoned down to reception and explained what had happened and that I wasn't actually booked in for a euthanasia session – it was my mum, I thought I needed to get that straight. They were very apologetic and sent me up a complimentary bottle of cava.

Nice room, but the choice of movies is not to my taste: *Schindler's List*, *Love Story*, *The Diving Bell and the Butterfly*, *Nil by Mouth*, *The Killing Fields* – all a bit downbeat.

It's not nice being abroad for bonfire night, so Mum and I

Zürcher Eintopf.
for tea.

share a couple of sparklers in our room and set off the smoke alarm.

Zürcher Eintopf for dinner, Chrabeli for pud.

November 6th

Big buffet breakfast with Mum, then a guided tour of the town. Stopped off for an ice cream and generally had a good time.

Back to the hotel for a nap, then back down the shops to get some souvenirs.

Bought Dog a cuckoo clock and a large Toblerone.

Had a quick look in the lake for any Nazi gold – but nothing.

Went to a folk night in the evening in one of the log cabins and sang our hearts out.

The good thing about this hotel is that no one tries to make friends with you.

Teigwaren and chips for dinner, Basler Leckerli for pud.

November 7th

Breakfast in the room. A little disappointing. Had to phone down twice to get some cold milk for my Frosties, and by the time it turned up my egg had gone cold.

I meet Mum in the lobby for the cable-car ride. She says she's enjoyed 'the holiday', as she calls it, so much so that she's changed her mind about the euthanasia part of the trip.

I've got mixed feelings really because I've enjoyed the trip too and it's been great spending some quality time with Mum, but I think part of that enjoyment came from us being nice to each other because we both thought these were her last few days on earth. Also I'm a bit worried that she's going to get back home to Bexhill and change her mind. Which of course would be expensive, plus I can't keep taking time off work for euthanasia trips that go nowhere.

I think on balance she's probably made the right decision.

There was a bit of a near miss in the afternoon, stemming from what can only be described as 'a mix-up'. Basically Mum thought I'd let the hotel know about her change of heart re. the euthanasia aspect of the holiday, and I thought she had. At three o'clock this afternoon, while Mum was having her kip, she woke up with a start to find a Swiss doctor administering a lethal injection. I walked her round the lobby a couple of times and took her outside to get some fresh air, and fortunately she managed to shrug it off – apart from a twenty-minute spell when she said she felt 'a bit wobbly' – and she now seems right as rain. The lady at the check-out desk insisted that we still had to pay for the injection. I point out that it had been unsuccessful, and she says that she could easily arrange for another one at no extra cost. She's got me over a barrel and she knows it. We both figure it would be a good idea to check out of the hotel before anything else untoward happens.

Flight home a bit bumpy, and Mum jokes that it would

be funny if after having decided not to go through with the suicide the plane crashed and we were all killed.

The flight was delayed by twenty minutes, which meant by the time we got home the Ocado delivery man had been and gone and not left our stuff. There's nothing else for it: Mum needs to swallow her pride and get back down Londis.

Lunch on the plane, I the chicken, Mum the beef.

November 8th

The honeymoon period in Mum's mood seems to be over and she says she's depressed again. I knew she'd do this! Women! I can see her point though.

Eric Smythe-Wilkes tells me that while we were away Lay Dee and co. had a big party with over a hundred guests. A couple of local traveller families turned up, a fight broke out over a flagon of cider, the police were called and Lay Dee and several of the cousins spent the night in the cells.

I get home to some rather unhappy news from Shirley at Madam Tussauds. It seems the central-heating system has been playing up in the non-Jewish/Muslim sector of the exhibit and last night it got so hot that those portions of the Harry Hill effigy which were fashioned from rendered pork fat have melted. When the caretaker opened the room this morning there was my double with no legs, and next to me George Bush's, Mel Gibson's and Salman Rushdie's shoes were all soaked in lard.

'We are a victim of Victorian plumbing, I'm afraid. We will be putting it right, but until then we have put you behind a desk up against a wall.'

'OK, thanks for letting me know,' I say. At least my face will still be on show.

'It does mean you will have to come in to have your legs measured again.'

I hung up and ignored all her attempts to contact me. I'm sorry, but even I am not shallow and desperate enough to go through that particular humiliation again.

Pork chop and two scoops of mash for dinner – purely by chance.

November 9th

The British Museum has announced today that it has purchased Jordan's discarded breast implants for the nation for an undisclosed sum. They will, it says, go on permanent display in a specially adapted caravan in the forecourt of the great institution, along with some of Jordan's outfits, including the gold bikini bottoms she wore on *I'm a Celebrity . . . Get Me Out of Here!* Other exhibits in the Jordan Experience will include a rare unsigned copy of her and Peter André's debut album *A Whole New World* and Gareth Gates's socks. Visitors will apparently be guided through the author's life while listening to the Andrew Motion poem 'Jordan in a Field of Maize', read by Nigel Havers.

I try to book my tickets but the line is engaged . . . all day . . . and night.

Lay Dee got in late last night after her second session with Pete the dental hygienist from Pevensey. Her face is very swollen and she has a black eye. I know it's early days but there is definitely an improvement in her looks. Sadly she's refusing

401

to go back and see him and has been turning the air blue with her language, none of it complimentary about Pete.

Later on, Pete himself calls me from the accident and emergency department of the Conquest Hospital, Hastings, saying that on no account would he see Lay Dee again, and further was threatening legal action. He wouldn't go into the exact nature of his injuries, but I could hear a nurse in the background saying something like, 'The proctologist should be with you shortly.'

Well, I shall certainly not be recommending him to any of my celebrity friends. We'll take a view on what more needs to be done for Lay Dee once the swelling subsides.

I'm really getting into some of the shows on the Filipino channel Astro Wah Lai Toi. I mean, apart from anything there's hours of high-level table tennis, but the regular soap *Ming Tong Pang* is brilliant. Obviously I'm not entirely sure what's going on, but it is set around a pig farm that supplies the spare-rib trade, with all the drama and excitement that goes with it. Last night the lead, Mrs Pangaka, appeared to have lost a hat, and the foolish farmhand Tagal Kang had hidden it under a foldable stool. Great fun!

Chicken stir fry for tea, tinned lychees and condensed milk for pud.

November 10th

Went to the premiere of *Alvin and the Chipmunks – The Squeakquel*, and against my better judgement took Lay Dee instead of Mum. I say that because she is not quite the sophisticate that, say, Holly Willoughby or Fearne Cotton is, and I was worried that she might play up and bring a little unwelcome publicity my way.

Mum was very disappointed too and accused me of being disloyal.

'You know I like Alvin, Simon and Theodore!' she said.

It's true, she does have all their records and all the toys from the McDonald's happy meals relating to the first film, but all I got was a 'plus one'.

I should have taken her. Lay Dee behaved disgracefully! For a start she wore those hot pants, the ones from the website that attracted me to her in the first place. Now don't get me wrong, they're fine as a carrot to dangle on a dating website like Manila Envelopes, but not at a black-tie, red-carpet do. They're far too tight for her as well. From the back she appears to have about eight buttocks – it looks less like a fashion statement and more like a biology lesson in mitosis. She snored through much of the film, occasionally saying, in a very loud voice, 'What he been in before?' when a familiar face took to the screen. 'Which one Sigourney Weaver?' she bellowed. I had to explain that SW wasn't in the film, it was Sharon Stone she was thinking of, and she wasn't in it either.

At the drinks do after the screening she hooked up with Kerry Katona, and they got on like a house on fire.

I got the last train back to Bexhill alone, leaving Lay Dee as she piled into Kerry's stretch limo.

Sandwich on the train.

November 11th

The tabloid papers are covered in photographs of Lay Dee

in those hot pants dancing on the bar of the Garrick Club. She's identified variously as 'exotic beauty' and 'weird Chinese woman'. All point out that she was with '45-year-old baldy-bonced floppy-collared loon Harry Hill'. The phone has been ringing off the hook with journalists asking how close we are, what our plans are and would we do a feature? No, we wouldn't, I say.

Kerry Katona phoned at half past three in the afternoon asking to speak to Lay Dee. When I said she couldn't, she accused me of stealing her Polos. She said she had a whole packet of Polos which she uses to freshen her breath so people won't know she's been drinking and that somehow I had taken them to get her into trouble because I do not approve of her relationship with Lay Dee.

It's true, I did take her Polos, although it was not a whole packet as she stated but just two.

November 12th

The *Daily Sport* features a double-page interview with Lay Dee, with pictures. I don't know how she did it because I was on guard outside her room for most of the day. She goes into quite explicit details of our love life.

'Frigid Saturday Night Entertainer Let Me Down,' shouts the headline. 'He won't *baldly* go where no man has gone before,' it says.

I wouldn't mind, but as outlined earlier the situation is quite the opposite. I accept that nothing physical has passed between us, but it's not for want of trying on my part. Chocolates, trinkets, four whole bags of Haribos, a liqourice stick and more Flakes than I can care to number – I mean, what has a fellah got to do these days to prove that he's genuine?

We are still awaiting a follow-up appointment with a specialist who reckons that there is something wrong with the dental veneers she had put in by Peter the trainee dentist from Pevensey. I think that's what he said – something about a real veneer disease, anyway.

Mum comes off quite badly in the *Sport* piece and is furious.

The fact is, I didn't necessarily want people to know that I was temporarily living with Mum.

Printed at the bottom of the article in small italics it says that Lay Dee was paid for the interview and that she planned to give a proportion of it to a charity of her choice.

When I quizzed her on the nature of the charity, she showed me a paper lifeboat pinned to the hem of her hot pants and winked.

November 13th

I had an odd conversation on the telephone this morning.

'Hello?' I said.

'No, *OK!*,' came the reply.

'Yes, I'm fine.'

'Hello? It's *OK!*'

'Yes, it's super. Now what is it you're after?'

So, after that initial misunderstanding, the editor of *OK!*, one Robina Croker-Staples, said that she'd seen the 'very favourable' item in the *Daily Sport* and wanted to know whether me and Lay Dee had any marriage plans. Well, I was just about to launch into a tirade of abuse about press intrusion and how Lady Di would still be around today if she hadn't been chased into a tunnel by the Duke of Edinburgh driving a white Fiat Punto when she dropped this bombshell: 'Because, of course, if there was a wedding planned, we at *OK!* would be happy to pay for it.'

'Eh?' I said, bringing myself up short.

'Yes, this is the sort of thing we do,' she said. 'We pay for people's weddings.'

'Well, that's very nice of you,' I replied, warming to this plucky investigative journalist. After all, she was only doing her job, carrying on the rich tradition of John Pilger and Bob Woodward and the other one. Where would we be without them? John Profumo would be prime minister and Richard Nixon no doubt would still be running America and South-East Asia would still be awash with the blood of young GIs.

After chatting some more with the fragrant Robina it became clear that she would only pay for the wedding if she could have a copy of the wedding photos. This seems very sentimental but also quite sweet, so I agree. She says they would also like to help with the planning of 'the big day'. What a stroke of luck!

While it's true that I wasn't sure about popping the question to Lay Dee – and in fact had started to violently dislike her at times and had found myself on occasion imagining what it would be like if something terrible was to happen to her, like a car crash or wardrobe falling on her – I am quite fond of her in a funny sort of way. Like you are fond of, say, a loose floorboard or painful tooth.

Besides, I'm not getting any younger, and Lay Dee certainly isn't. It would be nice to think that one day we might be able to start a family and hear the pitter-patter of tiny feet around the house and it not be the feet of her cousins.

In short, the offer of a payment for the wedding seems as good a reason to get married as any and I readily agree.

Straight away the phone rang again.

'Hello?' said a voice.

'You're too late, I've sold it to *OK!*,' I said.

'No, hello, it's Mum. They've got some cut-price kippers at Londis – should I get them?'

'What's the sell-by?'

'November 15th.'

'OK. What's the use-by?'

'November 16th.'

'Get 'em, but get a Glade plug-in too, 'cos the smell tends to hang around.'

Brisket for dinner.

November 14th

Mum still very wistful about Dominic the manager of Londis.

'He was probably my last stab at love,' she says.

'Nonsense,' I say, 'you're an attractive woman.'

'No, I'm not!' she snaps back.

'OK, that I accept, but you're relatively good company and own your own house.'

'Ah,' she says, looking at her shoes, which are for some reason in the microwave. '*Used* to own my own house.'

'Oh, Mum, what have you . . .'

'I remortgaged to pay for the geothermal-energy system.'

'Geothermal what?'

'Geo meaning "earth", thermal meaning "heat". Dave, you know, the nice man who laid the drive and . . .'

'Put the tin foil on all the windows, sold you the solar panels . . . yes, Mum, I know Dave.'

'Well, he's going to sink pipes in the garden three hundred feet down into the earth's core, which will provide all the hot water we need and run a sophisticated air-conditioning system in the summer.'

'How much?'

'Well, as he explained, this sort of advanced system doesn't come cheap . . .'

'How much?'

'£80,000 – but don't worry, I can pay for it in instalments!'

'I thought you might be able to. Mum, you need to cancel your geothermal-energy order, otherwise with your bank balance you'll never find a bloke!'

I'll kill that Dave when I see him next.

As she frantically went through the paperwork, I explained to her the advantages of internet dating, and she's agreed to have a go.

We sign her up to Maid in England, a dating website that specialises in older single women looking for men who live abroad. We spend the rest of the day working out a suitable dating profile for her. We come up with this:

Semi-solvent widow seeks easily pleased fellah for cuddles, possibly more. BSOH.

BSOH stands for Bad Sense of Humour – well, some of her gags really stink.

On my own romantic front I plan to pop the question to Lay Dee tonight.

Kippers for breakfast, chicken curry for dinner. The house smells appalling.

November 15th

Asked Lay Dee to marry me, and she said yes. Well, what she actually said was, 'Yeah, fine, we get joint bank account, you give me Abbey National book, I buy nice dress, you buy me ring.'

I explained that wouldn't be necessary as *OK!* would be paying for everything. A dry kiss and then we were off to our separate rooms.

Mum has already had a reply to her online dating experiment. She calls me into her computer room: a small card table with a huge monitor on it as wide as it is deep, and next to it on the floor a giant grey plastic box, which is the computer. It has 400k of memory and is tremendously slow. She bought it off Dave last year, who suggested she should get on the information superhighway. He explained that it was a snip at £4,000 – cash – and very kindly ran her down to the Hastings branch of Santander in his van to get the money out. For six months after that she couldn't 'get a picture on it', despite sticking a bent coat hanger in the USB socket. I did try and explain that it wasn't a TV, but she wasn't having any of it. 'The gentleman said we'd be able to get YouTube on it and trace our ancestors, like on the telly with Fiona Bruce.'

In the end I went round and set it up for her, but like I say, it is very slow.

She has taken rather a shine to the details of a man in Zimbabwe. However, the photo is taking a long time to load. He does sound nice, though; in fact, if I was a woman I would probably go for him. Funny how we both go for the same type.

He is coming over on a trip in a week's time, and Mum has arranged to meet him at the Coffee Pot cafe in Hastings. She decided against Bexhill as she didn't want tongues to wag until the relationship was on a firmer footing.

Economy burgers and potato salad for dinner, Austrian rum dessert cake for pud.

November 16th

Robina Croker-Staples phoned today and asked who I had in mind to take the role of best man. I said I was thinking about my cousin Dennis from the ironmonger's. He's always been very reliable, not just in the supply of ironmongery, but once or twice he's fed the dog when we've been away and once spotted a build-up of milk on the doorstep and interceded with the milkman on our behalf ('I just thought they might be planning a big rice pudding,' the milkman had said when challenged about the growing throng of milk bottles).

'Not sure,' said Robina. 'I'm sure that in his own way Dennis is a perfectly good man, but you must remember that you are a big star now, Harry, and your choice of best man should reflect that. Had you thought about Sam Kane?'

'Who's he?' said I.

'Linda Lusardi's husband, the actor Sam Kane?' she said. 'He played Peter Phelan, the philandering hairdresser, in *Brookside* for a number of years.'

410

'No, not familiar with him,' I say.

'OK, he was in the celebrity Christmas special of *Fort Boyard*.'

'No.'

'Um, he played the part of Roddy in the national tour of *Boogie Nights*.'

'Oh, that Sam Kane!' I said. 'Of course, Linda Lusardi's husband.'

'That's right, Sam, Sam Kane.'

'Well, I don't know him.'

'But you'll get to know him on the stag night and on the day itself. We at *OK!* love Sam. He's very well connected and brings with him a coterie of showbiz friends that appeal very much to *OK!* readers. It would be great if I could confirm this today.'

'OK then,' I say breezily, but as soon as I come off the phone I feel as though I've been pushed into it. Plus, how am I going to tell Dennis?

The Ocado delivery man is getting a bit over-friendly.

'I notice you've gone from Andrex Velvet Soft to the twelve-pack economy toilet tissue. Slow month?' he asked me this morning.

'Um, no, not particularly,' I said, caught off guard.

'And I notice you've got prawns in there. Having a dinner party?'

'No, it's for a stir fry. Look, what's it to you?' I said, allowing my irritation to show.

'Just being friendly!' he said, swinging the empty crate up into the back of the van. Then, of course, I felt bad. Until he told me he'd had to make one of his substitutions.

'I'm out of lamb shanks so I've put in a Moroccan-style stew for two. It's got your meat of choice and should be just as warming.'

And off he went.

Actually the stew was delicious and we had the prawns as a starter.

November 17th

While talking to Robina Croker-Staples about the wedding buffet she mentioned Linda Lusardi being maid of honour.

'Now hang on a minute,' I said. 'I never agreed to that.'

'Sorry, I just assumed that with your choice of Sam Kane as best man tradition dictates his wife Linda Lusardi should be maid of honour.'

'Well, it's just that we were going to go for Dennis the ironmonger's wife Jean.'

'I've told Linda now and she's already paid for the dress, plus of course it will be lovely to see the two of them side by side in the photos.'

'I didn't think she did that any more?' I said.

'No, no, not her naked breasts, you fool! Sam and Linda, a lovely-looking couple – that will certainly enhance your wedding photos. But of course it's your wedding . . .'

'Well, if you've told her, I suppose.'

Some wedding this is turning into.

Out to H. Samuel in Bromley to buy an engagement ring. Why Bromley? Well, it has such a complete set of shops and a high street that's hard to beat. The first hurdle was trying to find a parking place. Lay Dee refuses to enter a multi-storey

H. Samuel the Jeweller

as, she says, it brings back 'bad memory!' It's not clear to me what the memory is of, but as her fiancé I must respect her wishes. It turns out my biggest mistake was actually taking Lay Dee with me, firstly because she kept wanting to stop for refreshments – Dunkin' Donuts, then Greggs the bakers – and secondly for what happened in the jeweller's shop.

We started looking at the rings. Naturally I had a price in mind. Sadly Lay Dee's eye kept being drawn by rings a little above my top whack of £900. Some, indeed, were over £1,000.

'No, darling,' I said, trying to wrest one particularly pricey bauble from her grasp. 'It's just not you.'

'Me likey!' she said.

A slightly unseemly tussle ensued, culminating in Lay Dee putting the ring in her mouth and swallowing it.

'There!' she said, opening her mouth wide to demonstrate that the ring was indeed on its way down her alimentary canal. 'Happy weddings!' And with that she walked out of the shop.

I had no choice but to pay for the thing. She really is naughty to have done that. We walked the four miles back to the car in silence.

When we got home she went straight to the kitchen and rooted around for a sieve.

Beef stew with dumplings for dinner, Dunkin' Donuts for pud.

November 18th

Mum went off on her internet date with the gentleman from Zimbabwe this morning. She did look nice, although I probably would have dispensed with the anorak. I waved her off as she set off down the drive on her disability vehicle, avoiding the crack that's reopened in the middle of it. It's been a real godsend, that vehicle, but it will take her a good two and a half hours to cover the fifteen miles between the two resorts.

After waving Mum off I stopped by her computer and glanced at the dating web page, just as the photo finished downloading (it has taken a week, during which we have been unable to make or take any phone calls on the house phone). Her new beau looks a heck of a lot like Robert Mugabe!

Mum returned from her date at midnight looking very flushed and agitated. I wasn't sure if it was anxiety or excitement. It seems the man she met in the Coffee Pot cafe in Hastings was indeed the president of Zimbabwe, Robert Mugabe. She said they had a very nice time despite the attention they were drawing from the locals, which was compounded by a forty-strong security detail outside the cafe and at key points along the prom. They each had a frothy coffee and sticky bun and chatted about their lives. Somehow Mum got onto the subject of the crack in the drive, and Bob said he would be able to get it fixed 'no problem'. After about an hour and a half he asked Mum if she would like to sit on his knee, which she accepted. They then went for a walk along the front. Stopping off at the amusements Bob produced a big leather pouch full of 2p pieces and placed a handful in Mum's hand. 'Help yourself, girlfriend,' he said, and guided her hand as she fed the tuppences into the slot on the game where coins are pushed ever nearer the edge of a precipice. At one point she was 24p up, but in the end she lost the lot. From there to the Crazy Golf, where Mum, knowing the course well, thrashed Mr Mugabe. In fact, he didn't finish the course, floundering at the windmill for a good forty-five minutes. Then on to the fun fair proper and three goes on the caterpillar roller coaster. Mum described how Robert shrieked with joy as the caterpillar passed through the painted metal apple, and how he begged her for another go after dismounting.

At this point hunger overtook them both and they retired to Bob's car – a wonderful P registration black Maxi Vanden Plas. She sat in the front passenger seat as Bob brewed up a couple of Cup-a-Soups with an attachment plugged into the cigarette lighter. He tuned the radio to Magic FM to create a pleasant relaxed mood and they quaffed their soups looking out over the English Channel.

What happened next becomes a little hazy and Mum hesitates to give me any hard details, her eyes filling with tears. It seems she started to become 'fuzzy-headed' as he drove up along the coast to Beachy Head. There . . . well, as I say, she's not certain what happened. She remembers only flashes – a skull, a candle, a tribal incantation and the acrid smell of pine-scented Magic Tree air freshener, then Robert's hand reclining the plush velour seats as Neil Fox intoned pleasant-ries from the speakers in the doors.

She managed amidst the fug of it all to release the door and stumble out onto the main road, where by chance cousin Dennis the ironmonger was flying his kite. A stand-off between Mr Mugabe and the ironmonger ensued, with Mugabe eventually backing down. Dennis then returned Mum home, towing her disability vehicle behind the van.

'I think we need to upgrade your computer, Mum,' I said, rubbing an essential herb into her bare shoulders.

'No,' she replied, 'that is the top of the range. It's the one they've got in the space shuttle, Dave told me.'

Casseroled chicken with herb provençale and potatoes parisienne for dinner, jammy dodgers for pud.

November 19th

There were several nasty emails from Robert Mugabe in Mum's inbox this morning, which I deleted before she had a chance to see them. I then relegated his address to spam. To think had I been born a woman it could have been me in that Maxi Vanden Plas. A shudder passes through me at the thought.

A reporter from the *Bexhill Gazette* calls trying to verify a story about Robert Mugabe and my mum being spotted in the Coffee Pot cafe. Thinking quickly I explain that the gentleman in question was not in fact Mr Mugabe but a look-alike organised by Mrs Riefenstahl of the Bexhill WI as a singing telegram to raise money for a local charity. He seemed to buy it.

Lay Dee has insisted that we have the wedding-present list

at Hoi Chok Filipino Merchandise Emporium on the Purley Way, Croydon, but to be honest there's not much in it for me. The wedding breakfast is to be traditional Filipino fare, and I boil up some noodles and try and run Mum through how to operate chopsticks. I looked away for a moment and when I looked back she'd knitted an Arsenal scarf with them. Ingenious, yes, and with a little soy sauce on quite delicious.

We're still not sure whether Nan will be able to make it over from the Shia Muslim stronghold of Najaf for the wedding as she is now forced to obey a curfew.

Got a text from Sam Kane saying that I should meet him at Paddington station tomorrow evening at 3.30 for the stag night, when 'all will be revealed'. Very exciting. I hope he hasn't gone to too much trouble.

Noodle scarf and gloves for lunch, fruit salad for pud.

November 20th

The day of my stag night. To be honest I have been let down rather by my friends. My brother says he can't get a flight over from Thailand, Major Peter Andrews of the Devolution for Bexhill Party says he doesn't approve of interracial marriages, Neil the Ocado man is on a late shift, and when I went down to the ironmonger's to pick up Dennis he clearly wasn't ready.

'I've had a rush on. Would you believe I've had three plumbers in the last hour and a half asking for wire wool?' he said excitedly. 'I don't normally sell that quantity of wire wool in a month let alone in one afternoon – it's mad!'

'Can't Jean handle it?' I asked.

'Normally she would but I've had to go down to the lock-up and get some old stock because one of the plumbers is coming back in fifteen minutes. I can't tell you how unusual this is, Harry – it's bonkers!'

'But I'm due on a train to meet the best man, Sam Kane, in twenty,' I said, a note of urgency creeping into my voice.

Suddenly Dennis's demeanour changed.

'Oh well, if you've got to meet your best man . . .' He almost spat out the words 'best man' as he said them. 'You know what, Harry? The time was when you would have loved the fact that I've had a spike in demand for wire wool, time was when you would have shared in my good fortune, waited for that plumber and chewed the fat, speculated with me as to the cause of such a demand. You've changed. Go to your lah-di-dah fancy actor friend, Sam Kane, who once played the part of Roddy in the national tour of *Boogie Nights* or Phil, the philandering hairdresser from *Brookside*. But me? I've got a customer with a copper pipe to burnish.'

With that he turned on his heel and went out back.

'I'll have a word with him, Harry,' said Jean, appearing in the doorway. 'He's under a lot of pressure. He told you about the rush on wire wool, did he?'

'Yes, yes he did, Jean.'

'He'll catch you up. I'll make sure he gets there. Where should I tell him to meet you?'

'Well, that's just it, Jean, I don't know. Sam's supposed to be organising it.'

'Sam?'

'My best man, Sam Kane.'

'That bastard!' she said, visibly angry. Then, gaining her composure, 'Text me, I'll make sure he's there.'

'Thanks, Jean,' I said. 'Listen, I never meant for . . .'

'Sshsshh!' she said, caressing the back of my head with an adjustable spanner. I looked at her then as I had never looked at her before – the dry skin of her face, the cold sore playing around her lips, the bloodshot eyes, one with just the hint of a cataract, all sitting 'neath a baseball cap with 'Don't just do it, B&Q it' on it – and I realised that she was a woman and I a man. The reverie was broken by the sound of the shop door opening.

'Ding!'

'Hello, Roy,' said Jean.

'Hello, Jean. Listen, luv, you haven't got any wire wool, have you?'

I made my excuses and left.

I met up with my best man, Sam Kane, at Paddington station. At first I didn't recognise him. In fact, I approached three other men before I found the right one. To complicate matters one of them was actually called Sam, which wasted about twenty minutes as I explained my ideas for how the evening should progress.

'. . . then maybe go for a Chinese,' I finished up.

'Actually, mate, I'm waiting for my girlfriend, so . . .'

Which was all rather embarrassing.

When the real Sam Kane arrived with the photographer he didn't seem that pleased to see me, to be honest. It was almost as if he was treating the whole best-man thing as a sort of job! He explained that he could only really spare forty minutes as he had a performance of *Boogie Nights* to get to in Guildford. He suggested we go to the pub in the station and then to the Delice de France for a ham-and-cheese croissant.

We chatted distractedly, mainly about Linda and his time playing a paedophile on *Coronation Street*. He didn't really get animated until he got onto the subject of the role of government in regulating the internet. All the time Ray the photographer from *OK!* was snapping away.

'Throw your head back as if you're laughing, Sam!' he'd say.

'Let's see those fillings, H!' he'd say, prodding me with the end of his tripod.

We both had a half of bitter and then strolled over to Delice de France, but there was a huge queue and mindful of Sam's busy schedule I suggested we go to Costa Coffee instead.

'You got enough, Ray?' said Sam to the photographer.

'Just about. We can always use some of the stills of you at Bobby Davro's fiftieth.'

'Good. Right then, I'd best be off. Nice to meet you, H,' said Sam, patting me on the back. And with that he was off across the platform and away to entertain another boogie-hungry crowd.

'What a great bloke,' said Ray, putting the paper cup with white plastic baby's beaker lid up to his lips and draining the last drops of his cappuccino.

Just then a shadow fell across me. I looked up. It was Dennis. He'd been waiting in the loos for Sam to leave.

'Pub?' he said.

'Why not?' I replied. And off we went.

Steak bavette for dinner. Large biscuit on the train home.

November 21st

A photo of Mum sitting on Robert Mugabe's knee in the bay

window of the Coffee Pot cafe, Hastings, appears on the front page of the *Bexhill Gazette* under the heading 'MUG-abe of Coffee for Local Lady'. Phew, looks like she got away with it, but she got her fingers burned and I doubt very much whether she'll be going back for any more internet dates.

I went along to the recording of *Jools Holland's Hootenanny* and it was great to see Duffy again after all this time.

'How's your year been?' she asked in her husky Welsh brogue.

'Oh, pretty quiet,' I said, shifting uneasily on Lenny Henry's knees as I seemed to have been sitting on a hard bit.

'I missed you,' she said, flicking a deceased moth from her lapel. 'We should meet up in the new year.'

'OK,' I say. 'Where?'

'Cockfosters tube.'

'Whereabouts?' I said, leaning towards her.

'By the key cutters,' she said, producing a detailed diagram of all the entrances and exits. 'You go down this subway here and turn left, not right, otherwise you end up round the back . . .'

'Oi, look lively,' chipped in Lenny. 'You're on.'

And with that she was away and singing at the top of her voice a song about how horses love having their hair brushed.

At the end of the show, Jools sidled up to me as I was leaving and said, 'Oh, before you go, Harry, I've got something for you, a little early Christmas present.'

'But it's New Year's Eve, remember,' I said with a smile.

He handed me two Sainsbury's carrier bags containing my tin-frog jazz band.

'Don't ask me where they've been but believe me, if they could talk, quite a story they would tell!'

I bet!

Got back around midnight and watched *Ming Tong Pang* on Sky Plus with Lay Dee. It was nice, just the two of us – me on the sofa, she on the rocking chair. The first time it's been just the two of us for a while. We both laughed heartily at the foolish farmhand Tagal Kang as he tried to spy on Mrs Pangaka and kept falling off his bamboo ladder and into the mud, and later both had tears in our eyes as he was mortally wounded in an industrial accident at work.

In her grief Lay reached for my hand – and fell out of the rocking chair onto the rug, ending up with her head in the coal scuttle! We both collapsed in a big old heap of laughter. A scene worthy of *Ming Tong Pang* itself!

Cold turkey and salad for supper, Xmas pud for afters – all courtesy of the BBC.

November 22nd

Lay Dee's relatives have started arriving in Bexhill for the big day. There were sixty-three of them at the last count. That's in addition to the twelve who came over in the lorry and who are now staying in a Portakabin on the front lawn. The rest have been booked in, at some personal expense, to the Safety First Fixed Caravan Site, just down the coast in Cooden. There's a rumour that they have been turning up at the dog-food factory with dogs in an effort to turn them into cash, until someone explained that it's food for dogs and that they don't turn dogs into food. It's just a rumour, and just the sort of rumour that I have grown to expect from the bigots round here.

OK, Lay Dee was once caught trying to force a chihuahua between two slices of bread on the esplanade, but that was a case of mistaken identity. She thought the creature was a breed of monkey. I don't know, to be honest. It's difficult for me to (1) keep tabs on what she's up to, and (2) get a sensible explanation from her.

I'm coming round to thinking that I may well have to learn Filipino.

As Mrs Pangaka says, 'Press my buttons, Mr Winston!'

November 23rd

Bit of a to-do today.

The Ocado man arrived to deliver the shopping, and as he opened the van doors Lay Dee's relations (now numbering seventy-eight persons, housed in two static caravans, one on the drive and one on the lawn) set upon its contents, forming a human chain and passing stuff over their heads and into a waiting car, which then sped off to who knows where. The Ocado man was dazed but not injured, and I took him into the house, sat him down and gave him a stiff brandy. Then another, then another . . . by which time he was in no fit state to drive his van and I had to make up the day bed for him so he could sleep it off. As he dozed his phone kept ringing every five minutes – presumably people wondering where their groceries were. Where indeed!

I paid him off and I suppose he left at about eight in the evening, after *Coronation Street*, saying that unless we were able to control our 'lodgers', he would not be calling again.

Nan called to say that she has been refused permission to come to the wedding as it breaks the terms of her bail. She does, however, have an escape plan.

With the long nights in she has managed to knit an exact replica of herself and intends to prop this up in the window of her house and slip away under cover of darkness with the help of her ice-cream-man friend Abu, whom she's back in touch with. She must then make her way to a disused airstrip, where she will be met by my old friend Sir Clive Sinclair, who will transport her in his Heli-Clair over the border to Turkey, and from there she'll catch a flight into Gatwick. It's risky and although I begged her not to go through with it, I am kind of excited by the thought of it. If she gets caught it does mean she will probably be executed, but she knows this and she does love a wedding. Besides, she's had a good innings and is insured up to the hilt.

The Filipino posse rolled in drunk just after midnight and proceeded to stir-fry vegetables until the early hours while watching MTV.

A fitful night, the smell of hot soy sauce in my nostrils. Dreamt that I was in the killing fields of Vietnam waiting for a helicopter, and when it arrived it wasn't a real one but a wooden model with sound effects like in the show *Miss Saigon*.

Went downstairs at two in the morning and had a big piece of Parmesan cheese and a glass of water.

November 24th

Nan phoned, out of breath, from behind a rock. It seems her escape plan was not entirely successful. It started off OK. She cast off the knitted replica of herself and propped it in the armchair in the window of her Najaf villa, then slipped out of the back door and over the wall undetected, where Abu was waiting with his ice-cream van. Unfortunately Abu had not turned off the tannoy and as they set off towards the airstrip 'Greensleeves' blared out from the top of the van, alerting the security guards. A chase followed during which Nan managed to bail out and hide behind a rock, from where she was phoning me.

'What's the plan now, Nan?' I asked.

'Well, at the moment the guards are buying a handful of 99s and . . . oh! . . .'

'Yes?! Nan? Hello?'

'. . . and a Funny Face lolly.'

'So they don't suspect anything?'

'It seems not,' she said, slowly getting her breath back, 'and now they're leaving . . . yes, they've gone.'

'Right, get to the airstrip and get going!'

'Roger!' she said, and hung up.

You've got to hand it to the old vixen – ninety-one years old and still a player!

November 25th

I awoke to a shocking noise coming from the front of the house. I pulled back the curtains, and hovering outside my bedroom window, dangling from a rope, was Nan. She'd made it! Looking up, I could see Sir Clive waving from the cockpit of his Heli-Clair.

'Change of plan!' said the wizened nonagenarian as I hauled her to safety. 'What's for breakfast?'

'I'll get the frying pan,' I said, and we went downstairs for a traditional English.

Against all the odds, the old girl pulled it off.

The vicar, Trevor La Chemise, popped round in the evening to talk about the upcoming nuptials. He's a nice bloke, although his ministry has had its ups and downs. Mainly downs. He was the subject of a court case last year, the details of which I won't go into here,* but suffice to say he has ended up on some sort of register. The fact that he's still in his post has raised a few eyebrows locally, but as the bishop said, Jesus always encouraged forgiveness, plus there is an acute shortage of people wanting to become vicars and 'so long as he keeps his nose clean there's a job for him here in Bexhill'. Initially there was a bit of a backlash and attendances fell off, then Trev had the bright idea of giving double portions of wine at Communion and now he's breaking all box-office records for the church. We had a brief discussion about hymns and the order of service. Lay Dee was playing up, blowing kisses at him and peeking provocatively over her fan.

Fortunately he couldn't stay long because of his tag.

Trevor La Chemise's
Tag.

* Trev claims that it was an unfortunate combination of high winds and perished braces, but I'm not so sure – what was he doing on the netball court at half past two in the morning? I'm sorry, but I simply don't buy his explanation that he thought he'd seen a pine marten.

November 26th

Talking to Nan she admits that her Najaf bolt-hole hasn't been quite what she had hoped for. She accepts that she has upset the authorities and most of the locals, is often the target of stone throwing, and with the curfew spends most of her time in the house with her knitting, but nonetheless claims to miss her life over there.

'What do you miss most about it?' I ask.

'The people,' she says. She plans to return, to 'fess up to the authorities and throw herself on the mercy of the mullahs.

'They might well have me down for a stoning session,' she says. 'But I'm used to it now. Besides, sticks and stones may break my bones but names will never hurt me.'

I think she's missed the point there somewhat, but that's her decision. I cannot condone her actions but I applaud them nonetheless.

I introduced Nan to Lay Dee. They circled each other like two Alsatians, sizing each other up. I left them talking and went about my chores.*

When I went back some two hours later to see how the two of them were getting on, Lay Dee had got the karaoke machine out and the two of them were singing their hearts out. I stayed and watched as they worked their way through

---

* The bolt on the bathroom door is still sticking and doesn't seem to have responded to WD40, so I set about stripping it down. The downstairs shower still flip-flops between scalding hot and ice cold, and there is a little condensation inside one of the double-glazing panels in the rear bedroom.

427

the entire Beatles *White Album*, although I fell asleep during 'Revolution No. 9'.

It's great they are getting on so well. I don't know what it is. I think they see something of themselves in each other. Both are strong women, that's for sure. Both have had to struggle to make ends meet at some point in their lives and both have got – let's be frank – terrible teeth.

Chicken korma for dinner, coconut creams for pud.

November 27th

Took a moment today to look through some of the letters I'd received from Lay Dee during the time that the waves and the Home Office kept us apart.

They had various acronyms on the back. One was S.W.A.K.L.

'Shouldn't that have been S.W.A.L.K.?' I ask her.

'No. Sealed with a knowing look!' she fired back with a grin. Must remember that one.

'What about this one – B.U.R.M.A.? Be Undressed Ready My Angel, right?'

'No!' she barked. 'Burn under right mammary area!' It's true she used to store cigarettes under there during the uprising.

Ian the warden at the Nemesis rest home phoned to tell us that Uncle Bob has escaped from the ventilation system of his warden-controlled flat.

'Either that or he's died inside the complicated system of ducts,' he says.

Basically, every evening since his disappearance they have been leaving his meal inside one of the vents. In the morning

428

it would be gone, but for the last three mornings it's still been there, untouched.

'I've had to clear the three plates because they were starting to go off and the smell was being distributed all through the building by the ventilation system,' said the warden.

I feel we can probably expect him here any minute. He's bound to try and make his way back to somewhere that he knows, and so I pop down to the chemist for two litre bottles of Night Nurse, a funnel, some gaffer tape and a rope.

A little nervous about the big day tomorrow. Mum keeps coming up to me and singing the old song 'I'm Getting Married in the Morning' and prodding me with a wooden spoon.

In time-honoured tradition I am not to see Lay Dee the night before the wedding, so at about tea time she decamps to one of the fixed caravans with her favourite cousin.

'Last night of fun!' she gnashes at me, making a lewd gesture. 'Then ball and chain!'

She's got a great sense of humour – so important if the relationship is to last.

I had a restless night, partly nerves, but mainly because I was kept awake by the noise coming from Lay Dee's caravan. First just general carousing, but as the night wore on out came the karaoke machine. Her eclectic set list included Meatloaf's 'Bat Out of Hell', 'Milkshake' by Kelis, and Lady Gaga's opus 'Bad Romance'. She always finishes on 'My Way'.

As Mrs Pangaka of *Ming Tong Pang* might say, 'Kill the chicken! Eat his sunshine!'

Ham baguette, prawn-cocktail crisps and a Penguin for tea. Well, I wasn't really hungry.

The day of my wedding. My big day. The plan was for me and Mum to be picked up by Dennis in his beautiful P-reg Jaguar Sovereign, but in the end it seems it wouldn't start, so we turned to that trusty standby, Mum's disability vehicle, me steering, she wedged behind me like I was giving her a pig-gyback. Eric and Betty Smythe-Wilkes went out onto their front step and waved us off, which was nice.

We got to the church in plenty of time. Robina Croker-Staples from *OK!* was there to meet us with a photographer and a message of apology from Sam Kane to say that nei-ther he nor Linda would be able to make it to the service as Linda had an old hamstring injury that needed massag-ing, but they would be at the reception, albeit briefly due to a matinee of *Boogie Nights* and a personal appearance (for Linda) in Basildon high street. So cousin Dennis and his wife Jean stood in at the last minute. It seemed to me to be a little rough justice and Dennis was as pleased as punch.

'Have you got the ironmongery?' I said, making a little joke.

'Yes, you know I have an ironmongers shop, Harry,' said Dennis, missing the point.

'No, Dennis, I mean the rings!'

Well, that rammed it home and he laughed his head off for a good four minutes and thirty-eight seconds.

So there we were up at the altar, me and Dennis, then suddenly the organist struck up the opening chords to 'Here Comes the Bride' and Lay Dee, accompanied by her dad, started on her journey down the aisle. I turned and caught my first glimpse of her.

There she was grinning and waving to the various cousins and extended family, and she looked, well, different actually. The *OK!* team had larded a lot of make-up on her in an attempt to suggest cheek bones, but for my money it looked like she'd had her face grasped on either jowl by a sweep.

I felt a sharp jab in the small of my back and there she was next to me, a strong smell of pine emanating from her cleavage, where nestled a Magic Tree air freshener which must have fallen off the rear-view mirror of the car on the way in. I moved my hand to try and fish it out.

'Oi!' said the vicar, slapping the back of my hand with a prayer book. 'Plenty of time for that later!'

I must say even by her standards Lay Dee was very badly behaved all through the exchange of vows. She kept turning round and pulling faces at her family and friends, and when Trevor asked whether she would 'take this man to be your lawful wedded husband', she stuck her hand under her armpit and by pumping her arm up and down made a series of gastrointestinal noises. Much laughter from her side; outrage from Mum, Dennis and Jean and Major Peter Andrews on my side.

When the moment came to exchange rings she pretty much snatched hers out of Dennis's hand, put it on her finger and punched the air, shouting, 'Gotcha, long pig! Gotcha!'

It was at this point that I started wondering what I'd got myself into.

'You may now kiss the bride,' said the vicar.

As I leant in to get what was rightfully mine, she ducked, planted a huge smacker on Trev's face, then turned and ran out of the church.

From the church it was off to the parish rooms for the reception, where the picture editor of *OK!* had hung a huge blue screen.

'We'll get the photographs in front of that, Harry, then we can add a suitable background and some key *OK!*-friendly celebs later with the computer.'

Many of the guests had been invited by *OK!* and I was meeting most of them for the first time, apart from Richard Stilgoe, whom I'd met when I did my ill-fated *An Audience with Harry Hill*.

'Kriss Akabusi sends his apologies, but he couldn't make it as he's developed a snuffle,' said Jill from *OK!* I wasn't aware that Kriss had been invited. 'So he's sent his brother instead, who looks a lot like him.'

The photos took three hours, which left only forty minutes for the speeches and food. Lay Dee's side of the family piled into the buffet to the extent that there was really very little left for anyone else, and I found myself down at the hotel bar at half past nine in the evening buying a packet of nuts and a Twix.

Sam Cane's best-man speech was a tad desultory. It involved him pretty much reading my Wikipedia entry from his iPhone (yes, he hadn't even bothered to print it off) and a rather tasteless routine involving an inflatable sheep that he'd apparently bought while doing a summer season in Blackpool.

Nan heckled him halfway through and he used the old standby put-down line 'Is that a moustache or have your eye-brows come down for a drink?' – which got a good laugh, and which he used to cover his exit. After a cursory handshake for me and the missus, he grabbed a couple of bottles of wine and he and Linda were out of the swing doors as fast as their legs could carry them.

Uncle Bob, heavily sedated, snored all the way through the service. The medication started to wear off during my speech. He was grunting and oinking and struggling to break free of the ties that bound him to the chair, which was to be honest rather distracting. It upset the flow of the speech and I didn't get half the laughs I was looking for.

Lay Dee's 'dad', who actually looks younger than her, cornered me and kept shouting something about a dowry. I fobbed him off with the five hundred quid cash I had earmarked for sundries on the honeymoon.

My old friend Ken Ford, the bearded life model for the *Joy of Sex* books, sidled up to me in the bar and offered me a few tips for the wedding night. His beard smelt strongly of fish paste.

Still, it was a lovely day. At last it is all legal and above board in both the eyes of God and the state.

November 29th

The honeymoon has been a bit of a washout as we can't leave the country due to the fact that Lay Dee doesn't have a passport. In fact, that was one of the first things she brought up after she accepted my proposal. 'I want passport!' she said, and trooped down to the post office to get a form.

I had, however, done the next best thing – a night in the Novotel, Heathrow! Oh, what secrets will love's sweet bounty impart?

Well, not a lot as it turned out. Having waited in the bed watching the Discovery Channel for a good two hours while Lay Dee attended to herself in the bathroom, I finally went to check on her, and found her asleep in the bath, wrapped in the shower curtain and surrounded by fourteen empty miniatures. She looked so peaceful. Having put her in the recovery position, I decided to leave her there. I learnt a heck of a lot about the lifecycle of the sea lion that night. Still, we have the rest of our lives together for all that.

Got a text from Dog in the small hours: 'Conga Eel onyx Yom Kippur nudist.'

Which I took to mean: 'Congratulations on your nuptials.'

November 30th

Woke up on the floor, with Lay Dee in the bed. Not sure what happened, but to all intents and purposes it looked like she'd woken up in the bath and shoved me out of bed. You've got to admire her nerve! Could have sworn she was pretending to be asleep.

Lay Dee had breakfast in the room, I in the restaurant as I failed to complete the menu card and hang it on the back of the door handle before 4 a.m.

Returned back to The Close, Bexhill, in the afternoon, a little downhearted, while Lay headed off to the Purley Way to pick up the wedding presents.

As I park up outside the house I am a little aghast to see another static caravan arriving and being jacked up on breeze blocks. It seems that some of the wedding guests are planning to make a bit of a holiday of it.

Lay Dee arrives back mid-afternoon in a people carrier laden with all sorts of different-shaped woks, spatulas and a whole pig.

'Look what Daddy bought lucky boy!' she squeals, and so does the pig. One of the cousins grabs a rope and ties one end round the monkey puzzle tree in the front garden and the other end to a ring in the pig's nose. The Smythe-Wilkes are not going to like this!

December

BBC TV centre

December 1st

Another restless night. Lay Dee didn't come to bed at all, despite me scattering chrysanthemums on the counterpane. No, she stayed with her cousin in the fixed caravan. I gave up at about two and then was kept awake by the pig rooting around in the front garden. It's almost as if my life is turning into an episode of *Ming Tong Pang*.

A Pig

Call from Peter Fincham at ITV1 congratulating me on my nuptials and asking whether me and Lay Dee would be interested in taking part in *Celebrity Wife Swap*. Apparently they've got BNP leader and star of BBC *Question Time* Nick Griffin and his wife Bambi lined up. I'm not sure, but Lay Dee overheard me discussing the fee and is keen as mustard and tells me to sign up 'as present to me, lucky boy'.

I agree to go in for a preliminary chat.

Mum's mild curried chicken with sultanas for tea.

December 2nd

Had the preliminary chat for *Celebrity Wife Swap* today.

Actually, Mrs Bambi Griffin seemed very nice, and Lay Dee seemed to hit it off with Nick straight away, so it's agreed – we are to take part.

Had a meeting with the people from Waddingtons, the board-game makers, about Asylum Seekers and Ladders. It looks like fun. It's a fairly traditional board game: you move round on the throw of a dice and can land on squares that either promote your chances of gaining British citizenship or reduce them. For instance, here's a few they're suggesting:

The lorry you stow away in is refrigerated – go back three spaces.
Go on a date with Lembit Opik – advance to Go!
Your perfume is particularly attractive to sniffer dogs – go back three spaces.
Madonna expresses an interest in adopting you – advance to London.
Get caught walking down the Channel tunnel – go to a B&B in Dover.

It looks like good family fun and I tell them Lay Dee and myself are happy to lend our names to the project.

December 3rd

It's the first day of *Celebrity Wife Swap*.

As I waved goodbye to Lay Dee I whispered in her ear, 'Just don't fall in love with him.'

I arrived at the Griffins' mock-Tudor semi in Wales (why is it only Tudor buildings that we mock?) in the people carrier, and there's Bambi Griffin waiting on the doorstep with open arms. She gives me a big bear hug and a smoochie kiss, which I hadn't expected.

We get on like a house on fire, and after a lively lunch of ham and peas and a bottle and a half of English hock we play canasta. Then the fun was spoilt by a phone call from Peter F.

It seems that shortly after Nick arrived at The Close, Bexhill, Lay Dee attacked him with a bread knife.

As Peter F explained, 'While this is TV dynamite, we have to be sensitive, so the show's off. We might be able to use some of the footage as a DVD extra,' he adds.

Such a shame, and a nice little earner out of the window too. Bambi seems quite upset as she hugs me goodbye, and we promise to stay in touch.

I arrive home to a waiting throng of press men, and when Lay Dee appears at the door they go mad. Loving every minute of it, she hitches up her skirt and jumps on the back of the pig, riding it around the monkey puzzle tree and singing, 'I will do anything for love, but I won't do that.'

In the evening we were contacted by premier PR man Max Clifford, who has offered to handle all press interest and help us capitalise on Lay Dee's 'unique position in British life'. He says that 'If she plays her cards right, she could make a lot of dough out of this. You could be sitting on the next Susan Boyle,' and places a contract under my nose.

Beef goulash and Cadbury's chocolate fingers for tea.

December 4th

In the papers today Lay Dee is being hailed as a hero, and there is a lot of interest in her. Max has scheduled a full day of interviews:

6.30 a.m.: the *Today* programme, interview with John Humphries.

7.00 a.m.: GMTV interview with Lorraine Kelly focusing on her fitness regime.

10.00 a.m.: the Ken Bruce show, Radio 2, 'The Tracks of My Years' section – her favourite songs and reasons why she likes them. She chose 'Welcome Home' by Peters and Lee, 'Suite Pee' by System of a Down and the theme from *Follyfoot*.

12.00 noon: *This Morning* with Holly and Phillip to review this month's film releases with Mark Kermode.

2.00 p.m.: *Loose Women* – serious discussion about knife crime.

2.30 p.m.: meeting at Random House to discuss possible book deals – travel guide to the Philippines, a cookery book (good luck with that!) and autobiography.

3.00 p.m.: Steve Wright in the afternoon to talk about her upcoming autobiography. Other guests include Matt Monro's daughter and topical comic Russell Howard.

5.30 p.m.: Paul O'Grady – DVD-review slot.

8.00 p.m.: *The One Show* – Chinese food tasting with Nancy Lam and Brian Blessed.

9.00 p.m.: *How to Look Good Naked* (good luck with that!) with Gok Wan.

9.45 p.m.: Radcliffe and Maconie, Radio 2 (she's been primed with an entry for Britain's longest-running word-association game The Chain).

10.30 p.m.: *Question Time* from Basildon (other panellists: Sinitta, topical comic Russell Howard, Lord Tebbit and David Milliband.

11.30 p.m.: *This Week*, BBC2, with Andrew Neil, an item about immigration controls, with Michael Portillo, Diane Abbott and Timmy Mallett.

12.00 midnight: *The Sky at Night* with Patrick Moore, focusing on Uranus.*

To be honest, she struggled a bit. There are only a few shows where you can get by with her limited grasp of the English language.

It all went OK until Andrew Neil's show and the item on immigration, where once again she disgraced herself, this time by trying to strangle Michael Portillo with his own belt. Timmy Mallett had to step in with his mallet.

Unfortunately the story is now out that Lay Dee is an illegal immigrant.

December 5th

There is a huge outcry and general brouhaha in the papers and other media about Lay Dee's illegal-immigrant status. Peter the Pevensey dental apprentice has sold his story to the *Sun*, saying she had her teeth fixed on the NHS and supplying before and after photos. It's really not fair. We all know that I paid for that out of my own money as a matter of urgency. I must admit I shuddered when I saw her old gnashers.

The *Mirror* label her a gold-digger and have dug up a string of heartbroken middle-aged men who they claim she's turned

* Their joke, not mine!

443

over. The *Daily Sport* splash the front page with a lurid photo of what they suggest is Lay Dee coming out of a brothel in Manila arm in arm with Major James Hewitt (it's clearly been touched up – the photo that is, not the good major). The killer blow is delivered by the *Guardian*, who print a full-page picture of Lay Dee with a moustache, wearing a trilby and smoking a pipe, under the headline 'I'm *Not* a Lay-Dee!' Inside there are four further pages detailing her journey from man to wo-man. I am sure this cannot be true and I contact my solicitor with a view to bringing a libel suit.

Meanwhile, Jack Dee's denied all knowledge and gone into hiding.

Nick Griffin is calling for a general election, and Max Clifford is not answering my calls.

Coincidentally, I finally got the papers through from the Philippines and it turns out that Lay Dee, far from being thirty-nine as stated on the Manila Envelopes website, is sixty-three. Bang goes my chance of kids. Not sure how this leaves our marriage.

Tofu squares on a bed of basmati rice for dinner, Star Bar for pud.

December 6th

Finally got through to Max Clifford this morning.

'What do we do now, Max?' I say.

'She has no alternative but to sell her story, but to get any decent money out of it she's going to have to really stir it up.'

'You mean lie?'

'Yes.'

'I'm afraid we can't do that,' I say.

'Gimme dat!' shouts Lay Dee, grabbing the phone out of my hand. 'Any fing goes!'

Later, as I watch her walk the gauntlet of the world's top paparazzi and get into the stretch limo that awaits, with Max on the back seat, I start to examine my feelings for her.

Do I love her? No, not really. Did I ever? No. Will I ever? Certainly not. Good, I'm glad that's settled.

On reflection I probably should have examined my feelings a lot sooner. If I had I might have saved myself a lot of grief.

December 7th

Wrote to the Pope today asking for an annulment. I don't see that I have any alternative. Even if Lay Dee was to 'put out', the chances of her getting pregnant are next to nothing. Mum pointed out that there was a lady in Italy who had some sort of hormone treatment and had a baby in her sixties but was unable to pick it up.

If I'm honest I never really warmed to Lay Dee in the first place. I was fooling myself. I tried to make something of it, to look beyond the bad dentition and halitosis, the surly nature and aggressive outbursts, the stocky trunk and stubby legs, but sometimes the chemistry just isn't there.

It's a shame when love goes cold, especially after I bought that boxed set of *On the Buses* too.

December 8th

The good news is that all the fuss in the media about Lay Dee has helped to turn some attention towards me. Sometimes you just have to grab fame's spotlight with both hands and swing it round onto your own face.

The phone's been ringing off the hook with offers! Three months in panto in Birmingham (and it's great money – even more than Brian Conley got), an animation company are interested in me being the voice of a mouse or 'small mammal of your choice, but not the vole as Joe Pasquale's doing that', Channel 4 have enquired whether I'd be interested in fronting *The Philippines' Most Dangerous Roads* and, most exciting of all, Jana Bennett at the BBC has asked whether I'd like to 'come and do something for us'.

December 9th

I hot-foot it to Shepherd's Bush to meet with BBC head of vision Jana Bennett to discuss my plans for the future. The softly spoken Canadian is charm itself, and after to-ing and fro-ing with a number of ideas for shows that I've had in the bottom drawer for a while we settle on a quiz show in which divorced couples go head to head in an attempt to win back their kids. Rounds would include a general-knowledge section, a 'Things that used to annoy me about you' round, a 'Who got wot when we split up' round, a 'Name the mystery cousin' round . . . Basically it's the opposite to ITV's *Mr & Mrs* and we're calling it (drum roll) *Beat the Ex-Wife*. There is an opportunity for celebrity specials if the show takes off: think Anne Diamond and Mike Hollingsworth, Paul McCartney and Heather Mills, Jan Leeming could do a whole show with her five exes, there could even be a royal special timed to coincide with the Queen's diamond jubilee – Princess Anne and Mark Phillips, Fergie and Prince Andrew . . . I'm sure there are others.

By the end of the meeting Jana's cheeks were quite flushed with excitement and a rash had appeared on her neck. She said that she would need to check it through with compliance but that it shouldn't be a problem, and popping an antihistamine tablet added, 'Once it's got a green light from me nothing can stop it.'

All in all a very positive meeting.

Lasagne for dinner, fruit salad for afters.

December 10th

Terrible news.

When Mum was going through Brenda the cleaner's handbag today to get change for a fiver for the Betterware salesman (set of multi-coloured clothes pegs, pack of two scourers and a desk diary with a 3D image of Susan Boyle on the front) she came upon a photo which appeared to show Brenda at a wedding, and there at the centre, tying the knot so to speak, was my beloved Lay Dee. Well, I didn't know what to say or think. My mind was in turmoil and I had to take a valium and brandy miniature and lie down.

me, asleep

Finally woke up! I realise now I took six valium tablets and not one, and I'd forgotten I'd just had a slurp of Tixylix cough remedy to stave off this swine flu that's circulating and half a box of Zinfandel white, but I think it was the brandy miniature that just tipped me over the edge. I missed nearly a whole week!

Felt great when I woke up though. I thoroughly recommend it! That is until I remembered why I'd taken it in the first place: to forget . . . to forget about that photograph. While I slumbered, Mum had been sleuthing. She challenged Brenda with the photo, asking her to explain what was going on. At first Brenda denied that it was her in the photograph – even though by chance she was wearing exactly the same outfit as in the photo. Then she denied that the bride in the picture was Lay Dee. Then she denied that it was a wedding, claiming the whole photograph was a sophisticated collage formed for fun using Adobe Photoshop (2.4). After further pressure and a number of fivers Brenda gave in and confessed that Lay Dee is in fact her daughter and that she had attended the wedding between Lay Dee and one Man Lee, the proprietor of an electronics shop in the Tottenham Court Road, just eighteen months ago in downtown Manila, just off the ring road. Further, that Lay Dee was in fact born to her as a son, Bruce Chin, and four years ago had undergone gender realignment treatment in South America, involving the removal of certain items which now reside in a jar in the basement of the General Galtieri Centre for Medical Excellence, Buenos Aires.

Fortunately Mum had now put the valium up on a high shelf so I couldn't reach it, otherwise I might have done something very silly. I cannot believe it! My own Lay Dee, a man?! The *Guardian* was right all along!

Mum suggests I fire off an email to Manila Envelopes asking for my money back, but on closer examination of the small print on the contract there is a disclaimer in tiny, tiny writing: ' Some of our clients while outwardly appearing to be of one gender may be of another. Always check at base first.' I put down my magnifying glass and flung myself into my mother's arms in despair.

'Get rid of her, Mum!' I sobbed.

'If we do that, who's going to do the cleaning?' she said.

'Not Brenda, Lay Dee, you old fool!' I said.

'What, kill her?'

'No, just get her out of my life.'

'First we must establish the facts beyond all shadow of a doubt.'

'You mean?'

'Yes, we must get that pickled assortment sent over from Argentina and confront her with it.'

I suppose she's right, there's no need to be hasty.

At least now we have a plan.

Gherkin and two picnic eggs for tea.

December 17th

Went up to the loft to get the 'internally illuminated external Christmas Santa' (as it says on the box) to cheer myself up. When I plugged it in the bulb had gone. It's a small 12V bulb with a narrow screw thread unlike any I've ever seen before, and I suspect I'm going to have some difficulty tracking a new one down. I haven't told Mum yet. She loves that 'exterior illuminated Christmas Santa', as she calls it, and it has become something of a local attraction during the twelve days of Christmas.

December 18th

No luck getting the bulb for the internally illuminated external Christmas Santa. Took it to cousin Dennis at the ironmonger's, who explained that the voltage on it was closer to that of a boat but suggested I try the hardware store or possibly the car-parts shop further down. I carried the little broken bulb down to the hardware store, pretty sure that he wouldn't have a replacement. Sure enough, he said it was the wrong voltage,

The sort of bulb required for an internally illuminated, external christmas Santa.

but we had a laugh about the Santa being 'one of the family' and so on. He suggested I go to the lighting shop three doors down. I knew they wouldn't have the bulb but decided to pop in anyway as it was only a short walk. A similar exchange took place, and I found myself using the line about Santa being a member of the family, and we all had a laugh about it – me, the two shop assistants and a lady who was already in

450

the shop. As I left I thought I might just try the car-spares shop, and realised that really I was using the broken bulb as a conversation piece, as a way of chatting to people. The man in the car-spares shop was less friendly, offering only a curt 'no'. I tried the line about the Santa being a member of the family, but he just looked at me like I was mad.

What I would say to any lonely person at home with no one to talk to is that it might very well be worth getting hold of one of these bulbs as it is a great way to meet people. When you do get one, let me know where you got it, because I need one.

Jana Bennett of the BBC phoned in the afternoon. I could tell from her voice that something was up.

'Something's up,' she said.

She was very apologetic, but to cut a long story short, while the BBC's board of governors are happy with the concept of the show, recognising that it 'represents society's changing attitudes towards marriage', they are saying there is a problem with the title of the show, *Beat the Ex-Wife*.

They say that use of the word 'wife' excludes those couples who have opted not to marry, and also those people who have entered into same-sex civil partnerships, and did I have a problem with the show being called *Beat the Ex-Partner*? I tell Jana I'll think about it

December 19th

Nice letter from the Pope saying that Lay Dee is well known to the Vatican and the annulment wouldn't be a problem and would be automatically put through following receipt of the necessary monies.

The Vatican
Rome W1

Dear Harry

Thanks for your letter. I'm afraid Miss Dee or Miss Avril Sunshine or Miss Naughty Harris or Mr Bruce Chin as she is variously known is on our files and has been for quite a while. In fact, we have taken to circulating a photo of her to all our churches, telling our priests that on no account must they marry her to anyone without first checking with us here.

As the Führer used to say, 'Can we fix it? Yes, we can!'

The annulment will not be a problem, and I'm happy to enclose a bill of charges and the signed photo that you requested.

Yours through Christ,

Benny
Pope Benedict XVI

I wasn't sure about this Pope when first he took the robes of office after all that stuff about him being a Nazi in his youth and then the child-abuse scandal, but I'm definitely warming to him now. As Mum said, 'We've all done things we're not proud of.'

I have placed the signed photo on eBay, along with the *On the Buses* boxed set. I think I'll start the bidding at £5.

Talked to Mum about it and we have both decided to rest the internally illuminated external Christmas Santa for this year. Well, he's going to look a little bit sad, especially to those passersby and neighbours who remember him from last year all lit up. That gives us a year to track down a new bulb.

Creamed pork for dinner, coffee gateau for pud.

December 20th

I explain to Lay Dee that the marriage is over and show her the Pope's letter, which she grabs from my hand, screws up and stuffs into her mouth. I go to grab it back, and she topples over into the dog's bed. At this point Mum comes in and sees me and Lay Dee writhing around in the bed. She immediately grabs the bed and starts tugging at it, swinging us around and making it skate across the parquet flooring, all while shouting, 'No! It's wrong in the eyes of God!' I looked up to see the postman staring through the window at us, but when he realised I'd seen him he scuttled off.

Eventually I got the letter out of her gob, but it'll need ironing and I suffered a nasty bite to my pinky. 'You'd better get a tetanus jab for that,' said Mum. Lay Dee ran to her room and locked herself in.

While she's out of the way I take the opportunity to change the locks on the front door. I also remove the breeze blocks from under the wheels of the caravans, which were preventing them from moving, and tether the pig to the one nearest the road.

As night fell Lay Dee retired to her caravan for the night, as is her custom, and once we could hear the karaoke starting up Mum and I crept out into the front garden and woke the pig. Nan removed her false teeth and pulled a face so frightening that the hapless animal was startled and made a dash for the road, pulling the lead caravan along with it. With a little help from me, Mum and Eric and Betty Smythe-Wilkes it headed down the Bex Hill, with the cousins chasing after it. With the other caravans empty we hitched them up one by one behind the disability vehicle and towed them further up the close. There was a loud boom and a squeal as the lead caravan careered off the road and hit the climbing frame in the kids' play area.

Job done!

December 21st

Lay Dee banged on the door intermittently for three hours last night, before eventually throwing a brick through my bedroom window with a note attached saying 'Text me, yeah?'

Maybe in time we can be friends.

Went to the doctor's surgery for the tetanus jab. He suggested a very different jab as well, which I won't go into.

Mentioned in passing the bulb for the internally illuminated external Christmas Santa to Dominic at the Londis.

'Try down there,' he said, pointing. 'They should be between the twin-feed mechanical cylinder lubricators and corn-cob pipes.'

Sure enough, there they were, a pack of twenty-four. I took them up to the till.

'Just the one please, Dom,' I said, but he wouldn't split the pack up.

'But that bulb has lasted me thirteen years! It's only used over the Christmas period, and then only during the hours of darkness . . . and I turn it off before I go to bed!'

But the swine wouldn't budge, so I took the whole pack.

Fish fingers for dinner, two Ferrero Rocher for pud.

December 22nd

It is the National Society of Quantity Surveyors' annual dinner next week so I pick my dinner suit up from the dry cleaners. The girl on the front desk calls the proprietor, Ken, down, and he explains that there has been a problem. He says that because the suit was made in the seventies from an experimental man-made fibre, the entire suit has dissolved. He hands me a jar of black liquid and a label from the suit which says 'DO NOT DRY CLEAN'.

Diagram of Dinner suit paste
(shaded area shows re-fashioning
of trouser line to give them
a more contemporary feel)

'That'll be £7.99 please,' he says.

'Hang on a minute!' I say. 'I came in with a perfectly good suit and you hand me it back in liquid form and you expect me to pay you? You should be paying me, mate!'

He hands me £8.

'Got the one?' he says. I grab the dosh, the jar and the label and storm out of the shop, my dignity, if not my dinner suit, intact.

Mum seems to think that there might be something you could add to the jar of dinner-suit extract to make it back into cloth again, but I don't really want her to get involved. She goes into the front room to Google it, and comes back holding a bundle of VHSs.

She says that she's found out from an internet chat room popular with organic chemists that if you add VHS tape to the liquid it should turn it back into cloth.

We spend the next hour or so unravelling the tapes and stuffing them into the jar. We spread the resultant paste on a sheet of grease-proof paper in the shape of a dinner suit (actually I streamline the trousers slightly as those bell-bottoms were a little passé – see diagram). We leave it out in the sun to dry.

A hamper arrives from ITV with a note from Peter Fincham on a card with a photo of the cast of *The Bill* on the front and the legend 'Looking forward to another great year with ITV'. Inside he's jotted: 'Thanks for all your guidance. We make a great team, don't we? Luv [*sic*] Peter F and all the team at ITV.'

The hamper contains huge amounts of shredded paper ('Those are probably ITV's accounts for the year!' jokes Mum) but also two packets of digestives, a carton of juice, a slab of pâté, a jar of cranberry sauce and my favourite – a box of Zinfandel white! It's going to be quite a Christmas.

The Betterware salesman turns up with the catalogue, and on the cover is what looks suspiciously like my God Bed.

December 23rd

Got a postcard from Goa, India, from the dog: 'Spending a little time trying to find myself.'

456

The producer of *Grand Designs* phones, saying that they're dropping my windmill/station conversion project from the show because 'Kevin doesn't think the design is grand enough.'

Stuff him. Stuff the lot of them. I'll prove them all wrong. When that station is open and is one of the main stops on the way to Europe and beyond, they'll be laughing on the other side of their faces.

'Oh, hello, Mr McCloud! What's that? You'd like a coffee and a Danish for your trip to Bruges? Certainly. Oh! I've just noticed you're on our blacklist. Sorry, can't serve you. Thanks for shopping in Cuppa Cino!'

Picked up Nan from the airport – she does look well, nicely tanned, although there are still a few scabs on her face from the stones.

It's the day of the National Society of Quantity Surveyors' annual dinner. To my great surprise the dinner suit, once peeled from the grease-proof paper and trimmed, is pretty serviceable. The only problem with it now is that it is magnetic.

I'm an hour late because the magnetic sleeve of my suit has interfered with my wristwatch.

December 24th

Got a Christmas card today from Dizzee Rascal. 'Have a great Xmas, luv Dizzee. P. S. Sorry.'

I put it straight in the bin. Well, I can forgive but I can't forget (or if I'm honest, forgive either).

Hatched a plan this morning to shift the excess unusual-gauge light bulbs I bought off Dominic.

Mr. Dizzee Rascal

I phoned both Dennis at the hardware shop and the bloke at the lighting shop, putting on a voice and claiming to be from a supplier of electric light bulbs. I offered them a range of bulbs (I had the catalogue in front of me), placing special emphasis on the twelve-volt tungsten for external use – 'For instance, with an internally illuminated external Santa.'

Both of them took the bait and ordered one.

'Oh no,' said I, 'they only come in packs of eleven,' and both of the tight-fisted swines said they wouldn't bother. Well, at least I know where I stand. And Dennis a cousin too!

Spent the day getting a few last-minute presents for the family from the Londis, but I'm pretty much covered thanks to being organised early in the year. I've bought Mum a fridge and freezer defroster, and Nan a chenille mitt and static duster set; for cousin Dennis at the ironmonger's a retractable clothes line.

I know it was a drag getting a replacement bulb for the internally illuminated external Santa, but I must say as darkness falls on this Christmas Eve it is lovely to see it lit up in the front garden, although it does throw the cracks in the drive into sharp contrast, making them appear worse than they really are. Mum has peeled off the foil from the sitting-room windows and applied copious amounts of spray-on snow. Sadly several insects have become stuck in the goo and I watched for twenty minutes as a daddy-long-legs struggled to free itself. It will be spending its Christmas with us this year.

Nan dressed the tree not with fairy lights but with candles, as is her custom since she was a child. She badly singed the front of her hair in the process, and we have to turn the Glade plug-in up to three to get rid of the smell. As Mum applied Savlon to her eyebrows, I go round quietly snuffing out the candles.

At just gone midnight the doorbell went, and pulling on my dressing gown, jockstrap and slippers I went down to see who it was. I opened the door to see the shivering, wretched form of Uncle Bob! Somehow, like a terrier separated from its master, he had managed to find his way home. I took him in and woke Mum, and she made him a hot toddy and warmed a mince pie in the microwave, which unfortunately burnt the roof of his mouth. Nan agreed to budge up on the bed settee and we have allowed him to stay for Christmas!

December 25th – Xmas Day

Lazy start to the day. Opened our presents. Mum bought me a bunch of flowers and a bag of charcoal briquettes.

Nan set to mulling some wine: she heated up a big copper pan of Zinfandel white, added a little cinnamon, some thyme, some sage and some onion and crumbled in an Oxo cube – delicious!

Then, just as we had all sat down for Christmas lunch, the door burst open and in flew Amanda Holden and crashed into the electric fire, banging her head on the stone-effect surround. In all the confusion we had forgotten to position her trampet! She was out cold for a good twenty minutes. Seeing her disadvantaged, Uncle Bob tried to drag her upstairs, but I managed to bring her round by slapping her repeatedly around the face. Unfortunately her husband wasn't far behind her. He stormed in through the open front door and punched me on the nose, accusing me of being involved in a bigamous relationship with her. I tried to explain. I even showed him the trampet, but he wasn't having it.

'Come on, Amanda! We're leaving!' he shouted. 'You'll be hearing from my solicitor in the morning!'

'What, on Boxing Day?!' I sneered, and he punched me on the nose again.

Uncle Bob couldn't eat much due to the blood blister on the roof of his mouth from last night's mince pie.

We all agreed that the Queen's Speech – or Queen's Rap as it is now billed – wasn't as good as last year's.

I received a text from Dog in Goa in the evening: 'Hamper a lorry tie rack with yodel welk heron.'

Which I translate into: 'Having a lovely time wish you were here.'

Played charades in the evening but got stuck on Nan's interpretation of *Avatar*.

December 26th

At about 11.30 in the morning a patrol van from the Nemesis rest home turned up to take Uncle Bob back. I must confess it was me that tipped them off – well, we're paying good money for it. In fact, I even paid the twenty quid extra for a Christmas lunch that he never had.

'Come on, Bob,' says Ian the warden, stepping over the cracks in the drive and dragging Bob towards the van. 'It's your favourite tonight, pineapple chunks.'

'Pineapple chunks!' cries Bob, visibly relaxing.

'And we've got the entire last series of *Last of the Summer Wine* on DVD.'

'Compo!' he shouts. 'Clegg!'

As the warden explained that they're not in it any more, we waved them goodbye.

Mum got a bit tipsy and told me that my dad was not, in fact, in the original line-up of the Drifters. I alter my Wikipedia entry accordingly.

Cold turkey and all the pickles for lunch and dinner, cheesecake and/or trifle for pud and as many Toffifees as we could eat!

A Toffifee

December 27th

Popped into the Londis sale today but didn't buy much, just some past-its-sell-by ham.

A package arrived postmarked Buenos Aires, but to be honest neither of us have got the nerve to open it and have written on it 'return to sender'. I think I need to draw a line under the whole sorry episode and not dwell too long on the whys, wherefores and indeed mechanics of it. Better to have loved and lost, I suppose.

December 28th

I always tip the bin men at Christmas. Well, you never know what you want to dispose of, do you? I've gone a step further actually: I've found out the dates of all the individual bin men's birthdays and leave them a card and book token each on their special day.

I received an envelope this morning postmarked Sinclair-ville. Inside is an invitation to a bash celebrating the engagement of Sir Clive Sinclair to one Lay Dee. I hope they'll be very happy together!

December 29th

Great news! Eric Smythe-Wilkes our neighbour put his Christmas tree out for the bin men and left a chocolate decoration on it! I looked out of the lounge window and could see something glittery dangling from the dried-out spruce but assumed that it was a missed bauble. It was only when

A chocolate Bauble

walking past that I got a closer look and clocked that it was a choccy! I saw Eric sweeping the path and made conversation with him – 'Good Christmas?' that sort of thing – all the time knowing about the tasty fruit upon the festive tree by his bins. What a laugh! Naturally I waited till nightfall to sneak out and retrieve it. As I walked up the path the movement-sensitive light in his porch came on and he appeared at the window. I froze at first, then waved, and he came to the door.

'May I be the first to wish you a happy new year for tomorrow!' I flannelled.

'Thanks,' he said.

I left it an hour and a half and tried again. The light came on again and he was straight at the door like he'd been waiting there.

'What are you up to?' he said coldly.

'If I tell you, you'll have to agree to split the proceeds.'

'OK.'

'You left a chocolate on your tree,' I said, pointing over at the carcass.

'I don't think so,' he said, edging back indoors.

'Yeah, look,' I said, and put my hand on the tree where I had seen the chocolate bauble hanging. It wasn't there.

'You were saying?' said Eric.

I fished around in the tree, turning it over a couple of times, but not a sausage.

'Happy new year,' he said with a grin, and shut the door.

I stood for a moment, then returned home, humiliated. The swine had obviously picked it off for himself.

December 30th

The headline in the *Bexhill Gazette* today is 'Postal Shock for Bexhill Resident', and it goes on to detail how 'Elderly resident of the Nemesis rest home Mrs Harriet Hill has suffered what doctors describe as "a severe setback" after she received through the post a set of male genitalia in vinegar from a hospital in South America.'

I'll kill that postman.

December 31st

Saw in the new year watching *Jools Holland's Hootenanny*, but couldn't settle. The thought of Eric noshing down that choccy bauble kept creeping into my thoughts.

Start to think back over what has been, all in all, a rather uneventful year.

Must be more aggressively proactive in the year to come.

January 2011

Bexhill station

January 1st

Head up to London to see my accountant.

As the train speeds towards our capital city I look around me at the other passengers in the carriage.

A young couple with a child in a buggy, dead-eyed, their faces blunted by burden. The child points at me. 'Man!' she says over and over again in what is already an Estuary twang.

A lad with acne and a put-upon look wearing a 'Who's the Daddy?' T-shirt and a tattoo saying 'Courtenay' on his upper arm (and I'll wager it does not refer to Sir Tom). The hunter-gatherer instinct is long gone, his fingers soft, his thumb swollen from frantic texting, his eyes tiny and his skin pale from hours in front of a computer screen.

Two teenage girls sit chattering about last night's reality TV show in which someone a bit like them was bullied.

A bored commuter alternating between sighing and burping clutches a cup of coffee with a beaker-top like that of the baby in the buggy opposite and barks noisily down his phone.

And through the window, as I pass through green meadows and dense woods, what do I spy?

Why, a conker lying ungathered.

Oh great God in the sky, what is the point of it all?

The End.

January 2nd

I got a call from Stephen Page at Faber asking that the ending of the diary be 'a bit more upbeat'.

I point out that technically I've run out of days. He counters with 'What about the six days you were out cold between the 10th and 16th of December?'

So I agree to give it a go.

January 3rd

I head up to London to attend an awards ceremony.

As the train speeds me towards our capital city I look around me at the other passengers in the carriage.

A young couple, their eyes sparkling at the prospect of an exciting future for their little girl, who thumbs through a copy of Seamus Heaney's latest poetry anthology.

The child points at me. 'Conkers!' she says, drawing a conker from her pocket. We proceed to play the ancient game. She beats me and plays a young lad in a 'Read More Books' T-shirt and with a tattoo saying '*Cats* Rocks' on his upper arm.

Two teenage girls cheer them on.

A young entrepreneur sips thoughtfully from a flask of tea, and I spy through the window a red squirrel digging up his winter cache of acorns as a white horse gallops in the field beyond. I look at my train ticket – all this for £19.50, as I am travelling off-peak and hold a Network South-East card.

God, this country's great!

I send it off to Pagey. As far as I'm concerned, he can like it or lump it.

Acknowledgements

Thanks to Peter Fincham for allowing me to take his name in vain and to everyone else mentioned – who didn't.

Likewise to my mum and the people of Bexhill-on-Sea – a lovely town and perfect holiday destination.

To Stephen Page, Julian Loose and Ian Bahrami for their encouragement, and to Donna Payne and Lucie Ewin for layout and design.

Finally to my wife Magda for chipping in with the occasional gag and general inspiration.

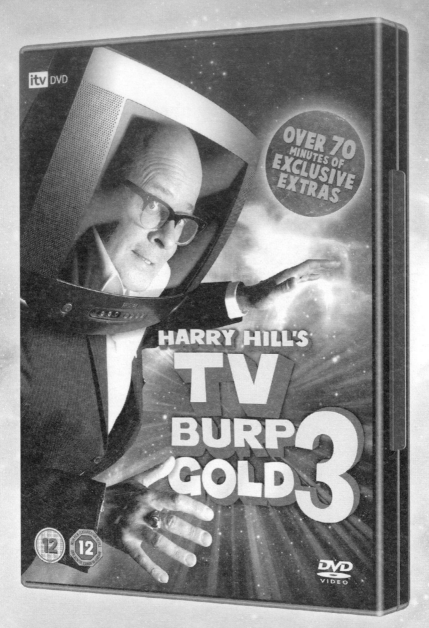